I0804305

The Aces of Fighting 17

17-F-6
17-F-25

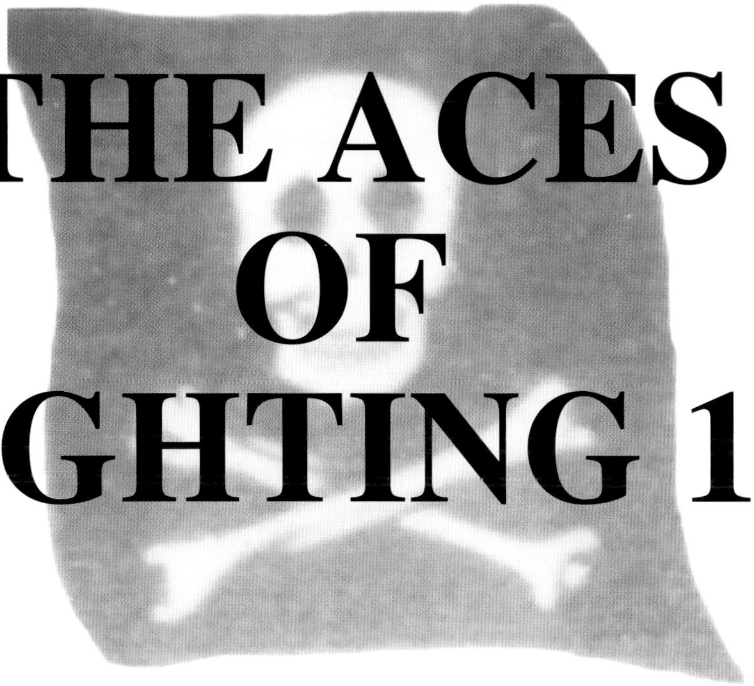

THE ACES OF FIGHTING 17

LEE COOK

Schiffer Military History
Atglen, PA

Book Design by Stephanie Daugherty.

Copyright © 2011 by Lee Cook.
Library of Congress Control Number: 2011937279

All rights reserved. No part of this work may be reproduced or used in any forms or by any means – graphic, electronic or mechanical, including photocopying or information storage and retrieval systems – without written permission from the copyright holder.

Printed in China.
ISBN: 978-0-7643-3947-9

We are interested in hearing from authors with book ideas on related topics.

Published by Schiffer Publishing Ltd.
4880 Lower Valley Road
Atglen, PA 19310
Phone: (610) 593-1777
FAX: (610) 593-2002
E-mail: Info@schifferbooks.com.
Visit our web site at: www.schifferbooks.com
Please write for a free catalog.
This book may be purchased from the publisher.
Please include $5.00 postage.
Try your bookstore first.

In Europe, Schiffer books are distributed by:
Bushwood Books
6 Marksbury Avenue
Kew Gardens
Surrey TW9 4JF, England
Phone: 44 (0) 20 8392-8585
FAX: 44 (0) 20 8392-9876
E-mail: Info@bushwoodbooks.co.uk.
Visit our website at: www.bushwoodbooks.co.uk
Try your bookstore first.

TABLE OF CONTENTS

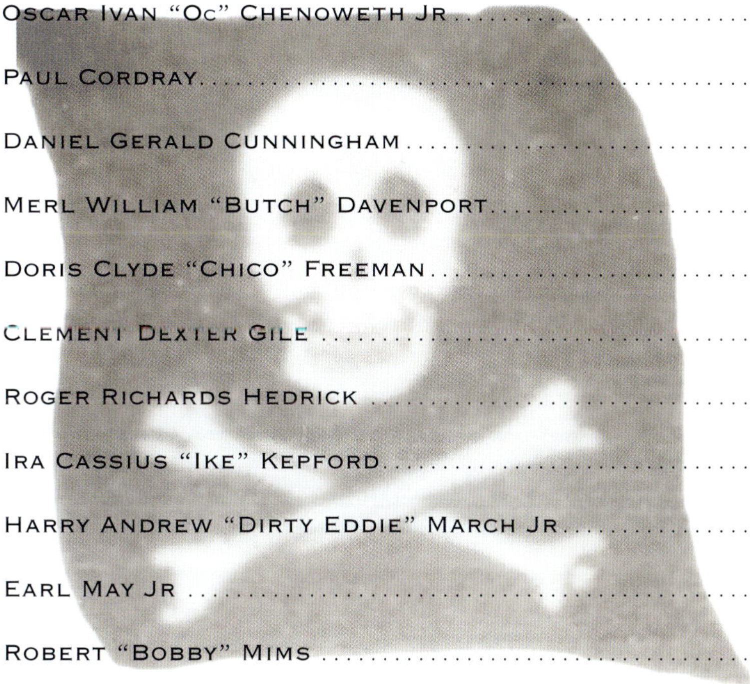

FOREWORD

More than sixty years ago it was my great privilege to fly with the best pilots in the world, the pilots of Fighting 17. The relatively few among us who became aces were the best of the best: Skipper, Rog, "Ike," Earl, Danny, "Dirty Eddie," "Timmy," and more…their young faces are still clear in my memory. We loved one another fiercely, our bonds of brotherhood forged in high-spirited fun, celebrated victory, and grievous loss. It is an honor to have known them. Thanks to Lee Cook, the world now will know and honor my shipmates more completely.

Lee has spent the last seventeen years of his life performing intensive research in the accomplishments of all the members of Fighting 17. He has attended more reunions and kept in more faithful contact with squadron members than most of us who survived. Just when I think that there could not possibly be any nugget that his first book, *The Skull and Crossbones Squadron - VF-17 in WWII*, didn't thoroughly cover, his diligent research mines even more gold. Thanks to Lee Cook's talent and persistence, history will come alive for future generations.

I'm confident that I speak for all my dear friends and fellow pilots – both here and in the hereafter – when I stand and lift a grateful glass to Lee in a toast, "*We of Fighting 17 wish you much success in your new literary endeavor. Carry on, Lee.*"

William L. "Country" Landreth,
Commander, U.S. Navy (Ret.)

INTRODUCTION

In the film "Top Gun" all the fighter pilots stayed together at one end of the bar and kept themselves apart from other pilots. "Country" Landreth said it was the same during the war. The fighter pilots were considered the elite and kept to themselves away from others, generating the feeling amongst themselves that they were an exclusive club. One of the standing jokes was "*I heard you nearly made a really good fighter pilot.*" This type of quip was made to a lot of the pilots who had obviously wanted to be fighter pilots but did not make the grade and were moved to other duties. The fighter pilots were the best and the "Top Guns" of their day, and the aces were the best of the best.

After the publication of my first book, *The Skull and Crossbones Squadron - VF-17 in World War II*, I talked about the possibility of an aces book with Schiffer Publishing in 1997 and the idea was born. I continued to research for many years, and as I had more time on my hands it became a full time occupation. With access now to the internet the focus of my research was locating families of Fighting 17 Aces. All have contributed greatly with original material and photographs and given their full support to this project. I also managed to obtain the service records of the aces from personnel and archival records and met and interviewed family members, along with surviving aces, in the course of my seventeen year research. I have had access to unique original material and located many previously unpublished photographs and information from the families of aces who served with Fighting 17.

With meticulous attention to detail I have researched Social Security records, marriage records and Census records to verify family details. I have had the approval, support and help of the aces' families.

This book is the culmination of seventeen years of dedicated and meticulous research and a goal I have had to honor the "Top Guns," the Aces of Fighting 17.

Lt. Cdr. Tom Blackburn, Commanding Officer of Fighting 17 and ace with eleven victories. *Courtesy of the Tom Blackburn Collection*

1

TOM BLACKBURN

11 VICTORIES

John Thomas "Tom" Blackburn was born in Annapolis, Maryland, on June 24, 1912, while his father was teaching at the Naval Academy.

The Navy was in Tom Blackburn's blood, and below is an excerpt from the entry about Tom in the 1933 U.S. Naval Academy "Lucky Bag", which gives some flavor of his character in his early days:

> *"Early in Plebe Summer, Tom blew in, lay down on the nearest bed, and said, "When do we eat?" His philosophy of life has not changed. Never stand up when you can sit down is his motto, and he has thrived on it.*
>
> *Academics were only a nuisance to Blackburn, and he joyously took them in his stride for four carefree years.*
>
> *Due to a never ceasing flow of good humor and a seemingly endless supply of skags, Tom was a welcome addition to any after - chow bull session and was at home in any company."*

Tom's nephew Paul Blackburn has carried out a lot of family research, especially regarding Tom's parents. Here he gives an idea of the Blackburn family upbringing:

> *"Tom's parents (Paul Prichard Blackburn and Nellie Gertrude Carey) were born, respectively, in Omaha, Nebraska, and Shenandoah, Iowa. Paul's father (Thomas Wakefield Blackburn) was a prominent Omaha Lawyer, who had also been a Newspaper Editor in Los Angeles and had run the education office of the Bureau of Indian Affairs in Washington, D.C. Nellie's father was a Cattle Broker of Protestant Irish stock. Through Thomas' political connections, Paul was appointed to*

the Naval Academy in 1899 after finishing his junior year at Central High School in Omaha. His young age and slight frame did not prevent him from doing very well at the Naval Academy, from which he graduated in the class of 1904. Paul went on to have a successful Naval career, notably as a submariner. One of his early assignments was to teach at the Naval Academy from 1911 to 1913. Paul retired as a Captain in 1939, but was recalled for wartime service and then retired a second time in 1945. Nellie, also a graduate of Omaha's Central High School, went off to prestigious Wellesley College, where she graduated in 1906 as a classics major. The couple were married in 1907.

Paul loved the Navy from the moment he arrived in Annapolis and throughout his life, and Nellie was a fervent supporter of both her husband and all that she felt was best in Navy traditions. Their first child, my dad (Paul, Jr.; I'm Paul III), told me he was essentially given no option but to pursue a Navy career. He was sent to Severn Academy, then a kind of prep school for the Naval Academy, and got into the Naval Academy on a Congressional appointment from Nebraska, just as his father had. A graduate in the class of 1930, and thus at Annapolis during Tom's Plebe year, my dad got his wings in 1931 and went on to have a very successful career, before retiring as a Vice Admiral in 1969.

Nellie was a loving but demanding mother, one who used her classical education to encourage her children to read widely and to explore the world around them. From early experiences in Guam, the Philippines, China and Japan (mostly before Tom was born) she developed a strong, respectful interest in the high culture of Asian civilization (but definitely not the dirt, disease, poverty, etc).

Disappointed that Paul's assignments to ships or U.S. duty did not afford travel opportunities for their teenage children, she decided in 1924 to take the three of them (Paul, daughter Elinor and Tom) off to Europe, where they saw the sights and then stayed in Lausanne, Switzerland, for a few months.

So what did all this mean for Tom? First, he grew up Navy through and through. No wonder the Lucky Bag describes him as having been so relaxed the day he showed up as a Naval Academy Plebe. His father was a graduate and had taught there, his older brother was on the scene in his final year, and even an uncle (Caspar Blackburn; 1916) was an Annapolis man (though through a World War I injury only briefly so).

Second, he and his older brother were quite different. Though also a flyer, my dad mostly flew PBYs and the like and did not become a "fighter pilot" - or buy into the hard - charging ethos that went with that pilot breed in those days. (I can't imagine that my father ever flew under telephone wires while in Pensacola flight school, as Tom told me he had done). My dad was less flamboyant, less charismatic, perhaps more interested in process and organization, than Tom. Those differences perhaps gave an extra edge to Tom's life - long propensity to flaunt convention, to go against the grain.

A final point about Tom's family background - my impression is that the three children were strongly encouraged by their erudite and sophisticated parents to engage in almost constant verbal competition and self - improvement exercises - word games, puns, witticisms, invented limericks, recitation of memorized verses or patches of Shakespeare, spouting of foreign language phrases, charade - like guessing contests and the like. Though the youngest of the three siblings, Tom I gather eventually proved the quickest among them (though the other two were no slouches). Tom demonstrated his remarkable intelligence by how he got into the Naval Academy. Unlike his father, uncle and brother, he decided that he did not want to benefit from the "favoritism" of a Congressional appointment to the Academy. He felt he should get in there by his own merits, or not at all, so chose to compete for the 100 or so places then made available through open written examination. Family lore has it that he came in 3rd in that nationwide competition."

En route to Operation Torch and the invasion of North Africa in November 1942. Tom Blackburn, Commanding Officer of VGF-29 on the USS *Santee* (4th from left). *Courtesy of the Tom Blackburn Collection*

Tom's nephew Paul vividly remembered two conversations he had with Tom while staying with him in Sanford, Florida, at the end of 1956:

> *"In one of them he vividly described his close brush with death on that raft off North Africa at the start of the war, while in the second he talked about the daredevils at Pensacola who were so crazy they took pride and delight in flying under bridges and even telephone wires. I think he may have said he flew under a bridge once, but am quite sure he never claimed to have gone under a wire."*

Tom was educated at Western High, Washington, D.C., and Severn School, Severna Park, Maryland. He began his Naval service on June 17, 1929, as a Midshipman and was commissioned as an Ensign on

June 1, 1933. From June 30, 1933, to June 26, 1935, he served on the USS *Mississippi* and was Aircraft Gunnery Observer with VO Squadron 3B from May 28, 1935, to January 23, 1936. He married Rosalie Reed in June 1935 in Coronado, California.

Following service on the USS *Mississippi* he started training as a Naval Aviator between February 20, 1936, and March 29, 1937, at N.A.S. Pensacola. He was promoted to Lt. (jg) on June 1, 1936, and qualified as a Naval Aviator on February 26, 1937.

He then served with Bombing Squadron Two (VB-2) on the USS *Lexington* from July 1, 1937, to June 16, 1939, and while serving there his son, Mark W. Blackburn, was born on September 14, 1937.

He was then assigned to Fighting Squadron Two on the USS *Lexington* from June 16, 1939, to February 24, 1941. While serving with Fighting Squadron Two his daughter, Patricia A. Blackburn, was born on April 13, 1940.

He reported as an Instructor to N.A.S. Miami on March 14, 1941, and served there until June 30, 1942. While there he was promoted to Lt. on April 1, 1941.

Tom Blackburn reported for his first combat assignment as Commanding Officer of VGF-29 on July 9, 1942. He was promoted to Lt. Cdr. on October 1, 1942, and flying F4F Wildcats off the USS *Santee*, they formed part of Operation Torch and the invasion of North Africa in November 1942.

Blackburn's first combat mission was on November 6, 1942, when his flight were unable to find their target due to poor intelligence. Due to worsening weather they were forced to land where they could, or have to make a water landing. Blackburn had to ditch, and was stuck in his life raft for nearly sixty hours before he was rescued. It was not the start to his combat career that he had envisaged. Upon his return to the States in late 1942 he was ordered to form Fighting 17, who were commissioned on January 1, 1943, and were to become the first Navy squadron to see action with Corsairs.

Tom had to train a group of new pilots into an effective fighting unit in a matter of months flying the new Chance Vought F4U Corsair, which was unproven to the Navy as a carrier fighter. At first they had no Corsairs until March, when the first ones were available from the factory. The pilots were then checked out on the new type and started flying the F4U in earnest. They experienced many mechanical difficulties and lost six pilots in training, as the F4U was unforgiving of pilot error.

Blackburn managed to get Roger Hedrick as his Executive Officer and they made a good team. Hedrick was an excellent shot and an experienced fighter pilot with over 2,500 hours in fighters prior to combat.

Opposite: Tom Blackburn taxiing out in "Big Hog" at Munda in November 1943. *US Naval Historical Center / M W "Butch" Davenport Collection*

Lt. Cdr. Tom Blackburn, Commanding Officer of Fighting Squadron 17, receives the Distinguished Flying Cross from Major General Ralph J. Mitchell, USMC, in a ceremony on Bougainville in February 1944. Behind them is the Fighting 17 scoreboard showing 130 Japanese planes claimed shot down by the squadron at that time. *Courtesy of the National Archives*

*"If ever a man was tailor made
to be an across the board
role model and leader of men
flying and fighting from ships at sea,
it was Tommy Blackburn."*

VICE ADMIRAL JAMES STOCKDALE

Tom Blackburn (back row standing 6th from left) with his squadron VGF-29 on the USS *Santee* prior to the invasion of North Africa in Operation Torch in November 1942. *Courtesy of the Tom Blackburn Collection*

Once the pilots had checked out and had enough hours in the Corsair the next phase was carrier qualifications, which were very difficult, as the F4U had very poor landing approach visibility and in contact with the carrier deck had a marked tendency of a high bounce.

Blackburn worked his pilots hard on all aspects of the training and stressed the importance of teamwork, as he knew this would pay off later in combat. Particular attention was placed on gunnery and combat tactics. Slowly the squadron began to master the ways of the Corsair and came to realize what an effective fighting machine it could be.

Once training was complete and the shakedown cruise on the USS *Bunker Hill* was over, in July 1943 they received new F4U-1As with improved design modifications and were then ready for combat. Once Fighting 17 arrived in Pearl Harbor the decision was made to take them off the *Bunker Hill* due to logistics. The Navy was unable to support one squadron of Corsairs in terms of maintenance and spares when all the other carriers had Hellcats. Blackburn made the decision to stick with the Corsair, as he and the squadron believed in the aircraft, and history has proved that he made the right decision. They were then sent to Ondongo, New Georgia, where the Marines had been operating Corsairs, and they had the spares and ground crew that could support the squadron.

By this time Blackburn had moulded a team of mostly new pilots, along with a small number of combat veterans, into a squadron he felt were ready to take on the Japanese.

The first operation was to support the Marines, who were landing on Empress Augusta Bay, Bougainville.

On November 1, 1943, Blackburn had his first contact with the Japanese while on patrol over the landing ships in Empress Augusta Bay, Bougainville. His flight was orbiting Cape Torokina at 25,000 ft when an enemy formation, estimated at about forty Mitsubishi Zeke fighters and Aichi Val dive bombers, was sighted over Mt. Sugarloaf. The Vals were at about 16,000 ft., the Zekes at 18,000 ft.

Blackburn, flying in #1 "Big Hog", dived on the leading Zeke from about 21,000 ft. When the formations were 2,000 ft apart, the Zekes apparently saw the F4Us and dropped their belly fuel tanks. The leading Zeke executed a right chandelle; Blackburn fired and hit him but did not destroy him. Blackburn recovered to the left, looked for his wingman, Lt. (jg) Doug Gutenkunst (who was Blackburn's wingman until he was killed in a mid-air collision on January 30, 1944), and in the process made a diving head-on run at a Zeke on his port bow. The Zeke turned up 20° and returned fire with 7.7 mm machine guns and 20 mm cannons, but broke sharply at 200 yards to the right and down. Hits were observed on the port wing and fuselage of the Zeke, which trailed white smoke. A 7.7 mm hit on Blackburn's left wing probably occurred on this run. The Japanese turned right 90° and headed towards Empress Augusta Bay, and they re-entered the melee. Blackburn made a run on a Zekes' tail, he at 16,000 ft, the Zeke at 15,000 ft, and began firing at 200 yards, and at 100 yards the Zeke burst into flames and went down. The pilot did not escape.

Blackburn then headed north, picked up Ens. Don Malone (the wingman of his second section) northwest of Cape Torokina, and both pursued the enemy northwest. Shortly after this, Blackburn saw what he believed to be one F4U headed southeast pursued one mile astern by a Zeke. The friendly plane was zig-zagging at 5,000 ft. Blackburn attacked the Zeke from above and in front but missed. The Zeke continued his pursuit, and over Cape Torokina began firing. Blackburn, then 700 yards astern, fired on the Zeke, who broke away, turned left and headed north at 3,000 ft. Blackburn followed (beginning his chase at fifteen miles astern) slightly below the Zeke. He closed to 100 yards, pulled up to the Zeke's level and fired. The Zeke burst into flames and crashed into the water. During this entire action Malone was flying wing on Blackburn. In his first combat Blackburn shot down two Zekes and damaged two more.

His next engagement was on November 8, 1943, when twelve F4Us were assigned to fly escort for B-25 Mitchell medium bombers in a strike against shipping in Matchin Bay. Because of the extremely bad weather surrounding the base and the early hour (dawn) none of the fighters were able to find the bombers. Seven returned to base. Five pilots led by Blackburn left Baga Island - the rendezvous point - and took a NW course to a point at sea fifty miles SW of Buka. By this time the weather had cleared. They turned east into Matchin Bay and Blackburn, "Dirty Eddie" March, and Whit Wharton took a course of 310° to Minan Island and swung right on a course of 40° to the Buka strip. Just before passing Minan Island they had observed a transport-type plane, probably a converted Ruth, circling to land.

Fighting 17 aces Tom Blackburn and "Dirty Eddie" March at Bougainville in January 1944. *Courtesy of the Tom Blackburn Collection*

The three Corsairs flew right along the Buka strip at an altitude of 50 ft and strafed a Zeke parked on the SW end of the strip, then strafed personnel on the edge of the strip. By this time Blackburn and March were on the tail of the Ruth, who was halfway up the strip, just lifting off at 10 ft. Both planes had perfect shots (range 200 to 25 yards), and the Ruth, hit in the wing roots and motors, burst into flames and crashed.

One of the most significant missions for Tom Blackburn and Fighting 17 was the Battle of the Solomon Sea on November 11, 1943. Fighting 17 were the first Corsairs in action from a carrier, and Blackburn's faith in the Corsair was vindicated.

Fighting 17 acted as cover over Task Force 50.3 (USS *Bunker Hill*, *Essex*, *Independence*, and their destroyer screen) east of Bougainville.

The action as far as Fighting 17 was concerned may be divided into two operations. The first consisted of a twenty-four aircraft cover, together with twelve F6F Hellcats from VF-33 over the Task Force from dawn until it was necessary to land aboard and refuel. During this period the carriers launched their strike on Rabaul. The second operation was to fly cover over the Task Force whilst the carriers received their returning aircraft before retiring to the south. It was during this second operation that the Japanese attacked the Task Force in four waves.

Tom Blackburn and Gus Wildhelm, skipper of VF (N) 75, at Bougainville early in 1944. *Robert Lawson Photograph Collection, National Museum of Naval Aviation / US Navy photo*

Twenty-four F4Us took off from Ondongo between 17:00 and 17:20. The visibility was poor, with broken cloud at 1,000 to 3,000 ft., and for some reason the *Bunker Hill* and *Essex* did not have their YE equipment (aircraft radio homing beacon) turned on. Tom Blackburn's and Roger Hedrick's flights did not find the carriers until 19:00. During their search, however, these flights were actually within fifteen to twenty miles of the Task Force.

The carriers launched their aircraft between 19:45 and 20:45. At 21:30 the shore-based fighters began to land aboard the carriers: eleven Corsairs aboard the *Essex*, twelve Corsairs aboard the *Bunker Hill*, and twelve Hellcats aboard the *Independence*. This landing operation was completed in fifteen minutes. The fighters were refuelled and rearmed, and took off from the carriers at 23:30. The four divisions then reformed, and were told to orbit base at 22,000 ft. At about 02:45 they were vectored out twenty miles on a course of 340° and told to orbit. At about 03:00, seeing heavy A/A fire from the Task Force, they turned and headed towards the ships at full speed. Blackburn saw two F4Us make runs on two Zekes and miss. He and his wingman, Lt. (jg) Doug Gutenkunst, started after the Zekes, who saw them and went into a steep dive. Blackburn followed the Zeke section leader, who did a right half roll at 8,000 ft. Blackburn pulled out at 6,000 ft. He saw the Zeke below him headed for a cloud three or four miles away. Blackburn closed from above, fired at about 500 yards, and missed. He closed to 300 yards, fired again, and saw smoke stream from the right wing. At this point the Zeke entered the cloud. Through gaps in the clouds Blackburn got in two more bursts, then his windshield fogged up and he broke off. At this point he was alone, his wingman having lost him.

Blackburn saw Kawasaki Ki 61 Tonys above him at 5,000 ft. (he was at 1,500 ft.), so he re-entered the cloud. One Tony followed, so Blackburn turned in the cloud and the Tony broke off. As Blackburn came out of the cloud he saw Roger Hedrick's and Mills Schanuel's F4Us on his port beam. Hedrick, mistaking Blackburn for an enemy, fired a short burst, then perceived his mistake and the three F4Us joined up. They swung around north of the Task Force, saw no A/A or enemy planes, and returned to Barakoma, being joined by Burriss over the Treasury Islands. All four landed at Barakoma at 04:40. Blackburn had shot down one Tony and damaged one Zeke.

On the first combat tour, the flight time per Fighting 17 pilot was an average of 100 hours, and they were ready for a well earned rest in Sydney, Australia, in December 1943.

They returned to action at the end of January based on Bougainville, and this time the combat was intense, as instead of the hunters, they became the hunted. Escorting bombers in daily raids to Rabaul, they encountered heavy anti-aircraft fire and were always outnumbered by enemy fighters. The Japanese knew when they were coming and how many, as they still had forces on Bougainville passing on the information to Rabaul. The primary task for Blackburn and the Fighting 17 was to protect the bombers. The first mission to Rabaul was on January 26, 1944, when Fighting 17 were assigned to cover SBD Dauntless dive bombers in a joint SBD and TBF Avenger bomber strike on Lakunai Airfield, New Britain. Fifty to sixty Japanese fighters were in the air around the target.

Twelve to fifteen Zekes were sighted over Rabaul, and these attacked the medium and low cover from 21,000 ft. Blackburn himself made contact as the formation was retiring from the target. He was at 4,000 ft. over the channel off Rapopo. He made a head-on run, scored hits on a Zeke's engine, made a quarter roll to the left and hit him in the left wing. The two planes crossed, and the Zeke dived out and went into the water off Matupi Island. Tom Blackburn was now an ace.

Due to pilot losses in the first few missions, Blackburn devised a new tactic called Roving High Cover. The purpose of Roving High Cover was to fly ahead of the bombers and break up the Japanese fighter attacks from above before they got to the bombers. He rotated the pilots so that they all had the chance to shoot some of the attacking fighters without having to worry about bombers. He could have taken this himself on each mission and amassed a high number of victories, but didn't. He shared this duty out so everyone got a chance at the enemy, which amply demonstrates the sort of leader he was. They called it the "Gravy Train."

On January 28, 1944, the first Roving High Cover mission was tried and was successful in a strike against Tobera Airfield. The score was 14.5 confirmed kills and four probables. This tactic not only saved a lot of Fighting 17 pilots, but also caused havoc among the Japanese, as their formations were disorganized and broken up before getting to the bombers. On January 30, 1944, Blackburn led the Roving High Cover and spotted twenty Zekes joining up over Simpson Harbor, Rabaul, at 20,000 ft. as the bombers were starting their runs. He came down on the second Zeke of the top pair in a beam attack ending astern and the Zeke exploded. Blackburn broke away and sighted two Zekes to the south starting runs on two Corsairs from 20,000 ft. Blackburn made a low side run on the second Zeke, hit it, and the Zeke went down in a diving spiral with Blackburn on his tail. The plane caught fire and the pilot bailed out. His shoulder straps must have burned through, as the parachute seat swung free. Blackburn recovered from his run and followed the bombers down the channel at 8,000 ft. There were many Japanese aircraft from 2,000 ft. to the 12,000 ft. cloud ceiling over Cape Gazelle. Blackburn made a high side run on a Zeke, hit him, and the Zeke spun.

As Blackburn and Doug Gutenkunst then swung back after the bombers they were attacked by ten or twelve Japanese. As he was climbing after a Zeke a Hamp got on his tail, but Blackburn took evasive action and eluded him. Blackburn pulled out over the SBD Dauntlesses and saw two Zekes at 5,000 ft. The leading Zeke broke away when Blackburn attacked, but he made a beam run on the second, scored hits, and left him smoking in a glide. He rejoined the SBDs and saw a Zeke heading for them at 7,000 ft., two miles astern. Blackburn swung back

Tom Blackburn flying in Lem Cooke's F4U-1A. The #29 aircraft later became famous as "Ike" Kepford's aircraft, but when the first tactical organization was introduced in the spring of 1943, Lem Cooke was allocated this aircraft. *Courtesy of the Tom Blackburn Collection*

and got a full deflection shot from below. He saw a flash of flame at the cockpit and stopped firing. The flame died out and Blackburn fired again. As he turned back towards the bombers the Zeke was in a 30° dive at 1,000 ft. Blackburn had scored two Zekes and three probables.

At the end of this mission Blackburn's wingman, Doug Gutenkunst, was killed in a mid-air collision. This hit Blackburn hard; for him, losing a pilot was like losing a son. He regarded all his pilots as his sons, and some, like Gutenkunst, had been with the squadron from the early days. Tom found losing pilots hard to handle, coupled with the stresses of combat flying. His next victories came on February 6, 1944, in a mission escorting B-25s against Lakunai Airfield. He and his division made the first attack on four of six Zekes who were over Rapopo and headed for the strike at 22,000 ft. He dived at 45° from 25,000 ft., fired from the five o'clock position, and the Zeke exploded. He recovered in a right chandelle to 23,000 ft. and saw a group of Japanese heading northwest after the bombers. Blackburn reformed his division and followed. Over Lakunai at 20,000 ft., the division jumped several Zekes who were climbing and heading south. Blackburn made a high side run from the left and saw the Zeke burn. Before he completed his recovery he made a pass at another Zeke and followed him down in a diving spin for about 4,000 ft. This was witnessed by his wingman, Lt. L. T. "Mac" McQuiston, who saw the plane burn. Blackburn recovered to the left in a tight climbing spiral to 2,000 ft. He picked up a group of Zekes and Hamps and pursued them to the north. He got in some bursts, and his wingman downed one Zeke. Blackburn again reformed his division, and the F4Us headed northeast after the bombers. They were attacked by a single Zeke without results, and shortly after saw four fighters climbing over Rabaul and heading towards them. Blackburn, unwilling to be sucked out of the main fight, kept on his course and pulled away from them.

As the division was above the clouds over Duke of York Island, they jumped eight or ten Zekes who were climbing for altitude. Blackburn caught one unaware and saw him smoke and pieces fly off. His section leader, Lt. (jg) Bobby Mims, had dropped back, and the other F4Us headed after him. The reformed division was pursued by four Zekes or Hamps, but climbed away from them at 160 knots. When they had gained altitude the Corsairs turned back. Two of the Japanese fighters had disappeared, and the other pair broke away in opposite directions. Blackburn followed one in a radical dive, but recovered in a right chandelle. He saw the Zeke turn sharply to the right and climb vertically, rolling at the top and pushing his nose to the level position; virtually a stalled out Immelmann, this roll-off-the-top maneuver was obviously intended to suck the F4Us into a disadvantageous position. Blackburn fired at long range and saw his tracers go into the Zeke but could observe no damage. He joined up with his division and sent his second section home because of oxygen shortage, which was needed for combat at high altitude. He and his wingman saw B-24 Liberators, a later strike retiring from the target. The B-24 escort (P-38 Lightnings) were chasing Zekes off the right flank. Blackburn headed for that melee, and en route he picked up a lone Hamp. The pilot apparently had relaxed from combat, lit a cigarette, and rested his feet on the instrument panel. Blackburn crawled up his tail and set him on fire. He and his wingman then headed home. Blackburn was credited with three Zekes, one Hamp, and two Zeke probables.

The last contact Fighting 17 had with the Japanese fighters was on February 19, 1944, when they shot down sixteen aircraft. Fighting 17 never saw enemy aircraft in the air again.

On March 7, 1944, Fighting 17 flew out of the combat area and headed for home as the highest scoring squadron in the Solomon Islands. Under Blackburn's leadership the squadron scored 152 confirmed victories. Despite this record score, they completed their primary objective of protecting the bombers, as no bomber was lost due to enemy air attack. No ship they covered was ever hit by bomb or aerial torpedo, and they also proved the Corsair could be operated off a carrier under combat conditions.

Blackburn had developed innovative combat tactics, and along with his ground crew, Vought Representatives, and "Butch" Davenport made many F4U design modifications which became production line standards. The F4U became standard on carriers later in the war, and even flew in the Korean War in ground attack operations.

One other development which is not so well known is that Fighting 17 experimented with carrying bombs on the Corsair. The Corsair was a superb fighter bomber, and squadrons were formed later in the war to carry rockets and bombs in this role.

Blackburn was convinced that the F4U Corsair was the best aircraft for the Navy and carrier aviation, and persevered with it when others did not. He proved the Corsair could be operated in combat from a carrier and worked his men hard to iron out the many problems with the early F4Us.

As Skipper of Fighting 17, Blackburn led by example: he had the most flying hours of anyone in the squadron on both combat tours. On the second tour he had the most days flown (21) and most combat sorties (26) completed, along with the most missions (17) to Rabaul. He also had the most combat hours (81.8). He was awarded the Navy Cross, Distinguished Flying Cross, and Air Medal with two Gold Stars, and led Fighting 17 to a Navy Unit Commendation. Upon his return to the States Blackburn undertook many tours and events to promote the Corsair. On April 27, 1944, he was promoted to Commander, and from May to April 1945 he was assigned to the Bureau of

Aeronautics, Military Requirements Division. One of his assignments was being temporarily attached to the Staff of Carrier Task Force 58 aboard the USS *Lexington* at the Battle of Leyte Gulf in October 1944.

In May 1945 Blackburn was made C.A.G. (Commander Air Group 74) of USS *Midway* and served there until September 1946.

Blackburn had various assignments with the Bureau of Aeronautics and as Executive Officer of USS *Saipan*, and was promoted to Captain on July 1, 1952. He studied at the Naval War College and was on the Joint Strategic Plans Group. His most challenging assignment was as Commanding Officer of the large carrier USS *Midway* (CVA-14) from May 1958 to May 1959.

His last duty assignment was as Commanding Officer of the U.S. Naval and Marine Corps Reserve Training Center, Alameda, CA. He retired with a total active service of thirty-three years, one month, and fifteen days on July 31, 1962.

His good friend Boone Guyton, Chief Experimental Test Pilot for Chance Vought, had this to say about Tom Blackburn in 1995:

"Our association began in 1938 when Lt. (jg) Blackburn arrived at our dive bombing squadron VB-5 in San Diego Naval Air Station, for duty. He had been in the Navy for two years after graduating from the Naval Academy at Annapolis, Maryland. I was an Aviation Cadet at the time, one of the first class of this new breed for the U.S. Navy, and had been in the squadron for two years.

From his day of arrival, we became firm friends, flew in the same three plane section, made several war gaming cruises on our carrier, the USS Lexington, and engaged in social activities about the Naval Air Station together. He was, at the time married and I was, by Naval decree, a bachelor.

Despite Tom being an academy graduate, and I, as a short time (four year tour of duty) cadet, there was no rank barrier between us. Tom was that way. Many regular officers carried a resentment of sorts toward cadets, as college intruders without the correct portfolio for a true Naval Officer. Tom cared nothing about displaying his rank over cadets. He associated

Tom Blackburn, Commander of Air Group 74 (center), relaxing with friends in 1945. *Courtesy of the Anderson Family*

freely with us and enjoyed our company at all times.

The chemistry between us was always good, and our friendship lasted for the next fifty - three years. I should add, that as Tom later acknowledged, after his retirement from the Navy as Captain, he was out of touch with many of us for some twenty years. He became a patron of the drinking class, had a divorce and several short marriages and spent much time off the beaten path, raising grapes for a winery in California.

When he finally married - to a lovely Navy widow who brought him around properly - our old relationship returned and we visited each other and kept in contact. His later years were spent in Jacksonville, Florida, while I continued to reside in Connecticut.

During our two years of active duty together in the squadron, Tom and I enjoyed cavorting, and competing in the air when we could measure off against each other. This occurred in simulated dog fighting, or simply using our training flights when occasion arose to roust about the countryside in southern California, land at times in oddball fields and enjoy life.

Tom was a dogged, persevering fighter pilot, always boring in and never quitting. Several times as our one - on - one mock combat continued, we would end up in a tail chasing dog fight, until with a tired arm or dizziness from high "G" turns I would pull out and wave - "enough!" Tom never once did. You will no doubt find from contacts with his war time squadron mates, he performed that way in combat.

He was a stern but fair disciplinarian, demanding regulation from subordinates if they became sloppy in attitude or execution. This was as I knew him during the pre WWII days. You should also check this with Jolly Rogers shipmates, for, despite contacts at our Vought - Sikorsky plant and my assistance visits with his squadron on the Corsair, as they prepared for deployment, I was not in combat with them.

I like to think it was my continual urging, in later years, that convinced Tom to write his fine book Jolly Rogers. You will note his foreword in mine, Whistling Death, what Tom acknowledged about our relationship.

Tom Blackburn was an exemplary military person from a family of Naval Officers. I need not comment on his war record. It was one of the finest in the Navy's war in the Pacific. There remains great camaraderie in the squadron as yet, with reunions continuing despite reduced participants due to the attrition of ageing. I suggest you contact his former Executive Officer Roger Hedrick, in case you have not done so. He was a close associate of Tom's during the war, and himself a fine Naval Officer."

In his retirement Tom faced another battle, this time with himself and alcohol addiction. He eventually overcame this battle, just as he did the Japanese at Rabaul. Tom married Jamie in 1983. Jamie had known Tom for years before and had attended squadron reunions with him. Tom died on March 21, 1994, aged 81, and he was interred in the Arlington National Cemetery.

In addition to the Navy Cross, Distinguished Flying Cross, and Air Medal with two Gold Stars, he was also awarded the Presidential Unit Citation (USS Santee), American Defense Service Medal with Fleet Clasp (VF-2, USS Lexington), American Campaign Medal, European-African-Middle Eastern Campaign Medal with one Star, Asiatic-Pacific Campaign Medal with three Stars, WWII Victory Medal, Navy Occupation Medal (Europe), and National Defense Service Medal. He had eleven confirmed, five probable, and three damaged Japanese aircraft to his credit.

During one of Fighting 17's reunions, fighter ace Danny Cunningham said that when Blackburn didn't make Admiral in the early 1960s he wrote a letter of complaint to President John F. Kennedy:

"I had all the respect and admiration in the world for Blackburn. I think our squadron was good because he trained the hell out of us. We had the best fighter plane and the best Skipper in WWII. That's why we were successful. It's like any other business. It starts from the top.

He was one of those guys that did it,
then said now do it. . . .
I respected that he led by example
which inspired confidence.

FIGHTER ACE DANNY CUNNINGHAM

The Skipper was absolutely great. He was one of those guys that did it, then said now do it. He was an eager beaver, tough as hell and when he gave an order you did it. I respected that he led by example which inspired confidence. I was very grateful to get into a squadron like that and fly the hog. We loved the plane. He had the most hours of flying in the whole squadron. Blackburn stressed tremendous amount of gunnery training. Overhead, high side, flat side runs. We got pretty damn good."

Top ace "Ike" Kepford remembered Tom Blackburn:

"I felt real strong about Tom. When I came to the squadron as an Ensign, I didn't know anything. But Blackburn taught me a lot fast. He was a fantastic Skipper."

"Butch" Davenport had fond memories of his Skipper:

"We were fortunate to have Blackburn as Skipper because he was a second generation Naval Officer who knew how to get things done. He knew what to say and where to go to get equipment and supplies the squadron needed. This made him invaluable. You can have the best pilots and airplanes in the world, but if you can't keep them flying, you aren't worth a damn. Blackburn kept us flying."

In response to Tom Blackburn's comments that Roger Hedrick was the best fighter pilot in the squadron, Hedrick had this to say:

"The character of the pilots we had resulted from the many hours Tom and I spent reviewing the performance of each of these fellows during training. We weeded out (got rid of) some that we felt didn't have what they now call "the right stuff." But I also recall some who we took along with us and were unable to keep going in combat, and that taught me that you cannot with any certainty predict a person's reaction to lengthy stress. I believe we all, all of us have our limits. Some are more fortunate than others, can keep going longer, but at some point in time I think we all would probably break.

Next is the realistic strenuous training program which one Tom Blackburn devised, and insisted, successfully, that the rest of us carry out. And this sure helped produce the pilots experienced and confident in their plane and in their own ability to handle it and get the job done.

We had a high morale due to the proceeding I just mentioned, as well as the faith we had in our own band of brothers, and our Skipper who was a gung - ho, extraordinarily capable fighter pilot, who while demanding much of us, led us into combat, and to what believe me what I think was the edge of hell and back, so very confidently and successfully, and in who doing so day after day, personally logged much more combat flight time than anyone else in the squadron.

I have nothing but the highest respect and admiration one individual can have for another. Throughout the year and half or whatever that we were together, both in Miami and later in Fighting 17, I have found that he was undoubtedly one of the greatest leaders of men I have ever had the privilege of working with.

There was only one best, and that was Tom. In any category you want to name, and that's why we had the morale and we were willing to follow him 'till we packed it in."

As Vice Admiral James Stockdale put it:

"If ever a man was tailor made to be an across the board role model and leader of men flying and fighting from ships at sea, it was Tommy Blackburn."

Opposite:
Squadron Commanding Officer Lt. Cdr. Tom Blackburn after his return from a successful raid on Rabaul in mid-February 1944. The squadron was then based on Bougainville. *Courtesy of the National Archives*

Howard McClain Burriss in flight gear, probably in the summer of 1942. *Courtesy of the Burriss Family*

2

HOWARD McCLAIN "MAC" BURRISS

7.5 VICTORIES

Howard McClain Burriss had two nicknames: "Mac" from his middle name, and the name with which he signed squadron photos; and "Teeth," which was his call sign in the squadron. His family remembers "Mac" having the nickname "Teeth" even before his military service, as he had "pearly choppers" and a disarming smile that made him popular with the ladies. Howard McClain Burriss was the son of Oliver Howard Burriss and Shirley (Slack) Burriss. His mother was a descendant of Charles Swan (1749 - 1832), who was a private in Captain William Crawford's Company, the 5th Battalion, Washington County Pennsylvania Militia, who fought in the American Revolution. McClain comes from his mother's maiden name, Dora McClain, which originated from the Clan McClain from Scotland.

His other Grandmother was Carrie Wright, first cousin to aviation pioneers Wilbur and Orville Wright.

"Mac" was born in Washington, DC, on March 28, 1921, but grew up in Granville, Ohio. He was the middle son and the twin of a girl who died at birth. When his father died the remaining family moved back in with his mother's family in Granville, Ohio. His father died on February 18, 1932, in Ohio, when Burriss was ten years old. This was a couple of years after an automobile accident in which his father suffered chest injuries. His father was an ex-professional baseball player for a team in Perovia, and was Accountant Clerk for the U.S. Government Interior Department and exempt from military service in WWI due to an old physical disability. He was discharged from the Navy due to this disability and was a musician while in the Navy.

Howard "Mac" Burriss and his brother Charles. *Courtesy of the Burriss Family*

Howard "Mac" Burriss as a boy with a new set of clothes and watch. *Courtesy of the Burriss Family*

With the Great Depression and the sudden death of her husband, "Mac's" mother moved in with her three boys with her parents, which made a household of seven and at times eight. "Mac" always told his mother that he was going to get her a home of her own again one day. His mother did indeed buy a home of her own with "Mac's" life insurance money, which she called "Mac's House" until she died in 1986. "Mac" was educated at Denison University and Butler University. He had a very good singing voice and played the trumpet in his band, as well as in a musical group in the Navy. He was adventurous and travelled abroad to youth hostels before the war, and was very much a leader in his group, socially and otherwise.

"Mac" enlisted for four years in the United States Naval Reserve as a Seaman Second Class on January 2, 1942, whilst a student at Denison University. It was noted he was "*Direct, sincere and determined.*" He was 5' 9" in height and built like a middleweight boxer when at age twenty years nine months he reported to the Naval Aviation Cadet Selection Board in Chicago on January 2, 1942. He reported to Naval Reserve Aviation Base, Chicago (Glenview), IL, on January 29, 1942, for elimination flight training. On March 15, 1942, he successfully completed his elimination flight training and was recommended for appointment as an Aviation Cadet. On March 19, 1942, he reported to Naval Reserve Aviation Base, Dallas, Texas. He transferred to

Howard "Mac" Burriss in his letterman's sweater with his sister-in-law, Valeria Wells Burriss. *Courtesy of the Burriss Family*

Student government at Granville High School. Howard "Mac" Burriss in letterman's sweater sitting at the end of the front row. *Courtesy of the Burriss Family*

N.A.S. Corpus Christi on April 11, 1942, to accept his appointment as an Aviation Cadet. He reported on April 14, 1942, and was appointed an Aviation Cadet on April 16, 1942.

On October 9, 1942, "Mac" accepted his appointment as an Ensign in the U.S. Naval Reserve, and on October 16, 1942, he reported to N.A.S. Miami, Florida, for flying training. "Mac" was ordered to report to the Carrier Qualification Training Unit at N.A.S. Norfolk, Virginia, on December 3, 1942, and on completion of this training on December 19, 1942, was assigned to Fighting 17 when it was commissioned on January 1, 1943.

After nine months familiarization training with Fighting 17 flying the new F4U Corsair, the squadron went into combat in the Solomon Islands, firstly based at Ondongo, and then Bougainville for their second tour. He was promoted to Lt. (jg) on October 1, 1943, just prior to going into combat.

One of the major engagements in the squadron's first tour was the Battle of the Solomon Sea on November 11, 1943. Fighting 17 was assigned to fly combat air patrol over the carriers USS *Bunker Hill*, *Essex*, and *Independence* while a strike went into Rabaul. The Japanese sent 100 planes to attack this Task Force as a retaliation for this strike.

"Mac" Burriss soon proved himself an exceptional fighter pilot. When they realized that the enemy attack had been launched, Lt. Johnny Kleinman and "Mac," flying in the second section of Tom Blackburn's division, turned back towards the Task Force with the other Corsairs. They were spiralling down, looking for enemy planes, and saw two Zekes at 10,000 ft, although they were too far away to attack. They went down to the water, and almost immediately "Mac" saw a Betty bomber pursued by a group of Hellcats. "Mac" turned abruptly to intercept, losing Kleinman in the process, and closed in on the Betty, getting in a long burst from seven o'clock level, and the Betty went into the water.

"Mac" pulled up to the left, saw Lem Cooke's Corsair at 3,000 ft, and joined up with

Opposite:
Howard "Mac" Burriss went to Butler College in Indiana, where this photo is believed to have been taken. *Courtesy of the Burriss Family*

'Mac' was 'One of the best'
a quick thinker and courageous.
He was so bright and resourceful
he could make it if anyone could."

"TIMMY" GILE

Howard "Mac" Burriss with his mother Shirley Slack Burriss at his graduation from N.A.S. Corpus Christi, Texas, in October 1942. His mother took a flight to see her son receive his wings. *Courtesy of the Burriss Family*

him. The pair spotted a Kate torpedo bomber making a run on a ship. Cooke and "Mac" each made two beam runs; Cooke broke them off, but "Mac" made another beam attack, chopped back on his throttle, and ran right up on the Kate's tail. At about 1,000 yards from the ship the Kate burst into flames and went into the water. "Mac" pulled up and saw another Kate heading north right on the water. "Mac" came down in a beam attack, and simultaneously a Hellcat made a beam attack from nine o'clock. The Kate struck the water and exploded. "Mac" then climbed to 6,000 ft but saw no enemy aircraft, so he joined up on "Timmy" Gile and, being low on fuel, they both headed for home. "Mac" was credited with a Betty bomber, a Kate torpedo bomber, and another Kate shared with another pilot. This was achieved while flying close to a U.S. Task Force and during intense anti-aircraft fire.

Howard "Mac" Burriss at Ford Island, Pearl Harbor, in September 1943, just prior to combat duty in the Solomon Islands. *Courtesy of the Burriss Family*

Following leave in Australia in December 1943 he returned to action at the end of January 1944.

His next score was on January 27, 1944, and despite being hit and badly damaged he managed to shoot down a Zeke before having to ditch into the sea. He was picked up shortly after and taken back to base. "Mac" and his wingman, Ensign "Andy" Jagger, were jumped by several Zekes just as bombers were running in to the target. "Mac's" aircraft was hit by two 20 mm cannon shells in the accessory section, but he dived down and got on the tail of a Zeke who jinked forward and down with "Mac" behind him, closing to fifty yards. "Mac" saw him catch fire and go down. Meanwhile, Jagger got on the tail of the Zeke who had shot at "Mac." In the meantime "Mac" was at full throttle, and Jagger did not join up until they were off Cape Gazelle. "Mac" found that his oil pressure, the life blood of a big radial engine such as the Corsair's Pratt & Whitney R2800, was dropping, and he limited his speed to 160 knots. The oil pressure finally dropped to zero and oil came out of his Hamilton Standard prop governer. He chopped back on the throttle and his prop stopped. All this time he was at 1,000 ft. He opened his canopy and prepared for a water landing. At 500 ft he lowered the flaps at 120 knots and levelled off at 10 ft. He skimmed in to land across an 8 ft swell. He got out of the cockpit and on to the wing without any trouble, and the Corsair sank almost immediately. His chute kept him afloat in a sitting position. "Mac" undid his harness and inflated his raft. Before going in he had called the Skipper, as had "Andy" Jagger, and three Marine aircraft circled him in his raft. Tom Blackburn arrived and circled until the Dumbo (called on Dane Base by Tom Killefer just as "Mac" went in) arrived and dropped a smoke bomb. He was rescued and picked up after almost an hour. When "Mac" was shot down he radioed to the skipper. "*Hello there 'Big Hog' one of your piglets is going down.*" "Timmy" Gile said that this was typical of "Mac" showing his fine spirit.

"Mac" was recommended for an award, and the citation in part stated:

> *"On 27 January he was escorting a flight of our bombers which was intercepted by sixty to eighty Jap fighters. He was hit by fire from a Zeke, but courageously remained at his post over the bombers and shot down one Zeke. His own plane was so badly damaged that he was forced to make a water landing while returning to base."*

"Mac" wrote to his girlfriend, Barbara Bjelke, on January 28, 1944, and gave an indication of how he was feeling:

> *"Well Barb, our plane finally up and quit on me. I'm living right now on a little borrowed time I figure - the Japs finally got next to me - three of them hopped me right over Rabaul. I got one and the other two got me - Barb III really had holes in her. I got her out to sea a little ways when all the oil was pumped out and the engine stopped - down I went - she went down in about 5 - 10 seconds but I got out and into my little rubber battleship. I've never felt*

so lonesome in my life - over 200 miles into Jap territory. Fortunately my wingman had stuck with me and he got my position. They sent up a Catalina with a big fighter cover and they found me eventually. Was that a beautiful sight when I saw them coming over the horizon. I wasn't banged up very bad - go up and try again tomorrow. Hope I get a Barb IV pretty soon - like to use my own plane. Barb III did all right by me though - if she'd quit much sooner I'd be writing this thru Red Cross from a concentration camp. They take some aviators prisoner I guess tho none of our boys has lived after being captured that we know of - well all in a day's work. We haven't had any mail since we've been here but I trust I'll have some when it gets in - anyhow I have some good snap shots of you to raise my morale with - the ones Addie sent - guess I don't rate a photograph - hint - but the ones I have are good - well getting dark and we have no lights so good luck - Love Mac."

Howard "Mac" Burriss had been dating Barbara Bjelke, whom he met while attending Denison University. She was a beauty queen, and was devastated when she heard he had been shot down. He named all his aircraft "Barb." She is pictured with the family dog, Ferdie. *Courtesy of the Burriss Family*

"Mac" named all his planes Barb after his girlfriend. He was assigned Corsair #30 from June 1943 as Lem Cooke's wingman, which stayed the same when he first went into combat at the end of October 1943.

On January 29, 1944, twenty Corsairs were assigned as cover for SBD Dauntlesses in a joint SBD - TBF strike on Tobera Airfield, New Britain.

The bombers went in at about 14,000 ft. The F4Us had an element at 15,000 ft, another at 16,000 ft, and two Corsairs, all that remained of a projected four aircraft cover, at 30,000 ft. "Mac" and "Ike" Kepford were assigned as Roving High Cover to break up the enemy aircraft before they got to the bombers.

As the formation was coming in, "Mac" and "Ike" spotted twelve Zekes below them at about 24,000 ft over Cape Gazelle. They climbed and dived down on the enemy. Working as a pair, with first one and then the other protecting the other's tail, they accounted for four Zekes apiece, with the whole action lasting about ten minutes. Their attacks were mostly high

Howard McClain "Mac" Burriss at Ondongo in November 1943. *Courtesy of the Burriss Family*

sides and overheads, with sharp chandelles to regain their height advantage between passes. The Japanese were apparently caught completely by surprise, and it is certain that their intended attack on the bombers was broken up.

Both Burriss and Kepford were recommended for the Navy Cross. Kepford was awarded the Navy Cross and Burriss the Silver Star. The citation in part for Burriss stated:

> *"With utter disregard for his own personal safety and with no heed for the numerical superiority of the enemy he pressed home his attacks to the limit and by superb marksmanship succeeded in shooting down four Zekes. His tireless devotion to duty, his extraordinary heroism in the face of numerically superior enemy forces, and his audacious airmanship were in keeping with the highest traditions of the United States Naval Service."*

"Mac's" final mission was on January 31, 1944, when sixteen F4Us were assigned as cover on the TBFs in a joint SBD - TBF strike on shipping in Keravia Harbor, New Britain. The Japanese attacked the bombers before they reached the target.

"Mac" and "Andy" Jagger, flying as a medium cover section at 14,000 ft, were hit by Zekes about four miles southeast of the target. They broke off and dived away. As they were over Kabanga Bay another Zeke made an attack on "Mac," whose aircraft was smoking heavily, and he was preparing to make another water landing. "Andy" turned in and drove the Zeke away, but in doing so lost sight of "Mac." He believed that "Mac" made a successful water landing, as when "Andy" last saw him "Mac" seemed to have his aircraft well under control.

"Mac" Burriss was listed as missing in action and was never seen again. "Timmy" Gile spoke to "Mac's" family when he returned from combat to the States:

They take some aviators prisoner
I guess tho none of our boys has lived
after being captured that we know of -
well all in a day's work

HOWARD McCLAIN"MAC" BURRISS

"His engine was hit - was smoking and flames came out but flames went out and 'Mac' glided as far as he could. 'Andy' Jagger was also hit but not so badly - was protecting 'Teeth' when they were attacked by another Jap and in getting the Jap 'Andy' lost sight of Mac.'

The Skipper watched and felt sure that he saw 'Mac' get out and into his rubber raft. The PBY went up and picked up another pilot but could find no trace of 'Mac' as 'Mac' was nearer the shore and too many Jap fighters came up so that he was afraid to go closer. The PBY pilot said he always felt that he should have gone farther up looking for 'Mac.'

'Mac' was 'One of the best' a quick thinker and courageous. He was so bright and resourceful he could make it if anyone could."

"Timmy" Gile was flying in the same formation and had been a very close friend of "Mac." "Mac" had flown five missions over Rabaul between January 26 and January 31, 1944, encountering enemy aircraft on each occasion.

Barbara Bjelke's youngest daughter Christine remembered her mother talking about her boyfriend:

"My mother confided in me about a boyfriend she loved very deeply, who went off to war and was killed. She was devastated. When he went off to war, he didn't ask her to wait for him, but she would have. Her father took her to San Francisco when she was eighteen to help her forget about him. Seven years ago, she took my sister Ingrid and me on a sentimental journey to San Francisco and we stayed at the St. Francis Hotel, where she and my grandfather had stayed.

My grandparents didn't really like Howard because he drove fast, came to the house and just honked the horn for my mother and he drank a lot. But mother adored him. When I went with her to her 40th college class reunion in Granville, she went to his grave and had a moment. She thought of him as the love of her life. After Howard died, his mother called my mother, Barbara, and scolded her for not waiting for Howard. My mother explained that he hadn't asked her to do so.

My mother grew up in Granville, Ohio and attended Denison University in Granville where they met. She was a beauty. She was the May Queen at Denison and she and her sisters were known as the Bjelke beauties in Granville."

"Mac" was recommended for an award on February 13, 1944, and part of the citation stated:

"His tireless devotion to duty, his extraordinary heroism in the face of numerically superior enemy forces and his audacious airmanship were in keeping with the highest traditions of the United States Naval Service."

"Mac" Burriss, in addition to the Silver Star, was also awarded the Distinguished Flying Cross, Purple Heart, Air Medal, Navy Unit Commendation, Asiatic - Pacific Area Campaign Medal with two Bronze Stars, and the World War II Victory Medal.

OPPOSITE:
Skull and Crossbones ace "Teeth" Burriss, who scored 7.5 Japanese aircraft whilst flying with Fighting 17. "Teeth" was his radio call sign. This photo is of Burriss in Bobby Mims' aircraft at Bougainville in January 1944 and not his own aircraft, as stated in my book *The Skull and Crossbones Squadron. US Naval Historical Center / M W "Butch" Davenport Collection*

Oscar Ivan Chenoweth, Jr., at Bougainville in February 1944. He shot down a Zeke with VF-38, then added another 7.5 victories with Fighting 17. *Courtesy of the National Archives*

3

OSCAR IVAN "OC" CHENOWETH JR.

8.5 VICTORIES

Oscar Ivan Chenoweth, Jr., was born in Salem, Oregon, on July 16, 1917, the son of Oscar Ivan Chenoweth and Gertrude Mae (Pollow) Chenoweth. His father was a Major in the U.S. Army who served in World War I and World War II. He had a brother Weldon Chenoweth who died as a baby, a brother Gerald Robert Chenoweth, Lt. (jg) U.S. Navy, who died on January 26, 1943, and a brother John D. Chenoweth who died in 2009. Oscar's dad was a Public School Teacher in Dallas, Oregon, in 1920, and was then a Fieldsman for Nestle' food in McMinnville, Oregon, in 1930.

The family had moved to McMinnville, Oregon, and "Oc" graduated from high school in 1935. John Chenoweth remembers his brother:

> *"He was a bit reckless as a teenager, tried the unusual sometimes to limits, brought home lost dogs, had more than one girlfriend yet was responsible for his age. For example he drove a new car home from the factory, some 2000 miles well before modern highways, when only 15."*

"Oc" went to Oregon State University, and on April 5, 1937, he enlisted in the Oregon National Guard in McMinnville, Oregon. He was discharged with an excellent character reference on June 9, 1938. He graduated from Oregon State with a Degree in Engineering in 1939. He began his Naval service on October 15, 1940, and became an Aviation Cadet at N.A.S. Miami on December 23, 1940, and also served at Pensacola. On June 30, 1941, he was commissioned as an Ensign, and in July 1942 reported to N.A.S. Miami as a Flight Instructor. It was a very busy time for "Oc": he married Ruth Shelley on May 30, 1942, and became a Lt. (jg) on June 15, 1942. He then reported to Fleet Air Wing, West Coast, and Fighting Squadron Twelve as Material Officer in November 1942. He then joined Escort Scouting Squadron Twenty One as Executive Officer, where he was promoted to Lt. on January 1, 1943. On June 15, 1943, he reported to Fighting Squadron Thirty Eight as Executive Officer, Flying F6F-3 Hellcats out of Segi Strip on Munda. He scored one victory, a Zeke shot down five miles northwest of Ballale Island, in September 1943. His first combat tour ended three months later. Whilst on rest and recreation some time after the Attu Campaign he ran into Tom Blackburn, who he knew from Opa Locka, part of N.A.S. Miami, where they were both Flight Instructors. That's how he came to be with Fighting 17. On January 5, 1944, he reported to Fighting Squadron Seventeen as Operations Officer. He named his planes "Ruthless" after his wife Ruth, took over Lem Cooke's aircraft when he joined the squadron, and he was soon into action. On January 27, 1944, he was assigned as cover for two B-25 Mitchell squadrons on a strike to Lakunai Airfield, New Britain. When leading the second section of a division in the medium cover, "Oc" was weaving 2,000 ft over the bombers on their retirement when he saw six Zekes diving down from the vicinity of Rapopo. The leader made a run on Chenoweth's wingman, Ensign Jimmy Dixon, but did not fire. Tracers went by his wings, so "Oc" Split-S'd to the left and picked the Zeke up on the turn. Both were on their backs, and Chenoweth, firing from almost dead astern, saw his bullets smoke the Zeke. Chenoweth then kicked up to the right to avoid the Royal New Zealand Air Force P-40s who were the low cover. He saw the Zeke go into the water off Praed Point. "Oc" was credited with a Zeke destroyed.

Lt. Oscar Chenoweth (left) gives his account of a Fighting 17 attack to Lt. Basil Duke Henning, Air Intelligence Officer at Piva Airstrip, Bougainville. Lt. (jg) Earle C. Peterson (center) listens in. The squadron shot down sixteen of twenty-seven aircraft on this strike to Rabaul. *Courtesy of the National Archives*

His next engagement with the Japanese was on January 29, 1944, when he was assigned as cover for the SBD Dauntlesses in a joint SBD - TBF Avenger strike on Tobera Airfield, New Britain.

"Oc" and his wingman Jimmy Dixon followed the last division of SBDs down in their dive and levelled out at 4,000 ft as they retired. As they were crossing over the coastline they saw a lone Zeke trying to sneak up under the SBDs. "Oc" and Dixon made a section run on this Zeke as he tried to pull around into them. "Oc" fired first and saw his bullets hit. Dixon was firing by the time "Oc" had stopped, and put a second burst into him. The Zeke passed them on an almost opposite course. He was smoking and his left wing was dropping as he went into a cloud and was diving at a 45° angle. "Oc" was given credit for a Zeke probable.

Opposite:
L-R: Jimmy Dixon (sitting on jeep), Dan Cunningham, and "Oc" Chenoweth at Bougainville in 1944. *Courtesy of Vought*

He was a bit reckless as a teenager,
tried the unusual sometimes to limits,
brought home lost dogs,
had more than one girlfriend
yet was responsible for his age.

JOHN CHENOWETH

On January 30, 1944, "Oc" was part of the cover for a joint SBD - TBF strike on shipping in Simpson Harbor, Rabaul. "Oc's" division came in at about 24,000 ft and made contact with four Zekes slightly below them. All four Zekes dived away before the Corsairs could get at them. The division scissored down to 12,000 ft over the bombers, where five or six more Zekes were sighted. "Oc" and Dixon made a head-on section attack as one Zeke turned into them. The Zeke exploded. "Oc" then turned behind another Zeke and opened fire at 200 yards. It began to smoke heavily and went into a dive. The pilot bailed out, but his chute was set on fire by his own burning aircraft and he plummeted down. "Oc" turned left to pick up Dixon, and as he did so a Zeke pulled up dead ahead of him. The Zeke was very slow, so "Oc" was able to get in a heavy five second burst and the Zeke exploded. Chenoweth was credited with 2.5 Zekes on this mission, and was credited with another Zeke probable over Cape Tawui, New Britain, on February 3, 1944.

On February 9, 1944, twenty-two Corsairs were assigned as cover for the TBFs in a joint SBD - TBF strike on Vunakanau Airfield.

"Oc's" division was flying high cover and rounded a cloud over the target, dropping down from 18,000 ft to 8,000 ft, and waited for the Avengers to come across Kabanga Bay on the way to the rally point. The main body of TBFs passed by and the Corsairs circled, waiting for stragglers. "Oc" looked down to see three or four Zekes at 3-4,000 ft about 1½ miles behind the bombers. The Zekes were in a dive, looking to set up into position for stern attacks from below. "Oc" pushed over and fired on the leading Zeke from 2,000 ft to 300 ft and scored a number of hits. He overran and pulled away to the left. The Zeke pulled away to the left and Dan Cunningham, who was leading the second section, got another burst into him. The Zeke went into a flat spin and crashed. The third Zeke then fired on "Oc's" number four man, Ensign Lou Fitzgerald, and he broke away. The division reformed, and "Oc" turned into another Zeke low on the water who was making a beam attack on the TBFs. The Zeke turned away, and "Oc" and his wingman, Jimmy Dixon, chased him. This proved to be a mistake, as they both were jumped by Zekes, and only by violent evasive action were they able to escape without injury. The confirmed Zeke victory on this day made "Oc" Chenoweth an ace.

Chenoweth's last engagement with the Japanese came on February 19, 1944, when he and his wingman, Dan Cunningham, were assigned as Roving High Cover on a joint Dauntless and Avenger strike on Lakunai Airfield.

"Oc" and Danny were the only Corsairs on Roving High Cover to complete the mission. They arrived over the target area at 30,000 ft about twenty minutes before the bombers were due. They circled, letting down to 24,000 ft, when they saw six to eight Japanese fighters over St. George's Channel at 18,000 ft. "Oc" made an attack on a Zeke with Cunningham on his wing. "Oc" followed the Zeke down to 12,000 ft with Danny overhead at 18,000 ft as cover. He saw the Zeke crash on Cape Gazelle and then climbed to rejoin Cunningham. Their section made a second attack. "Oc" overshot, but as the Zeke pulled up he was an easy target for his covering wingman, so Dan Cunningham set the Zeke ablaze. They both rejoined into section formation and headed westward over Blanche Bay, where they spotted Zekes below them on the same course, and this time Dan Cunningham shot one down. In the recovery from the attack "Oc" and Danny were separated. However, "Oc" spotted a lone Zeke and made a stern attack. Unfortunately, as only one of his guns was firing the Zeke got away. "Oc" turned away, rechecked his guns, got them working, and headed straight for a group of Zekes loitering at 10,000 ft over the TBFs and SBDs between Duke of York Island and Rabaul. "Oc" made a stern attack and the Zeke caught fire, with its pilot bailing out at 4,000 ft. "Oc" then went back to Cape Gazelle and saw some more Japanese fighters low over the water attempting to sneak in on the retiring bombers. He turned into a pair (believed to be Tojos) and, keeping above them, the wingman rolled away in a desperate attempt to escape the Corsair's guns and did a "Split-S" manuever and went straight into the sea, an aerial

"Oc" Chenoweth at Bougainville in February or March 1944. He was credited with 8.5 Japanese aircraft destroyed in aerial combat, all but one with Fighting 17 in the Central Solomons in January and February 1944. *US Naval Historical Center / M W "Butch" Davenport Collection*

victory for "Oc" without even firing a shot. He then joined the cover on the SBDs.

Between January 27 and February 28, 1944, "Oc" Chenoweth flew twenty-nine combat sorties, of which fifteen were escort missions or fighter sweeps over the Rabaul area. He encountered enemy aircraft on ten of these missions and flew 72.3 hours of combat up to February 21, 1944.

He returned to the U.S. in May 1944 an ace with 8.5 victories. He was assigned to Naval Air Operational Training Command from June 19, 1944, to June 30, 1944, and then reported to N.A.S. Miami in November 1944 and served as a Flight Instructor until October 1945. He was promoted to Lt. Cdr. on October 3, 1945.

His other assignments were as Flight Deck Officer and Assistant Air Officer on the USS *Midway*, Executive Officer of VF-42, Commanding Officer of VA-44, and was later in the second class of test pilots to graduate from the Naval Air Test Center at Patuxent River, Maryland.

He then served as Assistant Operations Officer on the Staff of Commander Second Fleet and Executive Officer of VC-9. "Oc" retired from the Navy as a Commander on April 1, 1954.

After his service career Chenoweth worked for his grandfather Robert Shelley in self levelling dispensers. He then left to go to Dallas and work for Chance Vought in government sales. John Glenn was a friend of "Oc's," and they had dinner together just before the announcement of the first seven American Mercury Astronauts. "Oc" then worked as a Sales Representative doing service equipment sales, and also helped various companies increase their business. He had just started working with John Andrews, who was developing a salt water ice machine, when he died of a heart attack on May 19, 1968. He left a wife Ruth and three children: Janet, Gayle, and Oscar III.

In addition to the Silver Star, Distinguished Flying Cross, and Air Medal with two Gold Stars, he was also awarded the American Defense Service Medal, American Campaign Medal, Asiatic-Pacific Campaign Medal, World War II Victory Medal, and National Defense Service Medal.

Paul Cordray from Texas shot down six Japanese aircraft while serving with Fighting 17. He scored another with VBF-10 when he destroyed a Zeke on April 16, 1945, near Kikai Airfield, Japan. *Courtesy of the National Archives*

4

PAUL CORDRAY

7 VICTORIES

Paul Cordray was born in Grand Prairie, Texas, on September 4, 1919, along with a twin sister Pauline to Hurley S. Cordray and Jessie Mae (Holland) Cordray. He had an older brother John who was born on January 27, 1917, a sister Sue born in 1931, and a younger brother Don born in 1939. His father died in 1943 whilst Paul was in the Pacific. He spent his younger years on a farm, where one year he raised a prize pig. The family moved to Dallas, Texas, in 1929. Paul was educated at Winnetha Grade School and graduated from Sunset High School in 1937. He was interested in sports, and played football and basketball during his time at Sunset High. He was the Right End on their varsity football team, but was more noted for his basketball skills, for which he received a scholarship to East Texas State, Commerce, Texas, where he attended for two years. Paul enlisted in the Navy in Dallas in January 1942 and graduated from N.A.S. Corpus Christi, Texas, in August 1942. He was assigned to Fighting 17 at N.A.S. Norfolk in early 1943.

He was assigned Corsair #23 from June 1943, and also when he first went into combat at the end of October 1943 as section leader in "Timmy" Gile's division. This changed when "Andy" Anderson was shot down in November 1943 and Paul was assigned #19 as section leader in Roger Hedrick's division; he stayed there until Fighting 17 left the combat area.

Paul went into combat with Fighting 17 in November 1943. He first engaged the Japanese while on station over Empress Augusta Bay, Bougainville, on November 8, 1943, and was given credit for a Zeke damaged. He scored again with a damaged Zeke on November 11, 1943, in the Battle of the Solomon Sea.

Paul's first confirmed aerial victory came on November 17, 1943, whilst he was assigned to fly cover over U.S. shipping over Empress Augusta Bay. After hearing the ships were under attack Fighting 17 engaged the Japanese. As part of Roger Hedrick's second division flight with "Timmy" Gile and Dan Cunningham, Paul, together with Brad Baker, broke right to attack five Kate bombers and five Ki-61 Tonys. Gile got on the tail of a Kate low on the water, who eluded him in a climbing turn. Paul and Baker followed this Kate and Paul, in a stern attack, opened fire on the Kate, which then exploded.

The division then climbed to 12,000 ft about ten miles north of Cape Torokina. At this time they saw the bombers returning from the Buka strike. Five minutes later they saw a group of ten Tonys and Zekes at 8,000 ft, proceeding NNE over Point Tosair. The division crossed above the Japanese and went down to attack from the starboard side. Paul tried a full deflection shot at a Tony and missed. He then climbed and looked for Baker, but could not find him.* Paul continued his climb in three circles with two Tonys climbing inside him. At 10,000 ft the Tonys broke away to the right, so Paul reversed and got on the tail of the rear Tony, then opened fire with a short burst. The Tony began to burn and exploded when it hit the water.

The other Tonys had disappeared, so Paul climbed and headed north. He joined up with two Marine Corsairs and saw Zekes heading NW. This mixed Fighting 17 and Marine flight gave chase, but could not overtake the Zekes. They gave up the chase, but then saw three Tonys low on the water heading north, about 45 miles NW of Cape Torokina. The three Corsairs made individual attacks. Paul got on the tail of a Tony which took violent evasive action, making four flipper turns to the right. After the fourth turn he was able to close to 200 yards, from where he fired, and the Tony crashed into the water. He then rejoined the two Marines and proceeded to the Shortland Islands, from where he broke off and then returned to Ondongo.

Paul Cordray aged about eleven years old in Dallas, Texas. His family moved there from Grand Prairie, Texas, in 1929. *Courtesy of John Cordray*

*Baker was never seen again. Paul wrote home about the loss of his friend Brad Baker and was devastated by it, quoting "*One minute he was there the next he was not!*"

Leading Japanese fighter ace Tetsuo Iwamoto took part in the action at Empress Augusta Bay on this day, although it has not been possible to confirm beyond doubt that he was in combat with Brad Baker.

Paul was credited with shooting down two Tonys, his first confirmed victories, and this concluded his scoring for his first tour of combat.

After a much needed rest in Australia, Paul and Fighting 17 returned to combat at the end of January 1944.

OPPOSITE:
Paul Cordray as a young Ensign in 1942. This photo was probably taken at N.A.S. Corpus Christi, where he took his flight training. *Courtesy of John Cordray*

He also told of having to fly through the bullets from a machine gun that was pointed straight up by a ground gunner.

JOHN CORDRAY

His first mission of the second tour was on January 26, 1944, to cover the Dauntlesses in the joint Dauntless and Avenger strike on Lakunai Airfield, New Britain.

Paul was leading the second division in Roger Hedrick's flight and spotted enemy fighters diving to attack the formation. As the Zekes came down he just missed the target on a stern attack and saw a Zeke hit his wingman, Lt. (jg) James Miller. Miller spun but recovered, and then he and Paul scissored down to 6,000 ft. As they were following the SBDs and TBFs to the rally point (five miles east of Cape Gazelle), they spotted eight more Zekes to the south of the bomber formation. Paul got on the tail of one Zeke and gave him a long burst, but then pulled up in a sharp turn and lost sight of the Zeke. Another pilot who observed the action saw the Zeke crash in flames. Immediately after this Paul got a head-on shot at another Zeke, but could not estimate the damage inflicted. He was then joined by Miller and they went home with the SBDs.

Paul Cordray on the wing of #19. He took this number after "Andy" Anderson was shot down in November 1943. *Robert Lawson Photograph Collection, National Museum of Naval Aviation / US Navy photo*

Paul was credited with one Zeke confirmed and one damaged.

On January 28, 1944, Paul was again flying cover, this time for the Avengers in a joint SBD - TBF strike on Tobera Airfield, New Britain.

The high cover approached the target area at 30,000 ft. As the bombers made their attack Roger Hedrick saw Zekes coming in from seaward. There were twelve Zekes at about 24,000 ft. in a loose column, breaking off separately and making attacks in formation. Hedrick's flight of six aircraft came down on the Japanese in column and Hedrick made four passes. After his third pass a Zeke got on his tail and Hedrick zoomed up. Just as the Zeke appeared to be stalling out, Paul came up behind him and fired a long burst, making the Zeke catch fire and fall away. Paul and his wingman lost Hedrick as they recovered from this attack. After several passes Paul then saw a Zeke 300 ft. below him, so he set up for a beam attack, closing in to very close range and firing. Pieces flew from the Zeke, which caught fire and went down. James Miller, Paul's wingman, stayed with him throughout the action. A Zeke made a high side attack on Paul, so Miller turned in on a head-on shot and saw pieces fly from the Zeke's engine. The pair then dived down on five Zekes, each taking one. Miller's Zeke rolled away, but he got in a deflection shot from astern, seeing his tracers going into the Zeke's belly, which then blew up. Paul then made his run on his second Zeke with Miller on his wing, and the pair rejoined the bombers and headed back to base.

Paul scored two confirmed Zekes destroyed that day, which made him an ace with six victories.

On February 18, 1944, Fighting 17 were assigned as low and medium cover on a B-24 Liberator strike on Vunakanau Airfield.

Paul Cordray and Earl May were flying second section in "Timmy" Gile's division. Eight Zekes were spotted, and as "Timmy" attacked, Paul and Earl went with him in beam high side attacks. Earl missed, but Paul sent a Zeke spinning down, smoking and out of control. The pair then headed towards Vunakanau and got in a running fight with eight Zekes. As they made a section run, three

Zekes jumped Paul, who dived down below a layer of clouds at 16,000 ft. Earl called Paul to zoom up through the cloud so that he (May) would shoot the Zekes off his tail. Paul did not hear and continued his dive. Having finally eluded the three Zekes by diving to the deck he made for home. Paul scored a Zeke probable, which concluded his scoring with Fighting 17.

For the first tour Cordray flew 149 hours of combat. The second tour comprised 46 hours of combat with thirteen sorties in fifteen days, including twelve to "Fortress Rabaul."

In his time with Fighting 17 Paul Cordray was recommended for the following awards:

30 December 1943
Recommendation for the Distinguished Flying Cross:

> *"Between 27 October and 1 December 1943, Lt. (jg) Cordray flew forty six (46) sorties, flying one hundred forty-nine (149) combat hours. He participated in seven (7) strafing missions against enemy shipping and shore installations, three (3) of these missions being in the face of particularly intense anti-aircraft fire. He engaged enemy aircraft on 1, 8, 11, and 17 November. On November 8th he and his wingman engaged twenty-two (22) Zekes over Empress Augusta Bay, Bougainville, destroying one (1) and damaging one (1). On 11 November his division was the first to intercept the enemy attack on Task Force 50.3. On 17 November, in an action with twenty-nine (29) enemy planes over Empress Augusta Bay, he shot down one (1) Kate and two (2) Tonys.2*

Suggested Citation:

> *"For meritorious achievement while participating in aerial flights against the enemy in the Solomon Islands area during the period of 27 October through 1 December 1943. In an action over Empress Augusta Bay, Bougainville, on 8 November 1943, he and his wingman attacked twenty-two (22) Zekes destroying one (1) and damaging (1). In addition to the above engagement he fought in three (3) other actions against enemy aircraft, on 1, 11, and 17 November 1943, and participated in twenty-eight (28) patrols, eleven (11) escort missions, and seven (7) strafing missions, meeting heavy concentrations of enemy anti-aircraft fire on three (3) occasions. In thirty six (36) days he flew forty three (43) sorties, a total of one hundred forty-nine (149) hours of combat flying. This tireless devotion to duty, his great courage in the face of numerically superior enemy forces, and his skilful marksmanship were in keeping with the highest traditions of the United States Naval Service."*

J.T. Blackburn

14 March 1944

Recommendation for Gold star in lieu of Second Distinguished Flying Cross.

> *"Between 26 January and 7 March 1944, during which time he was based at Piva Yoke, Bougainville, Lt. (jg) Cordray, as division leader, flew twenty-seven (27) combat sorties, seventeen (17) of which were escort missions or fighter sweeps over the Rabaul area. He encountered enemy aircraft on ten (10) occasions: on 26, 28, and 30 January and on 4, 7, 9, 13, 17, 18, and 19 February. On 26 January, while escorting SBD's in a strike on Lakunai Airfield, his formation was intercepted by fifty (50) or (60) enemy fighters. In the action which ensued he shot down one (1) Zeke and damaged another. On 28 January the TBF's which he was escorting were aggressively intercepted by fifty (50) to seventy (70) enemy fighters. Despite the numerical superiority of the enemy he made repeated attacks and succeeded in destroying two (2) Zekes. On 18 February, while flying high cover on a B-24 strike on Vunakanau Airfield, his flight succeeded in disorganizing the enemy interception and he himself probably destroyed one (1) Zeke."*

conspicuous gallantry and intrepidity
in action while participating
in aerial flights against the enemy

SUGGESTED CITATION

Paul Cordray, Brother Don, Grandma Holland, and Uncle Wiley Holland in 1941. *Courtesy of John Cordray*

Suggested Citation

"For conspicuous gallantry and intrepidity in action while participating in aerial flights against the enemy in the New Britain theatre. As division leader he flew twenty-seven (27) combat sorties, seventeen (17) of which were escort missions or fighter sweeps over the Rabaul area, and on ten (10) of these missions he encountered enemy aircraft. While escorting a bomber strike on 26 January, his formation was intercepted by over fifty (50) enemy fighters. In the ensuing action he shot down one (1) Zeke and severely damaged another. On 28 January he was again escorting bombers when some seventy (70) enemy fighters made a determined attack on the formation, however, he led his division in repeated assaults on the enemy and in so doing he destroyed two (2) Zekes. Again on 18 February while providing cover for the bombers he and his division succeeded in disorganizing an enemy interception of the bombers, and in so doing he probably destroyed one (1) Zeke. His outstanding leadership which made his division a formidable one under all circumstances, his

OPPOSITE:
Paul Cordray enlisted in the U.S. Navy in his home town of Dallas, Texas, in January 1942. He is pictured here in his flight gear. *Courtesy of John Cordray*

Paul Cordray and his wife Mary Lou, daughter Gayle, and sons Mark, Gary, and Paul Jr. in 1961. *Courtesy of John Cordray*

> *never failing devotion to duty, and his flaming courage in the face of numerically superior and advantageously positioned forces were in keeping with the highest traditions of the United States Naval Service."*

Paul Cordray ended his time with Fighting 17 with six confirmed, one probable, and three damaged Japanese aircraft. He sent several letters home to his brother John, who relates:

> *"I received several letters from him during his first tour. He wrote about combat in its most frightening form. He told about facing a Zero head on and firing all his guns. He didn't say but one can only imagine his feelings as he flew through the debris after the Zero disintigrated.*
>
> *He also told of having to fly through the bullets from a machine gun that was pointed straight up by a ground gunner. He wrote that his worst experience was losing his wingman Brad Baker in combat, a dear friend. He also told me later about his second tour and the difference.*
>
> *In 1944 he came home on a thirty day leave from the Pacific. He was an ace and a hero. One of the first to return home and you*

can easily imagine the attention he received. He was asked to speak on numerous occasions. I asked him later just what he had to say. He said "I just ask for their questions."

I heard that while on leave he asked to date a "good girl." A dear friend introduced him to Mary and there must have been a whirlwind courtship because he went back to the Pacific married.

He married Mary Lou Cain on April 21, 1944 and he couldn't have been back in the States a matter of a couple of weeks before getting married."

Paul was one of a number of Fighting 17 pilots who was assigned to N.A.A.S. Green Cove Springs as a Flight Instructor after his return from his combat tour in April 1944.

Paul was then assigned to VBF-10 flying F4U-1Ds from the USS *Intrepid*. He was recommended for the Distinguished Flying Cross on April 4, 1945, whilst serving as Flight Leader on a carrier based fighter sweep of twelve aircraft in attacks upon the island of Ishigaki. He first led the attack to Niyara airfield, where five 500lb bomb hits were scored: two in the barracks area and three on runways. The flight then attacked seven ships in the seaplane base harbor in strafing runs, leaving one ship burning badly. A final attack was made on Ishigaki Airfield, where seven grounded twin-engined aircraft were strafed, destroying one and probably destroying three others. Intense anti-aircraft fire was encountered over all three targets. His last victory came when he destroyed a Zeke on April 16, 1945, after a fighter sweep was made over southern Kyushu on airfields near Kokubu and a target combat air patrol was flown over Okinawa. The aircraft were apparently kamikazes heading for the U.S. Task Force.

Paul took over the duties of Chief Flight Officer on August 16, 1945, and was detached at Alameda on November 15, 1945.

After the war he left the Navy and joined his old school buddy, Ed Gibson, and they both became Manufacturers Representatives.

Paul Cordray died of a heart attack on October 20, 1963, when he was only was 44 years old. He left a wife Mary Lou and four children, Paul Jr., Mark, Gary, and Gayle.

In addition to the Distinguished Flying Cross with two Stars and Air Medal with three Stars, Paul was also awarded the Asiatic - Pacific Campaign Medal with four Gold Stars, Navy Unit Commendation, and WWII Victory Medal.

He was an ace and a hero.

Chicago's Pride - Dan Cunningham, winner of the Navy Cross for shooting down four Japanese planes in one day on February 19, 1944. *Courtesy of the National Archives*

5

DANIEL GERALD CUNNINGHAM

7 VICTORIES

Daniel Gerald Cunningham was born on July 3, 1919, in Chicago, Illinois. His mother was an opera singer and artist, and his father was a veterinarian. All his brothers, Ed, Ray, and Tom, served in WWII.

Dan loved sports, particularly baseball, and he was a fan of the Chicago Cubs. He also loved ice hockey and was proud to have been a stick boy for the Chicago Blackhawks.

After graduating from Loyola University in 1940 with a Bachelor of Science in Economics he was employed by a newspaper publisher's association prior to enlisting in the Navy in January 1942. Dan received his wings, and after completing his training joined Fighting 17 early in 1943. His daughter Kimberley remembers him saying:

> *"He was worried about the job they would assign him - when he filled out a form for job preference - he listed - 1- fighter pilot, 2 - fighter pilot, and 3 - fighter pilot. He figured they might assign him to something completely different, just to spite him."*

The short and stocky Dan Cunningham had some real problems with the first F4U-1 Corsairs. He relates the story:

> *"With the old birdcages I couldn't see out they were so damn low. I used to bring out three parachute cushions. I put two on the seat which would lift me high enough up so I could see, but then my legs weren't long enough to give a full kick on the rudders. So I had to put one behind my back to push me forward to do that. The Skipper I think was getting ready to bounce me as I was too short and I said I'll prove it to you. So he*

Dan Cunningham as a young man in Chicago in the early 1940s. *Courtesy of George R Edwards*

said tomorrow morning we'll check out. I said okay.

I get in and set myself up with the cushions and he was standing on the wing. He said give full right rudder and full brake. I did that. Full left rudder and full brake. He kept doing that and I said see I can do it. He said as long as the cushions hold out you're alright. But without them you're lost. I said no question!

I finally said for crissake give me a chance Skipper and I'll show you. He was still shaking his head when he walked away. I didn't know then whether I was getting bounced or not. By the time we get into combat and flying in that F4U-1A bubble canopy, I'm sitting as high as anybody. He said later he was glad he didn't bounce me."

Dan would repay the Skipper's faith in him when he went into combat.

He was assigned Corsair #22 as "Timmy" Gile's wingman from June 1943, which stayed the same when he first went into combat at the end of October 1943.

He was then assigned to "Ike" Kepford's division as a section leader, and at the end of the tour flew Corsair #15 with Lou Fitzgerald as his wingman.

Dan first went into combat with Fighting 17 in November 1943 and scored his first victory on November 8, 1943. He recalls his first victory:

"On the way home we ran into a stray and got him and joined back up and one time I think I was with Paul (Cordray) and Paul made a run on him and he thought he was smoking. I blasted him, but I wasn't sure I got him either. So we stayed there and watched him go into the water. I said to Paul. "What do you want to do, Share him." He said. "No it's yours." I think that was my first one. As a wingman you don't get a lot of shots. If you are a section or a division leader you get a hell of a lot more shots.

Paul and I were flying one time and he said turn left Danny. I said alright and I went left and Hell, here I was going farther left, and here's a guy coming up our ass. What he wanted me to do was to draw him out then Paul would come around and shoot his ass down. But in the meantime he was using me as a clay pigeon, the son of a gun, because if I get too far this guy could get up my ass before Paul could get him. Finally he called me and said he's broke off Danny come on back. I said okay I don't like this because of being the clay pigeon.

Combat lasts about a split second long. If you don't get them and you try and look for them, there aint nobody there. It just happens so fast and is over so quick. It's usually real fast action, then you're the hell out of there."

After some time on leave in Australia with Fighting 17, Danny returned to combat at the end of January 1944.

On January 27, 1944, Fighting 17 was assigned as cover on one of two B-25 squadrons striking Lakunai Airfield, New Britain. Between sixty and seventy Japanese fighters intercepted the strike.

"Ike" Kepford was leading the second division of the high cover and was jumped on the first attack. He then attacked the Zekes, scoring one for himself. Dan also got one, as did Ensign Don McQueen.

Dan and Lou Fitzgerald were attacked by a Zeke from astern and Split - S'd away. They used full power and got over the bombers at the rally point. On the return they saw a flight south of Cape St. George. They headed toward it, and then Dan saw a single Zeke below him, so he made a high side attack on the Zeke, which rolled over smoking with its prop windmilling and went into the water. Cunningham and Fitzgerald then rejoined the bombers. Danny was credited with two confirmed Zekes on this mission.

Dan describes what it was like in intense combat over Rabaul:

"Up into Rabaul every damn day automatic as hell and our job was to cover the bombers. We weren't supposed to be shooting down planes. So it was only when they got these special hops devised when we had more planes in enough condition than were assigned to a mission then we could take them up, leave before the hop and be 5 - 10,000 ft over them and just wait for them. You would see the formation coming in and as they start reporting bogies at ten o'clock or two o'clock. If they said two o'clock we looked like hell in that direction to see what was over there and we start slicing through them before they got up there. Wherever they report bogies our only job was to slice through, break them up, obviously shoot them down and pull back up, if they didn't go to the wind which often happened. If there was four of them and you got two of them, the other two God knows where they'd go. You can't find them so they aren't going to hurt anybody by themselves. It was just good fun to be there and I guess it's like a heavyweight fighting a lightweight because they didn't have a chance - no way. Because if they tried to get away from us we could wax their ass - we could out dive them - we couldn't out turn them or dogfight them they could get on our ass if you tried to dogfight them but you didn't have to because we had the speed and no reason to ever get hit by an enemy."

February 19, 1944, was a big day for Danny, and he remembers this mission on Roving High Cover:

"On February 19th, the last day we saw enemy aerial opposition, there were two extra planes which were assigned to "Oc" Chenoweth and myself.

Dan Cunningham and "Butch" Davenport at Ondongo in November 1943. They both became aces with Fighting 17.
Courtesy of Vought

Dan Cunningham as a young Ensign with an Air Force buddy in 1942. *Courtesy of George R Edwards*

Paul and I were flying one time and he said turn left Danny. . . . and here's a guy coming up our ass. . . . he wanted me to . . . draw him out then Paul would come around and shoot his ass down. . . . he was using me as a clay pigeon, the son of a gun, because if I get too far this guy could get up my ass before Paul could get him.

DAN CUNNINGHAM

Dan Cunningham in flight gear, ready to go, at Ondongo in November 1943. He flew #22 on the first tour. *Courtesy of Vought*

We got assigned to what we called the Gravy - Hop. Say we had sixteen planes assigned to the mission if we had twenty in enough condition then four of us that weren't assigned to be on the raid could take those four and take off ahead of the strike and be up over the target usually at around 30 - 32,000 feet and wait for the strike to catch up. Then report bogies and our only job was to start diving through and if they didn't break up to do it again and keep going until there was no more up above. It was just a beautiful set up. It's like shooting fish in a barrel.

There was supposed to be four of us but the Skipper had to call two of them into the hop so it was just "Oc" and I on this thing. We were up there around 32,000 ft and you could just barely way off in the background see the bombers coming. Miles and miles before they got to us. With that "Oc" makes a dive and I says where is that son of a gun going?

I looked down and there's a Zeke. I says he's going to go pick a cherry and he'll come back. He dove and missed the guy. The guy pulled right straight up and I never did see "Oc." He just kept diving after another one. I said hell I got to go down and protect him and take this guy that he missed. So I went down there and cut the circle and he blew up. Then I look around for "Oc" and there he is doing the same damn thing going vertically down after another one. I said we'll see what happens here and he did the same damn thing he shot and the guy pulled right straight up and so I went straight down again and did the same damn thing. He blew up the same as the other one. I'm looking for "Oc" and I see he is down near the water and he is right on the ass of a Jap. I then look up and here comes a Zeke just screaming down. I thought that son of a gun is after me. I tried to get around on to him but apparently his wing blocked me out from his vision. He just kept right on down. All I had to do was jump right on his ass and he was real easy to knock out. So by the time I got through with that one I'm right down on the deck too near the water. There's no "Oc" no nobody around. I said what the hell am I doing down here on the water in their territory nobody else to protect me. If they want to jump me I'm dead. So with that I see the bombers had made their run and they're pulling out so I said I'm going to join them as they've got fighters over them to protect them. I saw some Japs close to the bombers and I got real close to one of them. I went right up his ass, I mean ten feet and I blasted away and pieces were flying everywhere. He's dead. There were three F6F's lolly gagging in the sky and three Zekes. They were fighting with each other someway. I thought I could climb up and come down and get at least one of those. I was low on fuel so I leaned back on the throttle and got home. I think I used 525 rounds. We carried I think 2400 so they were all four short bursts. See they had no armor plate or nothing, they just blew sky high every time you hit them. It was a big day. I was lucky in that it was the last day we had enemy aerial opposition. Had I been a day later I'd have been sitting there with three instead of seven."

Dan Cunningham was awarded the Navy Cross for this action and became an ace in his last air combat with Fighting 17. The citation for the Navy Cross was as follows:

"For extraordinary heroism as pilot attached to a Navy Fighting Squadron operating against enemy Japanese forces in the Solomon Islands Area from January 26 to February 26, 1944. Upon encountering a numerically superior force of enemy aircraft while escorting a flight of bombers on an extremely hazardous mission over the strongly defended Lakunai Airfield, Lt (then Lt. (jg) Cunningham unhesitatingly maneuvered his plane into advantageous striking position and, fighting skillfully and with daring aggressiveness, shot down two of the enemy fighters. On another occasion, while preceding a bomber strike against Japanese shipping and harbor installations, he and another pilot engaged sixteen hostile Zeros and, fearlessly pressing home a brilliant, powerful attack, destroyed four of the enemy planes. Lt.

Cunningham's superb airmanship, gallant disregard for personal safety and unflinching courage in the face of overwhelming odds were in keeping with the highest traditions for the United States Naval Service."

Cunningham had 148 hours of combat flying for the first tour. When he returned for his second tour he completed nineteen combat sorties in sixteen days, twelve of them over Rabaul, and had 64.6 combat hours.

Dan was a national hero after becoming an ace. The Navy brought him back to the States, and after a ticker tape parade in Chicago, sent him on a tour of the States selling War Bonds. He then married Irene Sheridan Cunningham

After a short leave he was assigned as a Combat Instructor at N.A.A.S. Green Cove Springs. He joined VF-10 in September 1944 and then VBF-10 in January 1945. He was awarded the Distinguished Flying Cross for combat actions over Japan and Okinawa from March 18, 1945, to April 17, 1945. The citation stated:

"For heroism and extraordinary achievement in aerial flight as pilot and division leader in Bombing Fighting Squadron Ten, attached to the USS Intrepid, in action

against enemy forces in the Japanese homeland on March 18 and 19, 1945. Leading his division in strikes against enemy airfields and shipping, Lt. Cunningham pressed home rocket and strafing attacks in the face of intense anti - aircraft fire to destroy three grounded hostile aircraft and contributed to the probable destruction of eight and the destroying of ten others. In addition, he personally destroyed a 1500 - ton enemy merchant ship and directed his flight in damaging attacks on oil tanks, buildings, two railroad trains and six power launches."

Dan was involved in missions against Japanese forces in the vicinity of the Ryuku Islands and the Japanese homeland from March 24 to April 13, 1945. He departed from the squadron in Okinawa in September 1945 to return to civilian life.

Dan and Irene had a boy and a girl: Irene Jr. and Danny Jr. He divorced from Irene, and in September 1954 married Dolores May Brettman in Pensacola, Florida. They met while both were working at Equitable Life Assurance Society. They eloped, as her father didn't approve of Danny. They lived in Evanston, where their daughter Kimberley was born on May 8, 1956.

Dan bought a seat on the Chicago Mercantile Exchange, where he traded pork bellies and soybean futures.

Cunningham's brother-in-law, George Edwards, remembers Dan:

"Although we were married to sisters my visits with Dan were very limited. Being a pilot myself, I had great respect for those who made WWII carrier landings. A Navy pilot in those days required the utmost skill, before the days of a canted deck, which now permits a pilot to do a go around. The WWII options were hitting the stern, grabbing a hook or going into a barrier. Dan, being an ace with seven kills to his credit commanded even more respect.

I had the pleasure in the late 50's to fly to Chicago, land my Bonanza at the Glenview Naval Air Station, and pick Dan and my father-in-law up and fly them to the Air Force Museum in Dayton, Ohio. Art Beard an Air Force Test Pilot who became a friend when I was recalled in the Korean War was stationed at Wright Patterson Test Center and he had invited me to have a personal guided tour of the facility.

This was the only opportunity I had to fly with Dan. I let him have the controls and it was immediately apparent he was a natural as a pilot. It was a memorable experience for me which I still cherish.

After the war, he worked for the Equitable Life Insurance Company, where he was a member of the Million Dollar Round Table. (An honor for those who sold that much insurance in a one year period). He later acquired a seat on the Mercantile Exchange and traded in the futures market.

I found Dan delightful company and fun to be with. He had the reputation of being jovial, but with a quick temper."

After around twenty-two years together Dan and Dolores were divorced. Dan had some difficult family relationships and some tough times. His son was a world class swimmer who took his own life. After his divorce from Dolores he married Ruthie, and was with her until he died on February 24, 2006.

In addition to the Navy Cross, he was also awarded the Distinguished Flying Cross, three Air Medals, Navy Unit Commendation Medal, Asiatic - Pacific Campaign Medal with three Stars, and WWII Victory Medal.

Opposite:
Dan Cunningham with his aircraft #15 showing seven Japanese flags on Bougainville in 1944. He flew #15 on the second tour. *Robert Lawson Photograph Collection, National Museum of Naval Aviation / US Navy photo*

I finally said for crissake give me a chance Skipper and I'll show you. He was still shaking his head when he walked away. I didn't know then whether I was getting bounced or not.

DAN CUNNINGHAM

"Butch" Davenport, Fighting 17 Engineering Officer and ace with 6.25 Japanese aircraft to his credit. *Courtesy of the National Archives*

6

MERL WILLIAM "BUTCH" DAVENPORT

6.25 VICTORIES

Merl William "Butch" Davenport was born on March 14, 1918, in Sterling, Michigan. He was educated at Wayne University for three years and started his Naval serivce on January 6, 1941. As the first Navy squadron to take the F4U Corsair into action, Fighting 17 were responsible for many design modifications. As the Engineering Officer "Butch" Davenport, along with ground crews, worked with the Chance Vought Field Service Representatives, such as Ray DeLeva, to improve many aspects of the first Navy Corsairs. These modifications became standard on production models of later aircraft. Two of the significant design improvements were the landing gear oleo and a wing spoiler to improve stall characteristics. He also experimented with fuel conservation techniques that improved the endurance of the Corsair in combat.

"Butch" was assigned Corsair #31 in June 1943, and went into combat with this aircraft in Lem Cooke's division with "Ike" Kepford as his wingman. He was then promoted to lead a division and then a flight for the start of the second tour. After many months of training "Butch" went into combat with Fighting 17 in November 1943, and although his nickname was "Butch," he was also known as "Mother."

His first combat was on November 6, 1943, when his division, which was flying at 2,000 ft. ten to fifteen miles offshore from Cape Moltke, Bougainville, observed a Betty bomber at 300 ft. on a course one mile to the east of them. As they turned to intercept it the Betty apparently spotted them and turned north. "Butch" made the first run, followed by Wally Schub and Bob Hogan, although their attacks were practically simultaneous.

During the action the Betty took evasive action, S-turning in order to give the dorsal gunner good

"Butch" Davenport and Plane Captain Charlie Dixon (aged 16) with #9 at Bougainville in 1944. Dixon was given this responsibility by Davenport despite his young age. *US Naval Historical Center / M W "Butch" Davenport Collection*

shots at the Corsairs. All made low, high side attacks: "Butch" made three, Schub four, Hogan two, and Hal Jackson made one long attack on the Betty's tail, after which the Betty burst into flames and crashed into the sea. The four pilots shared the credit for the Betty.

"Butch's" most treasured memory was the recovery of "Andy" Anderson, who had been shot down in an engagement that involved the loss of several Marine pilots and Fighting 17's Brad Baker. All were presumed to have been lost, although Jack Chasnoff, Anderson's wingman, had seen him parachute. "Butch" relates the story:

"It just happened that I learned through the Skipper Tom Blackburn of an intelligence that they had up at Bougainville that the Japanese were coming down from Rabaul very early in the morning and were conducting strafing operations against the Seabees and Marines that were on this landing at Bougainville.

Opposite: "Butch" Davenport in front of the squadron scoreboard at Bougainville. *US Naval Historical Center / MW "Butch" Davenport Collection*

The cruise control techniques extended the range of the Corsair well beyond what was thought possible when it was introduced into service. Much . . . due to "Butch" Davenport's flight testing in operating at low altitudes with varying engine and propeller speeds and the lowest manifold pressure possible to produce both maximum endurance and greatest range.

I really liked to fly at night and I got clearance from Tom Blackburn to organize a flight of four up to Bougainville, taking off from New Georgia very early in the morning with the intent of intercepting these Japanese strafing missions.

My division of four F4U's left Ondongo at 03:25 November 18, 1943. While on the way to Buka at 04:25, I sighted a light in the water which appeared to be held in our direction without blinking. My division circled the light once at an altitude of 1,000 feet. During this circle a lightning flash revealed nothing about this spot but the light in the water.

After investigating by flying low and using the landing light, the object was found to be small enough to be a pilot afloat in the water. At this time, my division decided to leave the objective of the rest of the flight.

I then called Dane Base, told them we had sighted this light and asked him to take a bearing while I kept my emergency flash on and circled close by. When this had been accomplished, the division continued circling for a short time before the light blinked out. We had planned on remaining close by, so when this happened, I made a half minute square (flying straight for a half minute before making a 90° turn) about the spot using 1650 R.P.M. and 25"Hg. manifold pressure.

The light did not reappear after a long interval so we decided to return to Dane Base for patrol -- for our secondary mission. At daybreak, I requested the bearing of the light from Dane Base (295° distance 32 miles) and proceeded out from Pt. Easy. At the end of the required time, nothing was sighted except numerous gas belly tanks, etc. We turned back and re - covered the area to Pt. Easy. As soon as we reached this point, since we were sure of the bearing; we took the same heading out again for seven minutes at 160 knots. At precisely this time, "Ike" Kepford, my section leader, sighted the pilot in his raft. This was at 06:00.

As soon as the pilot in the raft had been checked for comfort, and Dane Base had been called, the division split up making a big circle about the spot in the water, each at a different level up to 3,000 feet. At this altitude I used 1300 R.P.M. and 27" Hg. manifold pressure with 10° flaps, maintaining my flight level with 90 - 110 knots indicated.

"Butch" Davenport and Crew Chief George Mauhar in front of a Corsair. Robert Lawson Photograph Collection, National Museum of Naval Aviation / US Navy photo

By this time Dane Base had contacted the rescue boat Janie only to find it short of fuel and unable to make the pick - up. Dane then arranged for a PT boat and, at my request, called Base for a flight of our planes to relieve me. The division continued to circle and finally "Ike" Kepford and his wingman Mel Kurlander returned to Barakoma owing to lack of fuel, leaving myself and "Chico" Freeman to await relief. The latter had 110 gallons of fuel and I had 125 gallons at this time.

"Chico" wrote a poem as he was sure that in that life raft was one of our pilots. He wrote

a poem, a ridiculous thing and put it in a bean bag and dropped it over the side, and by God it landed within arms reach and Anderson picked this thing up and read the poem. Well we stayed there until the Dumbo picked up Anderson and we returned to New Georgia."

The poem was as follows:

"Howdy Jonah "Andy,"
Thought you might like something to read and look at.

Once upon a time there was a big bad wolf who, after he got tired of shooting down Zeke's Went into the ocean to seek a Mermaid so fair with long golden hair
Not finding her there
He swore with despair
All angry and clammy
The wolf's name was "Andy"
By "Chico." See you later."

"Butch" continues the story:

Since no relief arrived, we covered the spot until the PT boat arrived and picked up the pilot and raft at 09:00. "Chico" and I then headed for home at 1600 R.P.M., 24"Hg. manifold pressure, 120 knots, landing at Ondongo at 10:05 with 28 gallons of fuel remaining. The total time of the flight was six hours and forty - five minutes. "It was on the way back that we established radio contact with the Catalina and found out the name of the pilot, which was Anderson. They brought him back to a dug out hospital that they had on New Georgia. I didn't see Anderson I don't know why but I didn't see him after. A couple of people went over to visit him in the hospital. He was flown back to Guadalcanal and then the States. He was badly injured. One of them said "Andy" you can thank God for that flashlight that you had. Anderson said "I don't know what you're talking about, ***I didn't have a flashlight!"***

So here's the irony. One of the other pilots that had been shot down had a flashlight and his efforts resulted in the saving of Anderson. This is the irony and the aspect of fate is the hunter. You can't understand these things why they occur this way."

"Butch" and Whit Wharton went up to search for the second pilot. They took off from Ondongo at 16:40 and searched the area between Cape Torokina and Sandinsel Island and also the coast from Kuraio Mission to Cape Torokina. No sign of any pilot was seen. "Butch" and Wharton landed back at Ondongo at 20:00.

This report from "Butch" really sets the scene on how the Corsair could be operated to maximise its endurance. It also shows the teamwork in Fighting 17, not only in covering each other in combat but in trying to save a downed comrade who would otherwise have been lost. Fighting 17 developed cruise control techniques for the Corsair which Charles Lindbergh, who was then employed by United Aircraft later refined. The cruise control techniques extended the range of the Corsair well beyond what was thought possible when it was introduced into service. Much of this was due to "Butch" Davenport's flight testing in operating at low altitudes with varying engine and propeller speeds and the lowest manifold pressure possible to produce both maximum endurance and greatest range. Another of Davenport's significant missions occurred on November 21, 1943 when two divisions of Corsairs were assigned as cover for U.S. land forces on Cape Torokina, Bougainville where they were to be on station for two hours. When they arrived Dane Base vectored out the P-39 Airacobra low cover to intercept them which forced a breach of radio silence by the Corsairs.

Dane Base then directed the flight to climb to 20,000 ft. on a vector of 260° to intercept bogies reported to be at 10,000 ft. or 16,000 ft. "Dirty Eddie" March led his division out twenty-five miles on this vector. "Butch" could not establish radio contact with Dane Base, so he remained over Cape Torokina at 3,000 ft. Three bombs were dropped in the water off a nearby island, so Dane Base summoned March back to Cape Torokina and his division turned and dived at full speed.

At 13,000 ft. they passed a Ki 61 Tony on an opposite course, but the Corsairs' speed was too great for them to turn and engage. The Tony was later shot down by the low cover Airacobras.

Meanwhile the second division ("Butch," "Chico" Freeman, Ray Beacham, and "Andy" Jagger) were at 2,000 ft. on the edge of a cloud and to the west of Cape Torokina, thus being in the dark. They saw the bomb splashes and headed in towards Cape Torokina, where they saw six Zekes slightly below them and 500 yards off their starboard beam on a course of about 150°. The Zekes were not going particularly fast, and "Butch" swung his division in a 180° turn on their tails. As the division turned the Zekes saw him and dropped their belly tanks; four of them changed formation into a column ready to turn into a defensive Lufbery Circle. "Butch" and his wingman, "Chico" Freeman, climbed in a sharp turn to get into position and began their attack runs. "Butch" picked the leader of the four Zekes and came in on a flat side attack, closing to very short range, and he saw his bullets going into the cockpit. The pilot bailed out, injured, and was picked up by a PT boat.

He then saw a Zeke at 1,000 yards making a beam attack at him, so "Butch" turned into the attack and the Zeke passed below him without getting his sights on him. After completing a 360° turn he saw another Zeke above him in a climb and started after it but could not catch him, so "Butch" rolled his Corsair over on its back and down in a Split-S. At that moment he saw a Zeke on "Andy" Jagger's tail, so he went after it and fired. The Zeke pulled up and "Butch" lost him, so he turned back and saw a Zeke above him on his left and on an opposite course. He turned in and fired, and saw the Zeke start smoking and crash into the sea. He then joined up with "Chico," and they circled the Japanese aircraft in the water. They went back on patrol over the bay and then headed back to base.

The success of this operation can be explained by the fact that it had been carefully planned. The enemy had made two previous dawn attacks and "Butch" had studied the reports. On the evening before his flight he went over all the available intelligence data and decided that the best place for an interception was slightly inland from Cape Torokina at an altitude of 2,000 ft. This would enable him to catch

"Butch" Davenport's aircraft wrecked at Bougainville. *US Navy photo Robert Lawson Collection*

the Japanese as they came down over the mountains behind Empress Augusta Bay. "Butch" and "Dirty Eddie" March agreed that the latter's division should stay up as cover in a position to deal with any different type of attack. "Butch" also believed that the attack would come just at dawn and planned to be on station before that time. Events proved him to be correct, as if he had arrived on station at the time assigned him, he might very well have been too late, and if he had gone out and up with March on Dane Base's vector he would certainly have missed the interception. All six Zekes encountered were shot down. Davenport was credited with two Zekes, Freeman with two Zekes, and Beacham and Jagger each scored one Zeke.

Shortly after this engagement Fighting 17 finished their first tour and were given a much needed rest in Sydney, Australia. They returned to combat flying out of Bougainville in late January 1944.

Sixteen year old Plane Captain Charlie Dixon remembered "Butch" Davenport:

> *"Most of the mechanics had left when I met "Butch" Davenport, they got the rest from C.A.S.U. 12 out of Guadalcanal. When we got to Bougainville I was picked by "Butch."*

While on Bougainville when "Butch" went out on a strike we would have the planes ready and ride the wing (the pilot could not see out the front of an F4U) with a signal with our hands until we got to the strip and I would crawl off and give him a prayer signal then each Plane Captain would walk the length of the strip and wait until they came home. I could tell my #9 as "Butch" messed up one wing and it was white on the bottom, we had a little tent and played poker until they arrived and picked us up on a wing and back to the revetment to park, while "Butch" would tell me if something was wrong and then he went to officers country and I would head for my tent. There were five of us there in a foxhole and at night we would crawl in it when the siren went off, and put a poncho over us (rain coat). If you could not see the stars it would be like armour plate. Even with a war going on there still is something to laugh about.

One morning our squadron was escorting B-24's from Guadalcanal to Rabaul a jeep pulled up and a stranger got out and told me he was going to use my plane. I strapped him in and crawled on the wing and rode to the strip. I waved him goodbye and followed the other guys to the end of the strip to wait under the tent 'till they got back. We played cards and finally the planes came back. I waited and waited and all the planes and Plane Captains were gone, after about thirty minutes. I walked back to the tower, climbed up the tower and asked where #9 was. They laughed and told me he wouldn't arrive until morning, he went to Vella Lavella to get some booze, he left with the squadron and made a left, the pilot name was Dixon. We were not kin he was twenty four and I was sixteen.

One trip "Butch" came in and said to tighten a Zeus button on the engine cowling. The next strike he went out on was bad news, he asked for my screw driver and got on his belly and crawled out on the nose and tightened it himself. Other than that we got on okay I had old number #9 shining from then until he left."

Charlie Dixon describes a Plane Captain's duties:

> *You are a pilot's bell boy; I took care of #9, #33, and new #9. I fuelled up the plane, checked the oil and kept the cockpit clean with no cigarette butts anywhere ("Butch" did not like that). Every morning before a strike I turned the plane up and checked it out, supercharger, prop pitch of 2700 rpms. I had a Marine ordnance man to handle the guns, my job was to tape the six gun holes up with masking tape to keep the coral dust out.*
>
> *They usually escorted B-24's from Guadalcanal to Rabaul. In the morning "Butch" arrived (and rest of the pilots) I put his chute in the plane and strapped him in (I had a hard time lifting it) I just weighed 116lbs and barely sixteen years old. Can you believe a pilot would let a sixteen year old kid from Corbin, Kentucky check his plane out then go hunt some Japs!!*
>
> *"Butch" and I got along real good although he tore my butt a few times after a strike. I gave him a prayer signal he gave me thumbs up before a mission."*

On January 30, 1944, Davenport was assigned as part of the TBF Avenger cover for a joint SBD - TBF strike on shipping in Simpson Harbor. Tom Blackburn spotted twenty Zekes joining up over Simpson Harbor and attacked them.

"Butch," leading the second section of Blackburn's division, went down after Blackburn in the initial attack. He started a run on a Zeke from nine o'clock and swung in astern. His first burst missed, but he closed the range and hit. The Zeke caught fire as he Split S'd out. "Davenport's" next two passes were unsuccessful, and as he saw his wingman Ensign Ed Beeler heading away he followed. A Zeke got on Beeler's tail and "Butch" dived from 3,000 ft. above and fired. The Zeke half rolled and "Butch" rolled with him, firing throughout, and the Zeke went down in flames. "Butch" then joined up on Beeler and two other Corsairs and went back over the bombers. "Butch" was credited with two Zekes confirmed destroyed after this mission.

On February 5, 1944, "Butch" was one of twelve Corsairs that were assigned as part of the

Can you believe a pilot
would let a sixteen year old kid
from Corbin, Kentucky
check his plane out
then go hunt some Japs!!

PLANE CAPTAIN CHARLIE DIXON

SBD Dauntless cover on a joint SBD - TBF Avenger strike on Lakunai Airfield, New Britain.

As the formation was between Duke of York Island and Crater Peninsula, about twelve Zekes were sighted at about 15,000 ft. Five of these Zekes made overhead runs on the Dauntlesses just before they pushed over into their attack dives. "Butch," whilst leading a division of the low cover, was able to lower his Corsair's nose, and with a 40° deflection shot hit the second Zeke, which caught fire and crashed. None of the attacking Zekes scored hits on the SBDs. "Butch" was credited with one Zeke shot down which made him an ace.

"Butch's" last victory occurred on February 10, 1944, when leading three Corsairs on a Roving High Cover mission supporting a strike by B-24s on Tobera Airfield. He made contact with six to eight Zekes at about 24,000 ft. diving in column on the bombers as they were turning out to sea after their initial run. "Butch" led his three aircraft down on the Zekes. He got on the tail of one at about 20,000 ft. and saw his bullets go into the cockpit and fuselage; the Zeke spun down in flames. Ensign John "Fatso" Ellsworth also shot down a Zeke, and then the division joined up with the low cover and after the strike headed for home. "Butch" scored one confirmed Zeke, which concluded his scoring with Fighting 17.

On his first tour "Butch" had flown a high 163 combat hours when the average for the squadron was 100 hours.

By the time enemy opposition had been cleared over Rabaul, "Butch" had flown eighteen combat sorties in sixteen days, twelve of them over Rabaul, and flown 57.4 combat hours.

After his combat tour "Butch" returned to the States, stayed in the Navy, and later became a Test Pilot at N.A.S. Patuxent River. He was also one of the first Navy pilots to attend the Empire Test Pilot School at Boscombe Down in England.

On November 20, 1946, at Wright Patterson Air Force Base, Ohio, "Butch," now a Lt. Cdr, flew an F8F Grumman Bearcat, taking off in a distance of 115 feet from a standing start and climbed to 10,000 feet in 94 seconds. This was a record "Butch" held for a long time. "Butch" amassed 7,500 flight hours during his six years in the Navy, and continued to fly after leaving the service in 1949, regularly flying his Piper Comanche around the country. He recalled the difference in aircraft technology:

> *"The plane has navigation and flight equipment that I would have traded my soul for in WWII. Modern aviation equipment is far superior to anything we had during the war."*

His service in the Navy had included assignments at N.A.S. Pensacola, on the carriers USS *Bunker Hill* and USS *Saipan*, N.A.S. Corpus Christi, N.A.S. Patuxent River, Office of Commander Navy Europe in London, N.A.S. Atlantic City, and Aircraft Development Squadron Three. "Country" Landreth remembers his friend fondly:

> *"Butch" has gone now. He came by here in California flying his own airplane. He stayed overnight and it was a wonderful visit.*
>
> *We didn't know it at the time as he was still in good shape and was out jogging before the sun came up while he was here.*
>
> *Later it dawned on us that he was going around saying goodbye to all the guys in the squadron he could find, because he subsequently died of cancer. Even though he had a daughter in the experimental cancer clinic up in Washington State (University of Washington).*
>
> *He tracked down every possible lead for a cure to treating his cancer including his daughter's studies.*
>
> *So without saying so I think he was going round and having a last visit with everybody."*

"Butch" Davenport died of cancer in Dexter, Michigan, on September 19, 1989.

He was awarded the Distinguished Flying Cross, Navy Unit Commendation, American Campaign Medal, American Defense Service Medal, Asiatic - Pacific Campaign Medal, and WWII Victory Medal.

Opposite:
"Butch" Davenport's aircraft #9, "Lonesome Polecat."
Courtesy of the Deveney family

Lt. (jg) D. C. "Chico" Freeman at Bougainville in 1944. "Chico" scored two victories with Fighting 17 and seven with VF-84 to achieve ace status. *Courtesy of the National Archives*

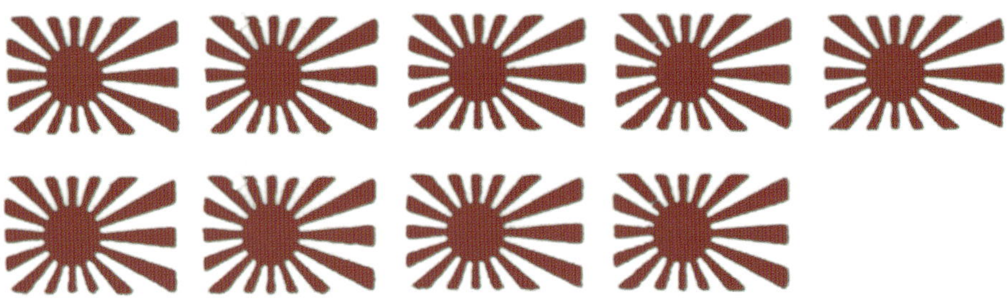

7

DORIS CLYDE "CHICO" FREEMAN

9 VICTORIES

"Chico" Freeman was born on April 18, 1920, in Los Angeles, California. His father and grandfather were also named Doris, which explains the unusual first name. His father was known as Clyde Freeman, and served in the U.S. Marine Corps in WWII. First Sgt. Clyde Freeman was a broker for A.W. Coote at the time of "Chico's" birth and married to Mary Jane Berkman.

"Chico" was called "Jack" by a nurse who took care of him during an illness when he was a baby, and since that time he was called "Jack" by all the family until such time as he started school, where he was known as Clyde Freeman, and later on he adopted the name Clyde Jack Freeman.

During his high school days he was an active member of the high school lightweight football team and played for three years.

Swimming was also a favorite sport of his. He felt at home near the water, and although he was never fast enough to compete on the swimming team he could swim for quite a distance.

"Chico" was educated at many schools and colleges in the Los Angeles area and entered University High in Los Angeles in 1935, graduating on February 3, 1939.

He studied from 1938 to 1939 at Manual Arts High School, attended Los Angeles City College in 1939, and then Oceanside - Carlsbad Junior College from 1939 to June 1940.

At Oceanside Junior College he participated in spring football and track. His summer jobs consisted of washing cars, digging ditches, selling articles and mining.

He spent the summer of 1940 on a Civil Aviation Authority flight training and ground school course. He then attended Los Angeles City College briefly before going to Ventura Junior College from 1940 until 1941. At Ventura he completed two years of college training and completed the sixty-four units required for graduation with a Degree of Associate of Arts.

He attended Santa Barbara State College in March 1941 but withdrew with an honourable dismissal.

Like many young men, after Pearl Harbor he applied to join the Navy in December 1941. On February 25, 1942, he enlisted in the U.S. Naval Reserve, and in May 1942 he accepted his appointment as an Aviation Cadet and reported to N.A.S. Corpus Christi, Texas, for training.

He was designated a Naval Aviator on October 8, 1942, was commissioned as an Ensign on October 30, 1942, and the same day reported to N.A.S. Miami for pre-operational training.

On December 12, 1942, he reported to N.A.S. Jacksonville for further advanced flying training, and on March 11, 1943, he reported to the Carrier Qualification Training Unit, Norfolk, Virginia. He was then assigned to Fighting 17.

In his fitness report in September 1943 he achieved a score of 3.6 as a Pilot, which was good, and it was noted:

> *"Ensign Freeman is an energetic, capable officer of excellent character and pleasing personality. He should develop into an excellent officer as he gains experience."*

"Chico" was assigned Corsair #24 in "Timmy" Gile's division as Paul Cordray's wingman in June 1943. When he first went into combat he was "Dirty Eddie" March's wingman. He was also "Butch" Davenport's wingman on many missions, and for the second tour flew as Davenport's wingman. His most famous Corsair was #34, "L.A. City Limits."

On October 1, 1943, he was promoted to Lt. (jg). He went into combat with Fighting 17 in November 1943, and his first aerial victory came on November 21, 1943, as "Butch" Davenport's wingman. They were flying in two divisions of Corsairs assigned as cover over U.S. forces on Cape Torokina, Bougainville. They saw six Zekes slightly below them. "Butch" swung the division in a 180° turn to get on the Zekes' tails. With "Chico" backing up "Butch" in his wingman

"Chico" Freeman at Bougainville early in 1944. *Robert Lawson Photograph Collection, National Museum of Naval Aviation / US Navy photo*

slot, they climbed together in a sharp turn to get into position from which to begin their attacks. "Chico" kept 200 yards separation between he and "Butch" and then followed him down to attack. "Butch" chose the third Zeke in the column as his target. "Chico" saw the second Zeke firing on "Butch," so he made a beam attack and hit the Zeke. The Zeke crashed into the water.

The third and fourth Zekes were then on "Chico's" tail, closing to about 75 yards when they commenced firing. "Chico" kicked the Corsair's rudder so it went into a sideslip, and one Zeke passed by as it overshot on his port beam. "Chico" then tried a sharp bank to the left and saw a Zeke still

Opposite:
"Chico" Freeman with his F4U-1A, "L.A. City Limits." This was his favorite picture. *Robert Lawson Photograph Collection, National Museum of Naval Aviation / US Navy photo*

"I think he would have made a million as a comedian. Oh God was he funny."

Fellow ace Dan Cunningham

An early photo of "Chico" Freeman with aircraft #7. He later went on to fly #34. *US Naval Historical Center / M W "Butch" Davenport Collection*

behind him, so he kicked hard left rudder and went into a half spin to the left. This maneuver shook the Zeke off.

He saw "Butch" not far off on the tail of a Zeke and turned to join up with him, but looked back and saw a Zeke start a run on him. "Chico" made a high, sharp chandelle to the left and turned 180°. The Zeke went straight ahead, so he completed a full turn and headed after him. He caught him just west of Mt. Balbi, fired a short burst from dead astern, and saw flames in the cockpit. The Japanese pilot tried to bail out, but the parachute was torn to pieces on the tail of the Zeke, which then crashed into the jungle.

"Chico" then turned back, joined up with "Butch" and resumed patrol. He was credited with two confirmed Zekes on this mission.

On December 19, 1943, he was recommended for the Distinguished Flying Cross. The citation stated:

"For extraordinary achievement while participating in aerial flights against the enemy in the Solomon Islands area. In a dawn action over Empress Augusta Bay, Bougainville, on November 21, 1943, he flew one of four Corsairs which attacked six Zekes, of which he shot down two. On 18 November he took part in the remarkable flight lasting six hours and forty five minutes which resulted in the recovery of Lt. (jg) R. S. Anderson. In addition to the above actions, he took part in numerous patrols, escort missions, and strafing missions, several of which were in the face of intense enemy A/A fire. In 36 days he flew 39 sorties, a total of 132 hours of combat flying. His devotion to duty, his great courage in the face of superior enemy forces, and his skilful airmanship were in keeping with the highest traditions of the U.S. Naval Service."

"Chico" Freeman in front of his F4U Corsair.
Courtesy of the Anderson Family.

After a short period of leave "Chico," along with Fighting 17, returned to action at the end of January 1944.

On February 7, 1944, Fighting 17 were assigned as partial cover for the SBD - TBF strike on Vunakanau Airfield. Due to the weather Tobera was selected as the secondary target. On the turn into the target the Japanese fighters attacked the high and medium cover. "Chico" was leading the section in the medium cover and came under attack. He was not hit, and got in a beam attack on a Zeke, closing in to forty yards. He saw the enemy plane fly through his tracers and a piece fly off as he passed. From 5,000 ft. he then saw a Hamp fighter at 3,000 ft. five miles east of Vunakanau. The Hamp took violent evasive action, but "Chico's" high side run put him dead astern. His first burst made the Hamp smoke, and it then entered cloud with "Chico" close behind. He got in another burst in the cloud but the Hamp disappeared. "Windy" Hill, who was Chico's wingman on the mission, was waiting above the cloud to rejoin "Chico" and did not see the Hamp appear. It is possible he was destroyed.

"Chico" was credited with one Zeke probable and one Hamp probable, which concluded his scoring with Fighting 17. On March 14, 1944, he was recommended for an award:

> *"Between January 26, 1944 and March 7, 1944, during which time he was based at Piva Yoke, Bougainville, Lt. (jg) Freeman flew thirty three combat sorties, eighteen of which were escort missions of fighter sweeps over the Rabaul area. He encountered enemy aircraft on eleven occasions: on 26, 27, 28, 30 and 31 January,*

"Chico" Freeman sitting on the wing of Corsair #34. *US Naval Historical Center / M W "Butch" Davenport Collection*

> *and on 4, 7, 9, 11, 17, and 19 February. During this period he ably led a section in a flight which accounted for twenty five enemy planes. On 7 February the TBF's which he was escorting in a strike on Vunakanau Airfield were intercepted by thirty or forty enemy fighters. Although under repeated attacks he remained over the bombers and probably destroyed one Zeke. After the successful retirement of the TBF's, he flew one of eight Corsairs which returned to the area in a delayed fighter sweep. In the ensuing action he twice attacked superior numbers of the enemy and probably destroyed a Zeke as it was making a run on another Corsair."*

He was awarded the Distinguished Flying Cross and two Air medals for his service with Fighting 17 and scored two confirmed and two probable victories. Fellow ace Dan Cunningham remembers "Chico's" humor:

> *"I think he would have made a million as a comedian. Oh God was he funny."*

"Butch" Davenport remembers his wingman:

> *"Freeman was born and raised in Los Angeles and on the tail of his airplane he had a big sign "L. A. City Limits." He was incorrigible, but a wonderful guy."*

On April 3, 1944, "Chico" was ordered to Fleet Air, West Coast, N.A.S. San Diego, and on May 3, 1944, after a well earned leave he reported to VF-84 under Roger Hedrick. After a period of training with VF-84 "Chico" went into action again in early 1945, flying off the USS *Bunker Hill.*

On February 17, 1945, whilst flying from the *Bunker Hill* on a strike to Nakajima Tama Musashino Engine Plant, "Chico" was flying as Roving High Cover. During the attack he saw and attacked a Ki 61 Tony; his bullets sprayed the fuselage and wing tank, and the Tony was seen to spiral and crash.

His fitness report dated April 7, 1945, marked him as a pilot 3.8 and rated him as Excellent. It stated:

> *"Lt. (jg) Freeman has satisfactorily carried out his duties as Personnel Officer. Constant improvement has been noted and since being ship - based he has been most energetic in looking after the welfare of the enlisted men. He is cheerful and willing and well above average in flying ability."*

"Ensign Freeman is an energetic, capable officer of excellent character and pleasing personality. He should develop into an excellent officer as he gains experience."

FITNESS REPORT IN SEPTEMBER 1943

His endless flow of wit and
his abundant store of good humor
always served to give his squadron
a lift when it was most needed.

Captain G.A. Seitz

On April 13, 1945, in operations over Okinawa while he was leading his division on a target combat air patrol, he pressed home his attack and destroyed a Sonia. For this action he was awarded the Air Medal.

On April 16, 1945, "Chico" destroyed one Japanese aircraft code named Topsy on the ground, and on April 17, 1945, he shot down a Kawanishi George over Okinawa to become an ace and was awarded another Air Medal for this mission.

On April 28, 1945, "Chico" scored two Nates and was awarded another Distinguished Flying Cross for his actions. The citation stated:

> *"For heroism and extraordinary achievement in aerial flight as division leader in Fighting Squadron 84, attached to the USS Bunker Hill, in action against enemy Japanese forces in the vicinity of Kikai, Nansei Shoto, April 28, 1945. Leading his division on a target combat air patrol, Lt. (jg) Freeman destroyed two of twelve hostile fighter aircraft encountered on his flight, thereby contributing materially to the success of the mission. His skilled airmanship, courage and devotion to duty were in keeping with the highest traditions of the U.S. Naval Service."*

His final victories were two Nates on May 11, 1945, which gave him seven confirmed Japanese aircraft to his credit with VF-84. "Chico" was awarded the Distinguished Flying Cross:

> *"For heroism and extraordinary achievement in aerial flight as a pilot in Fighting Squadron 84, attached to the USS Bunker Hill, during action against enemy Japanese forces in the vicinity of Tokyo, Iwo Jima, Kyushu and Okinawa, from February 16 to April 22, 1945. Undaunted by grave hazards, Lt. Freeman boldly penetrated hostile territory to execute twenty daring raids against strategic Japanese positions and, striking furiously at his assigned targets, inflicted severe damage upon the enemy, thereby contributing in large part to the success of his squadron during this period of intensive aerial activity. His brilliant combat tactics and utter disregard for his own personal safety reflect the highest credit upon Lt. Freeman and the U.S. Naval Service."*

"Chico" Freeman's final total was nine confirmed Japanese aircraft destroyed, including two with Fighting 17, and with John M. "Smitty" Smith he was the joint leading ace of VF-84.

He had just landed his Corsair after his successful mission destroying two Nates and was in the VF-84 ready room when a kamikaze hit the *Bunker Hill* and exploded, killing "Chico" and many of his squadron mates. He died at about 10:45 on May 11, 1945, and was buried at sea on May 12, 1945.

Captain G.A. Seitz wrote this about "Chico" on May 25, 1945:

> *"Lt. Freeman was one of our ablest fighter pilots, aggressive and determined in all his attacks against the enemy. His endless flow of wit and his abundant store of good humor always served to give his squadron a lift when it was most needed. We shall miss him greatly aboard this ship."*

In addition to the Distinguished Flying Cross and two Air Medals "Chico" was awarded with Fighting 17, he was awarded three further DFCs, the Purple Heart, five Air Medals, Asiatic - Pacific Area Campaign Medal, Navy Unit Commendation, Presidential Unit Citation, and World War II Victory Medal.

Opposite:
"Chico" Freeman leading a section of F4U-1As. *Robert Lawson Photograph Collection, National Museum of Naval Aviation / US Navy photo*

"Timmy" Gile, Fighting 17 ace with eight victories. He later went on to serve with VBF-10 as Executive Officer. *Courtesy of the Gile Family*

8

CLEMENT DEXTER "TIMMY" GILE

8 VICTORIES

Clement Dexter "Timmy" Gile was born on January 30, 1918, in Brookline, Massachusetts, and raised in Pittsburgh, Pennsylvania. Gile had the nickname of "Timmy." Gile's father was also named Clement, and so Gile was called "Timmy" for as long as anyone could remember.

He was the son of Clement Moses Gile and Anne Bunce Ryce and had two brothers, John and David. He graduated from Avon Old Farms School in Avon, Connecticut, in 1935. He attended Yale University in 1935 and graduated in 1939 with a BA Degree in American History. At Yale he was the Stroke of the rowing crew in his senior year in 1939 and, given his future squadron's nickname, was appropriately a member of the Skull and Bones Society. They traditionally gave people nicknames for life, and his nickname could have come from there. He was the leading Yale University ace for both world wars.

After leaving Yale he worked for the Schaefer Equipment Co, Pittsburgh, Pennsylvania, which sold railroad equipment. He worked there for a year and a half as a Salesman prior to joining the Navy.

On November 1, 1940, he enlisted as a Seaman Second Class, and on February 1, 1941, became an Aviation Cadet training at N.A.S. Jacksonville. He was commissioned as an Ensign on July 16, 1941, and then reported to N.A.S. Miami. On the completion of his training he became an Instructor at N.A.S. Miami. Promoted to Lt. (jg) on October 1, 1942, he specialized in gunnery and was noted as a firm and dependable character and a most capable pilot. He reported to Fighting 17 on January 4, 1943, as Gunnery Officer and was promoted to Lt. on October 1, 1943.

"Timmy" was assigned Corsair #21 in June 1943 as a division leader in Roger Hedrick's flight. This is where he was assigned for both tours of combat.

"Timmy" Gile (middle) with brothers John and David.
Courtesy of the Gile Family

He was soon in action on November 1, 1943, when on patrol with seven other pilots over ships in Empress Augusta Bay, Bougainville. Roger Hedrick's and "Timmy's" divisions took station as high cover over the bay. Cocker Base reported enemy aircraft SE of Cape Torokina. Hedrick saw an enemy formation over the island and turned to intercept it. "Timmy," who was leading the second division, was flying with Dan Cunningham as his wingman, and both dived on a pair of Zekes to the left of the pair attacked by Hedrick. "Timmy" got one in his sights and lost him, but found another immediately. He was in a 45° dive, speed about 270 knots, altitude 18,000 ft. As his tabs were trimmed for 200 knots and he was bouncing in the slip stream, he had great difficulty in keeping his sights on the target. Bullets were surrounding the Zeke, and several incendiaries were seen to hit the wings but did not catch fire. "Timmy" went past the Zeke, almost hitting him with his right wing. The Zeke dived into cloud and was not seen again. Dan Cunningham had followed "Timmy" down and also fired at the Zeke, getting some hits as "Timmy" went past it. With the Zeke in the cloud Dan rejoined "Timmy" at 20,000 ft., where they continued their patrol. Gile and Cunningham were given shared credit for one Zeke damaged.

"Timmy" Gile pictured in 1938. *Courtesy of the Gile Family*

His first confirmed victory came on November 11, 1943, in the Battle of the Solomon Sea, when Fighting 17 acted as cover over a Carrier Task Force. When the Japanese attacked the Task Force "Timmy" and Lem Cooke spiralled down to sea level about two miles north of the Task Force. They headed west and started a run on a Kate attacking a destroyer. They saw the Kate shot down by A/A fire and made a run on another. "Timmy" was too fast and overran, and at this point lost contact with Lem Cooke. "Timmy" then found a Kate heading for the *Bunker Hill*, made one run, and pulled up too high and too fast, but chopped back his throttle and made another pass from 250 ft. He got in two bursts and saw the Kate catch fire. He gave it another burst and saw the Kate explode. While "Timmy" Gile disclaims credit for saving the carrier from the torpedo attack, he was generally credited with doing so.

"Timmy" saw another Kate going west and headed after him, but an F6F Hellcat got in first, so "Timmy" turned back towards the ships. The attack seemed to be over, so "Timmy" joined up with "Mac" Burriss and both returned to Barakoma, landing at 04:30. "Timmy" had only twenty gallons left when he landed.

"Timmy" proved his prowess as an expert marksman in the action of November 17, 1943, over U.S. shipping in Empress Augusta Bay, Bougainville. Cocker Base reported that the ships were under attack. Roger Hedrick's division attacked one group and "Timmy's" division attacked five Tonys and five Zekes, "Timmy" and his wingman, Dan Cunningham, picked four Zekes in the center of the formation. "Timmy" made three identical passes, each pass being followed by a left chandelle to shoot down a Zeke on each pass. He shot down three Zekes, making only one run on each aircraft; all three caught fire and exploded, all within the space of one minute. Seeing no more enemy aircraft, they returned to continue with their patrol before returning to Ondongo.

Between October 27 and December 1, 1943, "Timmy" Gile flew forty-six sorties, 152 hours of combat flying. He also participated in four strafing missions, thirty-one patrols, and eleven escort missions.

After a two week rest in Australia with the squadron, "Timmy" returned to action on January 26, 1944, when the formation of SBDs which he was escorting in a strike on Lakunai Airfield was aggressively intercepted by fifty to sixty enemy fighters. "Timmy's" division was at 16,000 ft. over the SBDs when they were jumped by the Zekes. They dived down to 7,000 ft. and then headed for a melee over St. George's Channel off Rapopo. "Timmy" made attacks on four Zekes, and in a quarter stern run from eight o'clock set the fourth on fire. He looked for his second section but could not find them, so he and Ensign John M. "Smitty" Smith, his wingman, headed out after the SBDs. Twelve Zekes followed and one closed the range on "Smitty," got on his tail and hit him. "Timmy" chandelled to the right and made a run on the Zeke, who disengaged, made a 180° turn and headed back towards Rabaul. "Timmy" and "Smitty" then joined up. "Smitty's" aircraft had a hydraulic failure so they returned to base. This was "Timmy's" fifth victory, which made him an ace.

On January 29, 1944, "Timmy" was in combat over Tobera Airfield. He was the flight leader of

"Timmy" Gile with two varsity crew mates at Yale. *Courtesy of the Gile Family*

the low cover and turned back several attacks, but became separated from his division. He saw a dogfight going on ten miles southeast of Kabanga Bay, so he chandelled from 1,000 ft. to 5,000 ft. in a 180° turn and entered the melee, driving a Zeke off an F4U's tail. The Zeke headed for home at 200 ft. "Timmy" pulled up behind him, and at close range shot off his tail. He then followed the bombers and joined up. On February18, 1944, whilst on Roving High Cover over a B-24 strike on Vunakanau Airfield, "Timmy" led one of two divisions against eight Zekes and destroyed one of them.

The two divisions reached the target thirty minutes before the bombers. They approached from the south over Wide Bay at 32,000 ft. and made a wide circle of the area with Hedrick's division at 29,000 ft. and "Timmy's" at 26,000 ft.

When "Timmy" was over Blanche Bay he spotted eight Zekes at the same altitude in a climbing turn. The Zekes were in two well formed four aircraft divisions. The Zekes and Corsairs continued climbing, each formation seeking to gain altitude advantage. "Timmy" got to 30,000 ft. first and his division made section runs on the Zekes. The action then developed into a running fight. "Timmy" and his wingman, John M. "Smitty" Smith, made three unsuccessful attacks followed by chandelles to regain height advantage, but over Keravat they caught a Zeke at about 25,000 ft. The Zeke Split-S'd, but the Corsairs were able to make a division run from five o'clock. The Zeke caught fire, spun down, and was credited to "Timmy" Gile. The following day, February 19, 1944, the first division of the high cover, led by "Timmy," had to fight its way through about twenty Zekes and possible Tojos to get to the rally point off Cape Gazelle. "Smitty" scored first. Almost immediately after his attack the section made a similar run on a Zeke and "Timmy" got in a long burst, setting it on fire, and it was seen to crash. By this time the Japanese had withdrawn, and "Timmy" and "Smitty" continued their escort over the TBF Avengers as briefed. Between January 26 and March 7, 1944, during which time he was based at Piva Yoke, Bougainville, "Timmy" had flown thirty-one combat sorties, eighteen of which were escort missions or fighter sweeps over the Rabaul Area. He was awarded two Distinguished Flying Crosses for his actions with Fighting 17 and finished with eight confirmed victories.

After his tour he was marked 3.9 and rated as "Outstanding" by Tom Blackburn, and it was reported that:

> *"Lt. Gile is an industrious highly capable officer, well liked by all hands. He has a cheerful, pleasant personality and is of excellent character. He has shown great courage and high skill as a flight leader on daily combat missions."*

Yale varsity crew, where "Timmy" Gile was Stroke in 1939. *Courtesy of the Gile Family*

His daughter Toni remembers:

"In many ways I think this was one of the best times in Dad's life -- even with the deprivation and the danger -- because he loved to fly and I think the camaraderie of war is something that one can never replicate in peace time. I think the rest of his life probably seemed very tame by comparison. One of the few things I know about my Dad's war career is that the guys he served with and flew with were a wild bunch and got into all kinds of mischief. They were also clearly very close to each other and tried hard not to lose touch."

"Timmy" Gile with sailing buddies. *Courtesy of the Gile Family*

After sailing home "Timmy" was detached from the U.S. Pacific Fleet, Fleet Air Alameda, California, on April 3, 1944, and reported to N.A.A.S. Green Cove Springs on May 8, 1944, after a short leave. He served as a Flight Instructor from May 24, 1944, to July 31, 1944, and then reported to VF-10 in August 1945. On January 2, 1945, VF-10 became VBF-10, with "Timmy" Gile as Executive Officer.

It was said that "Timmy" was one of the best looking men in Fighting 17, and all the young Ensigns used to tag along with him because he was like a magnet to girls as he was so good looking - and some of the other Ensigns used to pick up the pieces he left behind.

"Timmy" Gile met Jean (June) Hill Tyner and they married very quickly. They actually had only around six dates before they were engaged. They were married on January 18, 1945, in New York City. "Timmy's" daughter Toni describes how they met:

"My mother was working in Miami for Pan Am and her job was guiding incoming airplanes down the runway. My father was on leave and had flown down to Miami to see his very close friend Fred Schaefer. When he taxied down the runway, he noticed my mother who was flagging in his plane. He apparently thought she was a knockout. When he called his friend Fred to tell him he had arrived, Fred told him he was going to have a party and that there would be some good looking women there for him to meet. He told Fred that the only woman he was interested in meeting was the one who had flagged in his plane. Fred said that he had no idea who that was but that Dad should come to the party anyway. When he got there, Fred introduced him to my mother.....and the rest, as they say, was history!"

"Timmy" and June had almost a month together after their marriage, and June went with him to California and then returned to New York when the squadron sailed to the Pacific on the USS *Intrepid*. On February 16 and 17, 1945 the squadron reported aboard the USS *Intrepid* (CV-11) at N.A.S. Alameda and departed on February 20, 1945.

On February 24, 1945, they arrived at Pearl Harbor and departed on 27 February on a brief shakedown cruise of Air Group 10, returning on March 1, 1945.

On the morning of March 18, 1944, the squadron participated in a strike on Oita Airfield, Kyushu. This strike was composed of eleven TBM-3s, thirteen SB2C-4E Helldivers, and twelve Corsairs from the Task Group. "Timmy" was leader of the VBF-10 element. The result reported by VBF-10 pilots was serious damage to hangars and assembly and repair buildings, and indeterminate damage to fifteen parked aircraft. In addition, a lugger and two barges were strafed and left badly smoking. "Timmy" received a burst of anti-aircraft fire while over the target which caused minor damage to his aircraft. He was also wounded with a shell fragment in his neck, for which he received the Purple Heart.

On March 26, 1945, "Timmy" led a sweep which included fourteen VBF-10 aircraft against Kikai and Amami. One "Tiny Tim" (air to ground rocket), thirty-seven five inch rockets, and seven 500lb bombs inflicted considerable damage to buildings at Urabaru Wan, docks at Somachi, and on a picket boat at Kasari Wan. On March 28, 1945, in a letter home "Timmy" stated:

> *"We've been busy as hell and I've been sitting on a parachute a great deal of the time. All of us are pretty tired and just a little nervous. This carrier aviation is pretty exciting when it gets rolling and somehow manages to leave me damn well wrung out at the end of the day."*

On March 29, 1945, in another letter home:

> *"We did hit Pearl Harbor but only got to Honolulu for part of one afternoon. The rest of the time we were right around Ford Island which is the N.A.S. right in the middle of Pearl Harbor. It's about 45 minutes from Pearl Harbor to Waikiki Beach and involved a lot of buses, ferries etc. and unless you've got a car or permanent situation in Hawaii, it's not really worth the trouble to go into town. We weren't in for very long and shoved off on an Essex class carrier quite soon after for places I can't tell you about."*

On March 29, 1945, "Timmy" was a Flight Leader on a fighter sweep of eighteen Corsairs over the Japanese homeland. They attacked seven Zekes and one Jack airborne en route to the target and destroyed all but one Zeke. Continuing to the target, the flight strafed eight small ships, leaving one in a sinking condition, two burning, and the others seriously damaged. Proceeding to Kagoshima Airfield, the hangar and shop area was bombed, strafed and attacked with rockets. One 500lb bomb and two rockets entered a hangar roof, and the structure was left burning; seven rocket hits were scored on an assembly and repair building. Two rocket hits and strafing runs were then made on a hangar at Chirau Airfield which was left smoking badly. En route from Japan, two small ships moored at a dock at Bono Nisaki were strafed and one was left on fire. Cumulative damage to the enemy was extreme. "Timmy" noted on March 30, 1945:

> *"I feel like a professional killer instead of an eager novice."*

On March 31, 1945, he stated:

> *"The nuggets are promising themselves to be every bit the pilots I've been sure they would be*

"Timmy" Gile with a tennis racket.
Courtesy of the Gile Family

"I feel like a professional killer instead of an eager novice."

CLEMENT DEXTER "TIMMY" GILE

"Timmy" Gile leading a flight of F4U-1s off Manteo, North Carolina, in the spring of 1943. *Robert Lawson Photograph Collection, National Museum of Naval Aviation / US Navy photo*

and have stood up against the test by fire in great shape. Occasionally they get a little lazy and start to straggle all over the sky but when I ask them to "Close up" and tell them I know it seems a little late but that I do feel it important, they take it in great shape and sock back into the formations I know they're able and willing to fly."

On April 8, 1945, "Timmy" noted:

"Maybe this goddamn war will be over when I get back. Germany tottering, Russia throwing up her non - intervention pact, Japan's cabinet resigning to a man, Okinawa invaded. The news is good."

On April 16, 1945, due to a kamikaze hit on the USS Intrepid, they departed from Okinawa for Ulithi in order to check the damage and arrived on April 18, 1945. They were unable to repair damage at Ulithi, so they departed for San Francisco via Pearl Harbor and arrived on May 19, 1945. From May 21 to June 4, 1945, the squadron was given leave. "Timmy" and June returned to some of their old haunts for a ten day leave and then went to the West Coast, a week in Palm Springs, and three or four weeks on duty, then "Timmy" returned to his carrier.

On June 29, 1945, the Air Group again embarked for Pearl Harbor on the USS Intrepid and arrived in Pearl Harbor on July 5, 1945. Shortly after departing Pearl Harbor on July 30, 1945, "Timmy" was diagnosed with acute appendicitis and had surgery on August 7, 1945, on the Intrepid.

"Timmy" was back flying in September, and on September 10, 1945, noted:

"Flew over a place called Chee Foo today. The Chinese name is Yent'ai. Anyway it is on the northern coast of the Shantung Peninsula and the idea was the same as the rest of these silly hops - to impress the populace with a show of force. The more I fly over China, Korea and Manchuria, the more I want to go home. Something's got to pop soon and it'll make a lot of difference."

On September 12, 1945, he was thinking of home:

"The ship is on its way to Okinawa. We get in tomorrow. I am through flying. I took my last

Taken in Chatham, Massachusetts, on Cape Cod at his mother's house looking out over the water. "Timmy" is holding his daughter Shelley. His other daughter Toni is standing beside him. They spent every summer on Cape Cod, where he loved to play golf, fish, and go out on the boat that he built. This is one of his daughter Toni's favorite photos.
Courtesy of the Gile Family

hop yesterday and as far as almost everyone is concerned, my Naval career is over!"

He further noted on September 13, 1945:

"We got into Okinawa today and are anchored in the harbor. There are lots of other ships here and some of them are leaving for the States soon and I hope to get on one in the next week. There were no small boats available today so the Air Group Commander didn't get ashore to find out what to do with those of us he plans to let off the ship, but he's going in first thing in the a.m. to get the word."

On September 26, 1945, "Timmy" disembarked at Okinawa and returned to the States; he was in the first group of officers to leave the squadron for civilian life. On his fitness report dated September 26, 1945, it was stated:

"Lt. Gile is an outstanding Naval Officer and an outstanding Naval Aviator. He has boundless enthusiasm and a bulldog type determination. His leadership as a strike leader in combat is commendable, and he has forcefully, aggressively and with great skill lead numerous successful attacks on enemy installations. He has a cheerful disposition and high moral code. He has contributed much to the successful tour of duty of this squadron. Lt. Gile is eligible for release."

He left the Navy on December 29, 1945, but stayed in the Reserves until October 15, 1954. He had logged 2500 Navy flight hours up to this time.

Yale University was dear to his heart, and he continued to be a very active alumnus. He was Class Agent for Davenport from 1963 until his death, a member of the Executive Committee, Chairman of the Special Gifts Committee for the 30th reunion, a Director of the Yale Alumni Fund for three years, on the admission committee of the Yale Club in New York, and Chairman of the 39th reunion class dinner.

"Timmy" Gile and the Gile family at brother John's wedding in Colorado Springs in 1955. Back, row left to right: David, John, and "Tim." Front row left to right are David's wife Patsy, Harriet ("Timmy's" stepmother), and Clement Gile Senior.
Courtesy of the Gile Family

"Timmy" and June Gile taken in Chatham, Massachusetts, after he came home from the war. *Courtesy of the Gile Family*

After the war from 1945 to 1948 he was the Vice President of Air Commuting Inc., a seaplane and helicopter commuter airline, qualified as a helicopter pilot, and spent three years in Lima, Peru, for Panagra. Then he went to work at Morgan Guaranty Trust Company and was a Vice President when he took early retirement in 1976 because of health problems

"Timmy" spent every summer with his family in Chatham, Massachusetts, where he played golf and loved to fish for the "*wily Bass.*" He built a speed boat called the Sea Robin and used it for waterskiing, trips to the North Beach, and all around the waters of Cape Cod.

Flying was always his great passion, and he maintained his instrument rating and flew a twin-engined aircraft N5888S that he co-owned until 1977, flying out of Westchester and the Chatham Airports. He was a great do-it-yourselfer and an expert at carpentry. He also played golf and a mean game of tennis, even though he didn't play very often. He loved bridge and classical music. Although he was a smoker all his life he was very fit and ran every morning, and generally took very good care of himself. He enjoyed almost perfect health until two years before he died. In those two years, he had triple heart bypass surgery and prostate cancer, followed by lung cancer. "Timmy"

. . . the guys he served with and flew with were a wild bunch and got into all kinds of mischief.

His daughter Toni

Gile died on November 21, 1978, in Rye, New York.

He had four children: Anne (Toni), Shelley, Jean (Robin), and Susan.

In addition to the two DFCs with Fighting 17, "Timmy" was awarded a further two DFCs, three Air Medals, Navy Unit Commendation, the Purple Heart, Asiatic - Pacific Campaign Medal with four Gold Stars, American Defense Service Medal, American Campaign Medal, and WWII Victory Medal.

On October 13, 1985, a Corsair FG-1 was dedicated on the deck of the USS *Yorktown* to honor" Timmy" Gile and his squadron-mate "Chuck" Pillsbury. The aircraft had been rebuilt with funds raised by Yale classmates to commemorate the two distinguished Yale graduates. The Corsair is still on the *Yorktown* at Patriots Point Museum in Charleston, South Carolina, but has been moved below decks on permanent display.

"Timmy" Gile in Antigua with his brother-in-law, John Tyner. *Courtesy of the Gile Family*

Opposite:
"Timmy" Gile in 1942. He served as a Gunnery Instructor at N.A.S. Miami in 1942 prior to reporting to Fighting 17. *Courtesy of the Gile Family*

"Timmy" Gile was an excellent carpenter, and he built this boat "Sea Robin" one winter. *Courtesy of the Gile Family*

9

ROGER RICHARDS HEDRICK

12 VICTORIES

Roger Richards Hedrick was born in Pasadena, California, on September 2, 1914, the son of Perry Lee and Mabel Richards Hedrick. Roger's parents were originally from Iowa. They moved to Chicago, where Roger's older sister, Helen, was born in 1905. Roger's father was a Civil Engineer working for the city of Chicago before Roger was born. His father "cleaned up" some unsanitary buildings by enforcing building regulations and the Mob didn't like it. As a result of that he was set up; money was stuffed in his coat pocket, and he was conveniently arrested. So he was either fired or resigned. He was later exonerated, but his work career was ruined. Roger inherited this sense of honesty and righteousness from his father.

Opposite:
Roger Hedrick, Fighting 17 Executive Officer and ace with twelve victories on November 4, 1949, at Newport, Rhode Island, aged 34. *Courtesy of the Hedrick Family*

Roger's father moved his family to El Centro, in Southern California down by the border with Mexico, a very barren and hot place. Perry started his own engineering business: building, irrigation, piping, etc. Roger was born on September 2, 1914, at the hottest time of the year in El Centro, so his mother and sister were spending the summer in Pasadena, which is where Roger was born. The family later moved to Hollywood, California, when Roger was in grammar school. Roger graduated from Hollywood High School, and attended that school with several famous movie stars of his era. He had small parts as an extra in a couple of movies.

Perry Lee Hedrick suffered a fatal aneurism in July 1931 when Roger was sixteen. This experience and living through the Great Depression shaped the rest of his life, as the Depression did for most other young adult Americans who lived through it. As the family company no longer existed, Roger's sister

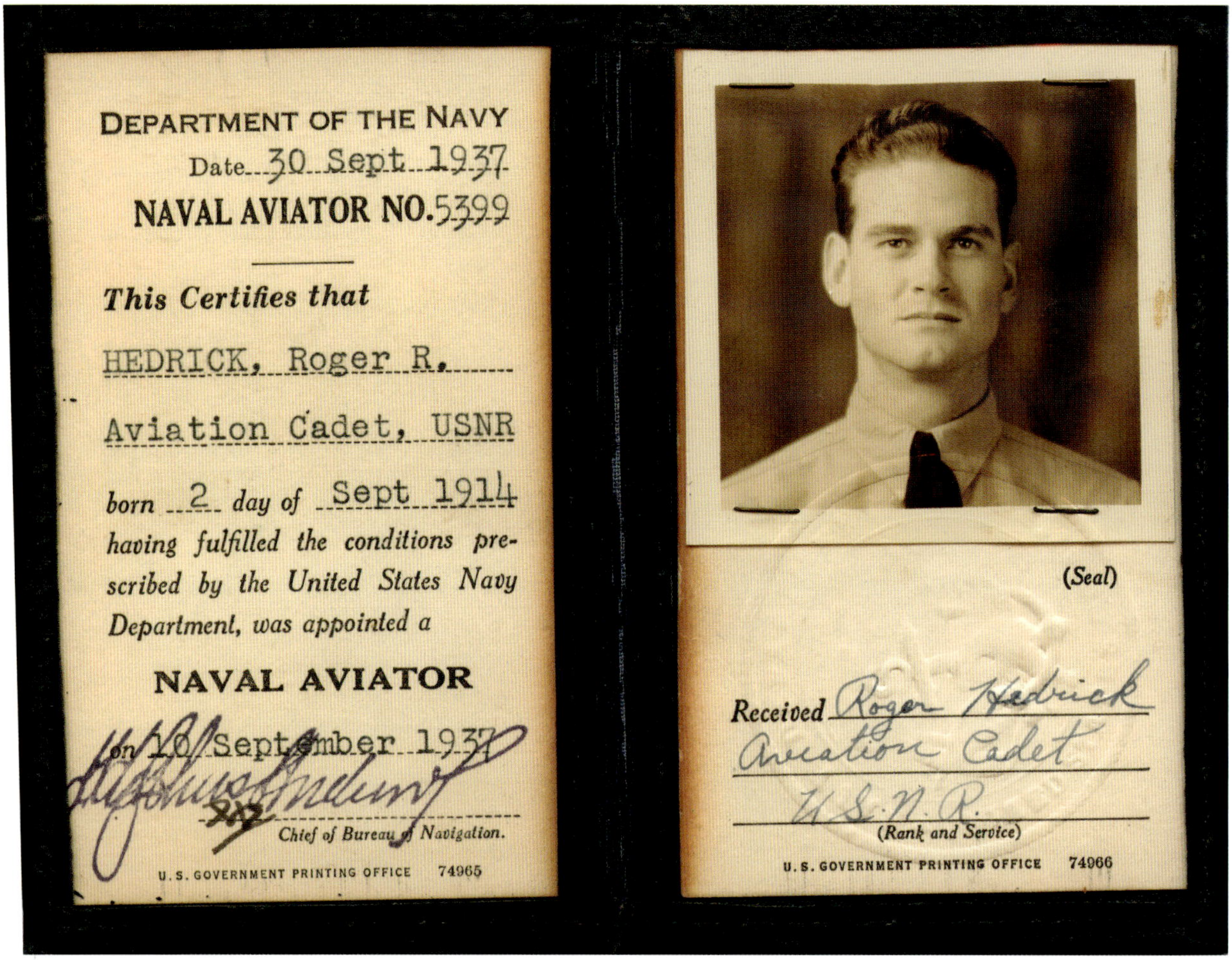

DEPARTMENT OF THE NAVY

Date 30 Sept. 1937

NAVAL AVIATOR NO. 5399

This Certifies that

HEDRICK, Roger R.

Aviation Cadet, USNR

born 2 *day of* Sept 1914 *having fulfilled the conditions prescribed by the United States Navy Department, was appointed a*

NAVAL AVIATOR

on 10 September 1937

Chief of Bureau of Navigation.

U.S. GOVERNMENT PRINTING OFFICE 74965

(Seal)

Received Roger Hedrick

Aviation Cadet

U.S.N.R.

(Rank and Service)

U.S. GOVERNMENT PRINTING OFFICE 74966

Aviation Cadet Roger Hedrick's Naval Aviator Certificate in 1937. *Courtesy of the Hedrick Family*

Helen, a school teacher, helped support the family, as did Roger's mother, who took boarders into their home to help pay the mortgage and Roger took what jobs he could, working in gas stations, etc. His plan to attend college quickly ended with his devoting all of his time after school to trying to help bring income to his mother to keep their home. According to his daughter Alida, the Depression had a profound effect on Roger:

> *"I really think his character was molded by the Depression. The very survival of one's family depended on your actions. He took that responsibility very seriously. He never took anything for granted. Any accomplishment was a victory not only for himself, but for those around him. He had a huge responsibility thrust upon him at age sixteen, during the middle of our country's most difficult economic times. There was not time nor room for frivolity. Every action taken mattered, had serious consequences. I assume that mindset carried through and became a part of who he was. Dad weighed every expenditure very carefully, always thinking of the consequences. I believe this mindset carried over into his decisions in the rest of his life - the "nuts and bolts" thinking that carried over to his Navy experience."*

Roger was able to attend Los Angeles City Junior College, which was basically free, and got two years of college education, graduating with a Degree of Associate in Arts.

Roger spent two summers at Citizens Military Training Camp in Monterey, California: first in

Roger Hedrick and Barbara Baril in Honolulu, where they met at a Tea Dance in 1938. *Courtesy of the Hedrick Family*

1931, when he was sixteen, the year his father died; and again in 1934, at age nineteen.

Held annually each summer during the years 1921 to 1940, the Citizens Military Training Camps differed from National Guard and Reserves training, in that the program allowed male citizens to obtain basic military training without an obligation to call-up for active duty. C.M.T.C. camps were a month in length and held at approximately fifty Army bases nationally. Roger entered the Navy on July 15, 1936, at age twenty-one. He joined as an Aviation Cadet because it was a good opportunity for a well paid career, and he was appointed a Naval Aviator on September 10, 1937, less than a month after turning twenty-three. He attended flight school at N.A.S. Pensacola in Class 95c from October 1936. On completion of his training he was ordered to VF-4 on USS *Ranger*, where he spent 3½ years as a fighter pilot. Whilst assigned to the USS *Ranger*, the following was noted on Hedrick's fitness report:

"Hedrick has accomplished his duties with complete thoroughness and uniform excellence."

"Awarded Navy "E" for excellence in Dive Bombing Practice."

"Awarded Navy "E" for excellence in Fixed Machine Gun Practice."

"Excellent combat material, very cool at all times."

In 1938, he was on a Naval tour that took him to Honolulu, Hawaii. There he met Barbara Baril at a "Tea Dance," and they dated for the two weeks he was in port, then corresponded for two years. He proposed via mail in 1939 and she accepted. She took a ship from Hawaii to Los Angeles in the spring of 1940, then a train to Norfolk, Virginia, where he was stationed, and they were married in Williamsburg, Virginia, on June 1, 1940. Whilst with Fighting Squadron Four he received a humorous award for "*Obstreperous and Malicious Conduct*" on July 21, 1938:

To Aviation Cadet Roger R. Hedrick USNR

Via Commander Fighting Squadron Four

1. At about 14:40 on June 14, 1938, the above mentioned officer with malicious and maladroit ineptitude did land an aircraft, namely, to wit, 4-F-17, at Palm Springs Airport with the wheels in a retracted position, and, in so doing, did demolish, destroy and render incapable for further flight said airplane. This infamous conduct, not only removed 4-F-17 from the eligible list, but impinged upon the ears of the peaceful residents of Palm Springs a terrific clatter and a considerable amount of dust.

2. For this obstreperous conduct, the board of awards presents the above named officer with the special Viewig Trophy for Low Altitude Inverted Flight and Asphalt Acrobatics.

First Endorsement
Fighting Squadron Four

Roger Hedrick at Guantanamo Bay in 1939.
Courtesy of the Hedrick Family

In 1941 Hedrick was about to leave the Navy, as he had been hired as a Captain by American Airlines. Shortly before he was due to leave the government cancelled his permission to leave. From May 1941 until January 1943, Hedrick served at the Naval Air Station, Miami, Florida, as a Gunnery Instructor working with Tom Blackburn. Blackburn remembered him when he was forming Fighting 17. On his fitness report dated October 23, 1942, while at N.A.S. Miami, Roger received a 4.0 mark as Instructor Fighter Gunnery Division, which is the highest achievable mark. Roger relates how he came to be with Fighting 17:

> *"I recall while we were in Miami, Joe Clifton once asked me if I would go with him when he was forming I think Fighting Twelve as his Exec., but having served with Joe and flown on his wing for a year or so in Fighting Four sometime before that; even though he was a Prince of a man and somebody else that I almost adored because he was such a kind, considerate guy, I felt there were certain areas where he and I perhaps didn't see eye to eye and I might be a fifth wheel (not needed). So I begged off and Joe was kind enough to let me remain on there in Miami until, fortunately Tom Blackburn selected me as his Exec., and that I think was the single most fortunate thing that ever occurred to me in the service. And gave me as a result of that, an education that stood me in good stead in later years and an opportunity to really learn from a*

After Roger and Barbara met, they dated for the two weeks he was in port. They then corresponded for two years prior to getting married in 1940. *Courtesy of the Hedrick Family*

guy who knew what the score was. My log book shows I had 2,900+ hours (with approx 2,500) in fighters prior to my first aerial combat in November 1943."

On his fitness report dated September 4, 1943, he achieved a mark of 4.0 as pilot and 3.9 for all other duties from Tom Blackburn:

> *"Lt. Hedrick is an excellent leader, showing ample qualities of leadership and good judgement. His habits and character are unimpeachable."*

After training for nine months with Fighting 17, Hedrick had the chance to demonstrate just how good an aerial marksman he was when on November 1, 1943, on patrol over U.S. ships in Empress Augusta Bay, a force of about nine Zekes were spotted at 23,000 ft. Roger took his flight up sun to get into position 1,500 ft. above the Zekes and came down in a 20° dive. He fired into a Zeke's fuselage (using only four guns, as his generator had gone dead on the flight up) and saw it burst into flames and crash. Roger was credited with one Zeke destroyed on this flight, and his notes below describe the combat:

"The first combat action that I actually experienced, my group was on station at Empress Augusta Bay. I heard the air controller on the beach broadcasting information as to a Japanese raid incoming from Rabaul which consisted of bombers and fighters escorting the bombers, and so of course I immediately speeded up our approach to Bougainville and climbing as rapidly as we could also. But unfortunately en route, or shortly thereafter, my darn generator went out on the plane, and as a result I turned off my radio to conserve power and climbed the rest of the way on up to the Treasury Islands without any radio. And at that junction in scanning the skies over Empress Augusta Bay, I saw a group of specks way off in the distance to the north of us. So before heading down to the beach area, I decided I'd better take a look at these because I couldn't believe any of our people would be up at that height. I think they were about 20,000 feet in that particular area. So still climbing to get above them, I swept out to sea to get up sun from them and came in for a closer look, and saw eight Zeros, the first Jap fighters that I had seen and this was still from some distance, but I was able to identify them definitely as being Japs.

Roger and Barbara Hedrick's wedding photo at Williamsburg, Virginia, on June 1, 1940. *Courtesy of the Hedrick Family*

So then I set up in a general slow, moderately slow high side run coming down astern of them, and giving the visual attack sign, rocking my wings, I came in on the center leader of the group and expected and hoped that the others in my formation would open fire when I did and I rocked my wings again just before I opened fire and as a result we would be able to get a goodly number of these eight planes.

I came in pretty close to my target, and fired, and as I fired, he immediately burst into flames. Well, the rest of the planes did a snap roll almost, and went vertically for the deck, and we took out after them. I later learned that the plane that I had hit had actually exploded after I had gotten past it. Incidentally, I still hadn't turned on my radio, of course, and warned the people and told them exactly what we had facing us.

I had the best look naturally, and some of them probably hadn't even had more than a glimpse of the formation before I opened fire and it was my total ignorance on the electrical capacity of that plane that prevented me from doing this, from opening up, giving the information. And now of course I regret very much that we hadn't because we might have had a much higher rate of success with those eight planes if I had. Anyway, we go following these planes down to the deck and mixed it up with them and whoever else was down in that area for a very considerable length of time. And I believe that the other pilots in my group, in addition to the plane that I had previously gotten, got an additional three or four planes before we had to head on back to Ondongo.

I recall what a real shock it was to me as we ended up just astern of the Jap planes. They had not spotted us as we came in. When I saw that first red meatball insignia on the side of one of the planes and to realize that at long last we were in combat with a chance to kill some of the enemy that had been inflicting such grievous harm on our friends since December 7, 1941."

On November 8, 1943, Roger's flight was assigned to cover landing forces over Empress Augusta Bay when he saw twenty-four Zekes and Hamps and fifteen Vals.

Roger chandelled across the enemy formation to get into position, and the Zekes immediately formed a loose defensive Lufbery Circle. In the attack Roger lost sight of his wingman, Mills Schanuel. He picked out a Zeke on the far side of the circle, made a high side run, and hit him. The Zeke dived straight down through the clouds with fuel streaming from the aircraft. By this time the other Zekes were in the clouds, so Roger went in to find them but with no success, so he headed NW at full speed to try to cut across their course. The action now developed into a running fight up the SW coast of Bougainville, almost as far as Buka. Roger spotted a six-aircraft flight at about 12,000 ft. He began his attack and the Zekes turned in towards him; he hit one of them on an opposite-course run. Pieces flew from the Zeke's engine, although it flashed by too quickly to determine the extent of damage. Roger made several passes at the remaining Zekes, finally catching one as he was recovering from a chandelle. He saw his

Roger and Barbara Hedrick in 1941. *Courtesy of the Hedrick Family*

So then I set up in a general slow, moderately slow high side run coming down astern of them, and giving the visual attack sign, rocking my wings, I . . . hoped that the others in my formation would open fire when I did and I rocked my wings again just before I opened fire . . .

Roger Richards Hedrick

J. C. Duke, Plane Captain AMM 3c, and Lt. Cdr. Roger Hedrick in March 1944 at Piva Yoke Fighter Strip, Bougainville. *Courtesy of the Hedrick Family*

bullets go in astern of the engine. Roger was credited with three Zekes damaged on this mission. Roger Hedrick describes the action:

> *I led four of the Hogs down on what seems to me now about thirty Jap fighters, all Zeros I guess, and I recall distinctly the thought that was in my mind, well, here's where we learn how good the Hog is. Well I was astounded when we hit these planes they immediately broke up into two big World War I Lufbery Circles. Well actually one circle had considerably more planes and therefore larger than the other. Now of course we had a good 5000 feet on them, the altitude advantage and the speed, we then came on back down hitting the outside of the circles and spraying the guys in the circle. Now I don't recall exactly how many passes, but it wasn't very many before the six of us, the other two planes had joined us of course, had them broken up into individual bunches or sections of flights, and it wasn't long either after that until we were broken up individually and a general melee was on ending up with us chasing them back toward Rabaul.*
>
> *I think one of the interesting things I made, again I don't remember how many, but a goodly number of head on runs against the Japs, and as you darn well know, a head on run, in order to get you deflection, you end up either standing on your tail or diving straight down, depending on how far away you start. But in any event, on several of those passes, three I think now, I was using the engine as a target, I saw large hunks of what I took to be a least two cylinders in size flying out of the planes.*

Opposite:
Roger Hedrick sitting in his aircraft #17 shown with nine victories. *Robert Lawson Photograph Collection, National Museum of Naval Aviation / US Navy photo*

The USS *Bunker Hill* on fire after a kamikaze attack on May 11, 1945. Roger Hedrick was Commander of VF-84 and later Air Group Commander on the USS *Bunker Hill*. *Courtesy of the Hedrick Family*

> *I remember seeing a couple of mine going down, not in flames, but streaming big buckets of gasoline, big streams of gas coming out where their tanks had been punctured. I was absolutely convinced we had by far, and know it to this day, the best plane that we could have had for that time and place. And if I did ever have any doubts, which I don't think I did initially, even as to the capability of that plane, they had been erased by this fight."*

On November 11, 1943, Roger was in action again as cover for a Task Force in the Battle of the Solomon Sea.

When the Japanese attack began Hedrick's division (himself, Mills Schanuel, "Andy" Anderson and Jack Chasnoff) turned towards the Task Force. They approached, descending from 18,000 to 12,000 ft., and saw four Zekes pursued by Corsairs. Roger and Mills attacked one who avoided them and headed North in a 45° dive with Roger right on his tail. Roger fired from 300 yards, and the Zeke caught fire just as it entered cloud. Roger and Mills then joined with Tom Blackburn and returned to Barakoma. Roger scored his second confirmed victory with one Zeke destroyed.

He was again into action when a flight of eight Corsairs were assigned to fly cover over U.S. shipping in Empress Augusta Bay on November 17, 1943.

It was reported that the ships were under attack, and all aircraft were directed to intercept the enemy. The Corsairs raced down to 6,000 ft., and when ten miles from Cape Torokina saw two groups of enemy aircraft heading NW.

Roger's division broke left and attacked one group consisting of three Kates and four Zekes, with "Timmy" Gile's division breaking right to attack the second group of five Kates and five Tonys. Roger's division closed rapidly on the Japanese and made an attack from dead astern on a Zeke, who made a slight climbing turn to the left before exploding. He then made two passes at another Zeke, although he missed, but then saw Jack Chasnoff shoot it down.

Roger then turned back to look for more enemy aircraft but saw none. He did see "Andy" Anderson parachuting down, so he circled Anderson, who was now in the sea, and signalled Chasnoff to join up. The pair then headed for Cape Moltke. Roger calculated the distance and bearing and turned south to Cape Torokina. Since his radio was unreliable he dropped a message giving Anderson's position. He then returned to relocate Anderson, but could not find him. Roger then left the area and returned to Ondongo. Roger was credited with a Zeke destroyed on this mission.

After leave in Australia, Hedrick returned to the intense combat over Rabaul at the end of January 1944.

On January 26, 1944, Roger, together with twenty-nine other Corsairs, was covering the joint SBD - TBF strike on Lakunai Airfield. Roger sighted his first Zekes midway between Duke of York Island and Lakunai. His flight was at 19,000 ft. and the Japanese at 22,000 ft. The group engaged his flight, and Roger got one shot at long range. As he recovered he saw six more Zekes in column above and behind him. He turned towards them and they rolled over and dived away. As Hedrick pulled up his wingman, Ensign John "Fatso" Ellsworth, lost him, and he found himself alone at 12,000 ft. directly over Rabaul. He saw three Zekes 300 ft. above him on an opposite course. The Zekes rolled over and made an attack in column formation. Roger made a 180° turn and passed close by them. He then started down to the rally point five miles east of Cape Gazelle and was over the channel at 6,000 ft. astern of the main SBD formation when three Zekes dived past the nose of his Corsair in pursuit of the bombers. Roger followed, and the leading Zeke realized this and zoomed up. Roger caught him at the top of his zoom climb, fired, and the Zeke's left wing root caught fire; as Roger pulled clear the Zeke went down.

Roger then joined up with a Marine Corsair and scissored over the SBDs. He got shots at two more Zekes who disengaged. The rest of the flight was uneventful.

Roger was in action again two days later on January 28, 1944, when part of the partial cover for the joint SBD - TBF strike on Tobera Airfield, New Britain.

The high cover approached the target area at 30,000 ft., and as the bombers made their attack Roger saw twelve Zekes at 24,000 ft. coming in from the seaward in a loose column, breaking off separately and making attacks in formation. Roger's flight of six aircraft came down in column first and he made four attacks, although he had only one gun firing. After the third pass a Zeke got on his tail, so he zoomed up. Just as the Zeke appeared to be stalling out, Paul Cordray came up behind the Zeke and fired a long burst, making the Zeke catch fire and fall away. Roger finally got four guns working and was ten miles astern of the retiring bombers at 4,000 ft. when he saw a Zeke two miles away, closing slowly on the bombers. The Zeke nosed over at a Corsair low over the sea and Roger fired, but at too long a range. The Zeke pulled up in an Immelmann and Roger followed. He closed to 100 yards and fired, hitting the left wing root and engine. The pilot bailed out and the aircraft caught fire. Roger strafed the chute, but believes that his shots bracketed it. This was his fifth confirmed victory, which made him an ace.

Two days later, on January 30, 1944, Roger was leading the flight assigned as high cover on a B-25 strike on a supply dump near Lakunai Airfield when he spotted twenty Zekes at about 30,000 ft. north of the target. The B-25s had just made their runs when four Zekes closed on Roger's division, which then dived away. During the dive "Fatso" Ellsworth, Roger's wingman, picked up a Zeke in the dive, and at 12,000 ft. set him on fire with a burst from dead astern. Roger and "Fatso" pulled up after another Zeke who looped and came head-on, still on his back. The Zeke dived with Roger following, and as the Zeke pulled up Roger hit him from seven o'clock slightly above and at very close range. The Zeke crashed steeply into the water.

Roger's last engagement with Fighting 17 against the Japanese was on February 18, 1944, when his flight was cover on the first of two squadrons of B-24s striking Vunakanau Airfield.

Roger made his first contact in the fight, which had been started by "Timmy" Gile's division south of Vunakanau. He and his wingman dived down from 29,000 ft. and he caught a Zeke in a stern attack at 18,000 ft., setting it on fire. He then spotted another Zeke below him and made another stern attack. The Zeke dived away, but Roger kept on his tail and fired until the Zeke exploded at 12,000 ft. Roger's wingman lost him in this run, so Roger headed back towards Cape Gazelle, and at the Cape, as he was circling, he saw eight Zekes climbing in a loose column at 15,000 ft. a few miles east of Tobera. Roger went in for a stern attack on the lead Zeke, which then caught fire. Roger, seeing no more

Zekes on his recovery, joined up on the bombers. Roger had scored three confirmed Zekes destroyed, and this ended his scoring with Fighting 17.

Fighting Squadron 17 was awarded the Navy Unit Commendation for operations at Treasury Island, Bougainville, Rabaul, and Green Islands, and Hedrick was personally awarded the Distinguished Flying Cross and a Gold Star in lieu of a second DFC. In May 1944 he was assigned as Commanding Officer of Fighting Squadron 84. He led that squadron in the Iwo Jima operation and first carrier strikes on Tokyo, shooting down three more Japanese fighters for a total of twelve confirmed victories. He participated in the Okinawa Gunto operation until the USS *Bunker Hill* was hit by two kamikazes on May 11, 1945. That aircraft carrier was awarded the Presidential Unit Citation for heroic service, as were her Air Groups 17, 8, 4, and 84 during the period November 11, 1943, through May 11, 1945. He was personally awarded the Silver Star Medal, Gold Stars in lieu of the third and fourth DFCs, and the Air Medal and two Gold Stars in lieu of the second and third Air Medals. The Air Medals were for operations against the Japanese (five strikes each) during the periods February 16 to March 23, 1945; March 24 to 30, 1945; and March 31 to April 13, 1945; and the fourth Distinguished Flying Cross was for completing twenty strikes on hostile shipping, airfields and installations during the overall period of February 16 to May 5, 1945.

On February 25, 1945, Hedrick was awarded the Silver Star. He describes the mission:

> *"A Jap 50 caliber round removed from my F4U-1D's gas tank after attacks, strafing and air combat, in Tokyo area on February 25, 1945 from USS Bunker Hill (CV-17) with A.G. 84. In which we (VF-84) destroyed fourteen enemy fighters. I shot down three and have camera gun film showing kills.*
>
> *My plane was hit several (9) times by A/A fire and damaged so I had no prop control (locked in hi speed) and no mixture control and also had to use two hands on the stick to keep the plane in level flight - elevator damaged - (muscles in my arms and shoulders quivered for two days afterward because of prolonged stress). I shot my last two planes down holding pressure on the stick with two hands.*
>
> *At one point of return to the Bunker Hill which was 150 miles off shore, had the rest of my flight slow down to conserve gas while I soared out ahead knowing I was rapidly running out of fuel and thinking about how cold the water looked (and was).*
>
> *I finally stood part way up in the cockpit and yanked on the prop control with all my strength and got it up into low speed and saved enough gas to make it back aboard ship. The prop control cable tube had been bent by a bullet and the cable stuck."*

Roger Hedrick in 1946. *Courtesy of the National Archives*

The citation for the Silver Star stated:

> *"For conspicuous gallantry and Intrepidity as pilot of a fighter plane in Fighting Squadron 84, attached to the USS Bunker Hill, in action against enemy Japanese forces in the vicinity*

of Tokyo, on February 25, 1945. Skillfully leading a flight of sixteen fighter planes in a sweep over Japanese airfields, Commander (then Lieutenant Commander) Hedrick directed his flight in the destruction of nine enemy airborne fighter aircraft and in the probable destruction or damage of five others, personally accounting for three of the hostile aircraft, two of which he destroyed after his plane had been hit by enemy aircraft fire. While three of his divisions made a strafing and rocket attack on Konoike airfield, leaving several hangars and oil storage tanks burning, he led his own division in the destruction of two grounded aircraft on another airfield. Carrying out his mission under unfavorable weather conditions, intense and accurate enemy anti-aircraft fire and against superior numbers of hostile fighter planes, Commander Hedrick, by his skill as an airman and his daring leadership, contributed materially to the success of his squadron. His devotion to duty was in keeping with the highest traditions of the United States Naval Service."

His fitness report noted on June 3, 1945, when he was Commanding Officer VF-84 and as Commander Air Group 84 when the Air Group Commander was listed as missing in action from April 27, 1945:

"Performance under combat excellent."

In July 1945 he assumed command of Experimental Fighting Squadron 200, and from October of that year until May 1946 had command, successively, of Fighter Squadron 200 of Composite Air Group, Operational Development Force, and of the Composite Air Group, Operational Development Group. He became a student at the Naval School, General Line, Newport, Rhode Island, in 1946, and in June 1947 reported to the Naval Air Station Jacksonville, Florida, as Officer in Charge of the Instructors Aviation Training Unit. From November 1948 to July 1949 he had similar duty at the Naval Air Station, Corpus Christi, Texas. In his fitness report in April 1949 it was recorded:

"Cdr. Hedrick is an outstanding Naval Officer. He is able, dependable, courteous, conscientious and of exemplary military character. He has maintained the Navy Flight Exhibition Team the Blue Angels at the highest proficiency."

Completing the course at the Naval War College, Newport, Rhode Island, in June 1950, he became Executive Officer of the Fleet All Weather Training Unit, Pacific, at Barbers Point, Hawaii, training night attack and night fighter pilots for the Korean hostilities. On September 19, 1952, he reported to the Naval Air Station, Whidbey Island, Washington, as Executive Officer. When detached in June 1954 he had brief instruction at the Naval Schools Command, U.S. Naval Station, Treasure Island, San Francisco, California, and the same month reported on board the USS *Boxer* (CVA-21), where he served as Executive Officer of that carrier until September

U.S. Naval Air Missile Test Center, Pt. Mugu, California, on April 12, 1957. VX-4 Annual Administrative Material Inspection. L-R: Roger Hedrick is the second officer from left - and the tallest. *US Navy photo via Courtesy of the Hedrick Family*

1955. Moving on to become Commanding Officer of Air Development Squadron Four, he worked with the unsuccessful F7U-3M Cutlass fighter, although this period is notable, particularly for the first deployment of the Sparrow 111 air-to-air missile. Hedrick served there until July 1957, and in August reported to the Bureau of Ordnance, Navy Department, Washington, DC, where he served as Deputy Director, Plans and Programs Division for development of the Polaris Ballistic Missile Submarine Weapons System. On November 1, 1958, Roger Hedrick retired from the Navy at the age of forty-four and was advanced to the rank of Rear Admiral on the basis of combat citations.

On his last fitness report on October 8, 1958, when assigned to the Bureau of Ordnance Special Projects Office Duties - Deputy Director, Plans and Programs Division, it stated:

> *"Capt. Hedrick is a thorough, conscientious and able Naval Officer, well versed in his profession. His military and personal character is above reproach. He meets people well and makes uniformly good impressions both in the service and among civilians. Willing to accept all the responsibility given him, he completes his tasks to my full satisfaction. Capt. Hedrick has recently submitted his request for retirement. I shall be sorry to lose him and the Navy will lose a splendid officer. W.F. Raborn Rear Admiral."*

Roger went to work for his brother as Director of Planning for a construction company that built and managed apartment buildings and settled in Arcadia, California. He retired from the company in 1975 at the age of sixty-two and bought a home overlooking the beach and Catalina Island, in Orange County, California. After fifty-three years of marriage his wife Barbara died, and in 1998 Roger decided to move to a retirement community. After a bad fall in his apartment he moved to a smaller sheltered community that had six residents.

Even though he was the consummate military man, he was a devoted family man. Up until his death, he was always concerned that everything was well in the lives of his three children, as his daughter Alida remembers:

> *"My dad was such an excellent role model, and person to emulate in so many ways. What you see is what you get person. I cannot lie, you can read my feelings on my face, and when I tell someone I will do something - I do it, and expect others to be the same way. I am way too literal - when someone says something is X, I believe them, because I wouldn't say that unless it is so. Dad absolutely led his life that way. Straightforward and to the point, no pussy footing around, no bull - just the truth as he knew it and my dad was a fighter, his dad was a fighter – it's in the genes. We don't give up."*

Roger's wingman Mills Schanuel recalls:

> *"I flew on Roger Hedrick's wing during the life of Fighting 17. This is true - from the day the squadron was commissioned in Norfolk to its decommissioning in San Francisco.*
>
> *Hedrick was the "nuts - and - bolts" engineer who made things work. In addition, he was a superb flyer. Never, no matter how hairy the combat situation, did I ever see him rattled or confused. Watching him carefully position his plane for a kill is something I will never forget. I feel that Roger Hedrick's contribution to the success of the squadron has not been fully appreciated."*

Rear Admiral Roger Hedrick died on January 10, 2006, aged 91 with his children Barbara, Rick, and Alida with him at his bedside.

His decorations and campaign medals comprised: Silver Star, Distinguished Flying Cross with three Gold Stars, Air Medal with two Gold Stars, Presidential Unit Citation Ribbon and Navy Unit Commendation Ribbon, American Defense Service Medal with Star; American Campaign Medal; Asiatic - Pacific Campaign Medal with four Stars; World War II Victory Medal; and the National Defense Medal.

Roger Hedrick was the second ranked U.S. Navy Corsair ace of World War II with twelve victories.

Opposite:
Roger Hedrick on July 10, 1954, as Executive Officer of USS *Boxer* (CVA-21). *US Navy photo via Courtesy of the Hedrick Family*

. . . we were in combat with a chance to kill some of the enemy that had been inflicting such grievous harm on our friends since December 7, 1941."

Lt. (jg) Ira C. "Ike" Kepford poses by the cockpit of his Courtesy of Vought F4U Corsair in March 1944. From November 1943 to February 1944 he shot down sixteen Japanese aircraft to become the Navy's then leading ace. *Courtesy of the National Archives*

10

IRA CASSIUS "IKE" KEPFORD

16 VICTORIES

One of World War II's great Navy aces, Ira Cassius "Ike" Kepford was born in Harvey, Illinois, on May 29, 1919, the son of George Raymond and Emma McLaughlin Kepford.

When "Ike" was a baby, his father worked as a head waiter in Cook County, Illinois, in a lunch room, and his grandfather, Cassius McLaughlin was a waiter at a lunch counter. George and Emma lived with her parents, and "Ike's" middle name came from Emma's father. Emma's grandmother was from Ireland.

The family moved to Muskegon when "Ike" was a few years old, and after settling in Muskegon his father George worked in garbage collection for the city service in 1930.

"Ike" was educated at Muskegon High School, where between 1935 and 1937 he lettered in three sports and was Captain of the football squad, leading the "Big Reds" to the State title in 1937. Although "Ike" had a reputation as a great blocking back, he was also on the team of Muskegon's State Championship basketball squad.

After he graduated from high school in 1938 he became a star football player at Northwestern University, where he lettered in football from 1939 to 1941.

One story from around this time was that "Ike's" family was so poor and struggling that his clothes could not be replaced and he had his sleeves wearing through. With holes in his elbows he cut his sleeves out, and due to the person "Ike" was everyone followed him and did the same, as they all wanted to be like him.

By June 17, 1941, "Ike" had completed thirty hours of flying time in a Civil Aviation Authority course. He enlisted in the U.S. Naval Reserve on August 18, 1941, where the report of the Naval Reserve Flight

"Ike" Kepford hamming it up. *US Naval Historical Center / M W "Butch" Davenport Collection*

Selection Board gave him a mark of 3.2 for potential ability as a Naval Officer and Aviator. It further noted that "Ike" was: "*Excellent officer material with a very good direct manner and was neat determined and rugged.*" He accepted his appointment as an Aviation Cadet on April 27, 1942.

After flight training at Naval Air Station Corpus Christi, Texas, and Miami, Florida, he was appointed an Ensign on October 16, 1942, and on October 23, 1942, was detached from N.A.S. Corpus Christi to report to Air Operational Training. "Ike" became a Naval Aviator on November 5, 1942.

He was detached from Naval Air Station, Miami, Florida, in December 1942 and reported to Carrier Qualification Training Unit, Norfolk, and then on to Fighting 17 on February 18, 1943. "Ike" remembered how he joined Fighting 17:

> *"When I checked in to Norfolk, Virginia I tried to find Fighting 17 and I'm fresh out of I think Miami, flying Brewster Buffaloes. I walked up and I'm looking for this Fighting 17 outfit and they sent me up to the second deck of this hangar. I walked in and there's a young looking burr headed intelligent guy and I walked in with this Manila envelope under my arm with my orders and boy am I green, and it's Tommy Blackburn and that's who I was looking for. He kinda looked up and said "Kepford." I said. "Yes sir I'm reporting for duty." He said. "Here's the handbook on that thing out there." I looked and there was one F4U sitting on the line. It was all we had to start with. "I'd like to have you check out in it." I fooled around and taxied that thing I think for two days!!*
>
> *On the ground you couldn't see but I did get it up and get it back eventually! That was one of the things I remember most."*

Another incident "Ike" remembers is as follows:

A rare photo of "Ike" Kepford in plane #7 early in the first tour. Most of the photos of Kepford were with his famous #29. *US Naval Historical Center / M W "Butch" Davenport Collection*

"I remember vividly. The F6F came out about the time we had some time in the F4U out at Norfolk. I hadn't seen one until I was out flying doing something and this damn fool jumped me. Just playing! It was a limey I didn't know why they had. I took him on and I finally got him and I drove him clear down and I guess we're going up the streets of Norfolk breaking some plate glass or something. But when I got back I had to go in and see Rog. I was two weeks in hack. But the problem was the Bunker Hill came in and they're lifting the airplanes on and guys were all leaving and packing. I'm sitting up here in the Base Officer's Quarters, nobody to talk to no nothing. I'm in hack solid man. I swear to this day I thought the guys had forgotten about me. I really did. At the last minute a couple of MP's came up with a jeep and I swear they were pulling up that gang plank when I got there. I had one parachute pack and that was it."

"Ike" was always associated with Corsair #29 as his most famous aircraft, but was assigned Corsair #32 in June 1943 as "Butch" Davenport's wingman in Lem Cooke's division. "Ike" moved up to section leader from #32 to #7, and by the time the second tour started was assigned #29. His wingman for the second tour was Don McQueen.

"Ike" went into combat with Fighting 17 in November 1943, and on a mission on November 11, 1943, demonstrated what a fearless fighter pilot he was.

Fighting 17 was covering a Carrier Task Force when the Japanese attacked with over 100 aircraft. Lt. Thad "Jug" Bell's division (Bell, Kepford, "Timmy" Gile and Lem Cooke) broke up just before the enemy attacked. Bell with 130 gallons and "Ike" with 120 gallons headed for home at 02:46.

They saw the ships begin firing, turned back, and let down fast. They entered the fight over the Task Force just after the dive bombers had started their dives. Bell and "Ike" followed them down. The Aichi Vals recovered very low, about 50 ft., just beyond the destroyer screen. They were in two loose columns; Bell picked the port column and "Ike" the starboard. The Vals kept their diving brakes down and were jigging, but Bell came down on one, saw it crash, picked up the aircraft ahead, and after a very short burst set it on fire and saw it go in.

The attack seemed to be over, although it was only the first wave, and Bell again started for home. He was fifteen miles from the Task Force when he looked back and saw a second attack. He turned but was too late to intercept. He was then very low on gas, so he gave the *Bunker Hill* a deferred forced landing signal. The carrier began clearing the deck when the third attack came in. Bell was unable to make any definite runs from 3,000 ft., and after the attack had been beaten off he joined up with "Ike" and landed aboard the *Bunker Hill* at 04:20. He refuelled and rearmed, took off at 05:45, and landed at Ondongo at 07:00.

"Ike" had broken off from Bell when they attacked the Vals. He got his first Val on a high side attack and saw him go down in flames. The Vals then headed for a rain squall. "Ike" made a flat side attack run from 500 ft., and after a short burst the Val

In this photo you can clearly see the extent of the damage to Kepford's F4U. This was caused when he ground-looped following a mission on January 30, 1944. *Robert Lawson Photograph Collection, National Museum of Naval Aviation / US Navy photo*

exploded. Just as he made this pass two Zekes made runs on him but missed. "Ike" pulled up into a right turn and headed for another Val. The Val went into a rain squall with "Ike" after him. The Val turned and "Ike" made a full deflection shot and saw the Val explode. He turned right out of the rain squall, and on an opposite course run on a fourth Val saw his bullets hit the wing.

It was at this stage that "Ike" joined up with Bell and they headed home. However, about fifteen miles from the Task Force they turned back to meet the second Japanese attack. "Ike" rocked his wings and got through the anti-aircraft fire. He spotted a Kate coming up aft of the *Bunker Hill*. He cut across and tried to get on the Kate's tail. As the A/A bursts were bumping him around he had difficulty in keeping his sights on, but finally he closed to 50 ft., fired, and saw the Kate roll over and go into the water. "Ike's" actions on this mission earned him the Navy Cross. The citation stated:

> *"For extraordinary heroism in aerial flight as a pilot of a Fighting Plane, attached to Fighting Squadron Seventeen, in action against enemy Japanese forces in the vicinity of the Solomon Islands, November 11, 1943. While covering United States Task Force Fifty Point Three in Empress Augusta Bay, Lieutenant (then Ensign) Kepford participated in an engagement involving approximately one hundred Japanese aircraft. Gallantly pressing home his attacks through intense anti - aircraft fire, he destroyed four enemy bombers and damaged another out of a formation of thirty. His courage and airmanship reflect the highest credit upon Lieutenant Kepford and the United States Naval Service."*

"Ike" was also recommended for the Distinguished Flying Cross after the first tour. The average combat hours for the first tour was 100 and "Ike" was well above this total. The citation was as follows:

> *"For meritorious achievement while participating in aerial flights against the enemy in the Solomon Islands area during the period of 27 October through 1 December 1943. In thirty six days he flew forty eight sorties, a total of 158 hours of combat flying. He participated in thirty one patrols and eight escort missions, and took part in nine strafing missions over particularly dangerous territory, meeting heavy concentrations of enemy anti-aircraft fire on*

six occasions. In addition to the above, he engaged the enemy on November 11, 1943 and succeeded in shooting down four enemy planes and damaging one other. His tireless devotion to duty, his heroic conduct under fire, and his skillful airmanship were in keeping with the highest traditions of the U.S. Naval Service."

Prior to the second tour "Ike" was promoted to Lt. (jg) on January 1, 1944. He returned to action on January 27, 1944, when twenty Corsairs were assigned as cover on one of two B-25 squadrons striking Lakunai Airfield, New Britain. From sixty to seventy Japanese fighters intercepted the strike as the bombers were leaving the target.

"Ike," whilst leading the second division of the high cover, was jumped on the first attack. They made their first runs in column on six Zekes 5,000 ft. below them. "Ike" got one, Dan Cunningham a second, and Don McQueen a third. Dan Cunningham flew with "Ike" Kepford on many occasions. He recalls this mission:

"I was on one hop with "Ike," leading his second section. When we joined up with the bombers we normally split into two's and started weaving. We never did. We were in pretty close formation and I'm working my ass off to hold my position and my wingman was doing the same but twice as hard. I'm watching him so tight that I didn't see what was ahead of us. All of a sudden "Ike's" shooting, his wingman's shooting and I'm right behind a Jap. I started shooting and my wingman started shooting. He went right up the ass of four of them with four of us and we blew the four of them out of the sky. I thought that was the neatest thing I had seen. I certainly enjoyed every time I flew with him. He was a good boy, good pilot, good shot, and had guts and God he was aggressive. Go! Go! I don't

"Ike" Kepford and his F4U-1A. Note the flaps burned by exploding ammunition cans. Piva Yoke, Bougainville, on January 31, 1944. *Robert Lawson Photograph Collection, National Museum of Naval Aviation / US Navy photo*

"Ike" Kepford and his F4U-1A at Piva Yoke, Bougainville, on January 31, 1944. *Courtesy of the Anderson Family.*

He clobbers him, looks up,
then there's all these Zekes above him and
they started making runs on him. . . .
That's when they had him cornered.
Finally he made the move and
turned to get home.
The Jap followed and his wing hit the water.

DAN CUNNINGHAM

Lt. (jg) Ira C. "Ike" Kepford stands beside his F4U-1A Corsair shortly after being rotated from combat duty in the Central Solomons. He became the U.S. Navy's then-leading ace, credited with sixteen victories. Note his .45 automatic pistol and sixteen Japanese flags painted on his aircraft. *Courtesy of the National Archives*

care whether you were playing softball, tiddly winks or anything else he wanted to win. That's all! That was his objective. That's why he was so damn successful and a hell of a nice guy."

The four climbed back to 19,000 ft. and then separated into pairs - "Ike" and Don McQueen made several passes on about twenty Zekes without success. "Ike" then heard Lt. (jg) Harold "Bitz" Bitzegaio call for help, and then made a high side attack on the Zeke and saw him burst into flames. He and McQueen climbed again, and "Ike" saw a Zeke on another Corsair's tail and probably destroyed him. The pair made a series of runs, ending at 8,000 ft. They then found the bombers, who were just leaving the rally point. On the way back, they beat off two attacks by a division of six Zekes. "Ike" became an ace on this mission.

On January 29, 1944, twenty Corsairs were assigned as cover for the SBD Dauntlesses in a joint SBD - TBF strike on Tobera Airfield, New Britain. "Ike" and "Mac" Burriss were the only Corsairs that remained from a planned four plane cover and were at 30,000 ft. Their job was to break up the enemy fighters before they got to the bombers. "Ike" and "Mac" spotted twelve Zekes below them and attacked, working as a team in an action that lasted about ten minutes. They shot down four Zekes each. Kepford and Burriss were both recommended for the Navy Cross. "Ike" was awarded a Gold Star in lieu of Second Navy Cross:

"For extraordinary heroism as pilot of a fighter plane in Fighting Squadron Seventeen in action against enemy Japanese forces in the Solomon Islands on January 29, 1944. Intercepted by a numerically superior force of Japanese planes while flying escort for a bomber strike over Tobera Airfield, Lieutenant, Junior Grade, Kepford and a companion engaged twelve enemy planes and, pressing home his repeated attacks, personally shot down four of the hostile aircraft. By his expert airmanship and courage in the face of tremendous odds, Lieutenant Kepford contributed materially to the success of the mission..."

On January 30, 1944, Kepford was assigned as part of the cover for the TBF Avenger's for an SBD - TBF strike on shipping in Simpson Harbor. He was flying at 15,000 ft. and was attacked by ten to twelve Zekes, who dived from 25,000 ft. coming down in pairs. One Zeke made a run on a Corsair, and "Ike" made a beam run from seven o'clock and set the Zeke on fire. The sky was full of enemy aircraft, and "Ike" had to weave radically as he went down after the bombers. A Kawasaki Ki 61 Tony Split-S'd and made a low side attack on him from twelve o'clock. "Ike" was badly hit in the right wing, but he kept firing with his left wing guns and the Tony caught fire. The ammunition cases in "Ike's" right wing had exploded and his wing caught on fire. He was joined by Mills

OPPOSITE:
The U.S. Navy's then-leading ace, Lt. (jg) "Ike" Kepford, over Bougainville in early March 1944, at the end of Fighting 17's combat tour. *Courtesy of the National Archives*

"Ike" Kepford and Jimmy Dixon playing chess. Taken while serving with VF-84 at N.A.A.S. Twenty-nine Palms in the fall of 1944. *Courtesy of the Matthews Family*

Schanuel, leader of his second section, and the pair returned to base. "Ike" could not get his right wheel down and made a one wheel landing. The aircraft was a write-off, but "Ike" was unhurt. "Ike" was credited with one Zeke and one Tony destroyed.

On February 3, 1944, "Ike" was part of the cover for a B-24 Liberator strike on Lakunai Airfield. The Zekes approached the formation on an opposite course, and when almost over the bombers made overhead runs on the B-24s. No passes were made at the fighters. "Ike" got in a full deflection shot at the number #2 Zeke in the second attack and it was seen to go down in flames. Although a group of Zekes was seen over Talili Bay during the retirement down St. George's Channel no further attacks were made on the formation.

"Ike's" most eventful mission came on February 19, 1944, the last time Fighting 17 saw the Japanese in air combat.

"Ike" led the second division of the high cover on the TBFs. His wingman, Don McQueen, had engine trouble off Buka Passage and was forced to return to base. "Ike" continued on as far as Cape St. George where, finding that the fighter cover was adequate, he also decided to turn back, as he did not want to go over Rabaul without a wingman. He began an easy turn to the right and saw something low on the water off Cape Siar. He went down to investigate and found a Rufe at about 1,000 ft. flying north. He dived down on it, and in a stern attack set it on fire. At this moment, he saw twenty Japanese fighters coming down out of a cloud at 16,000 ft. over New Ireland. Four came down on him in a loose column and the leader made a stern attack, but "Ike" lowered his flaps and the Zeke overran him. As the Zeke pulled up "Ike" got in a good burst and sent it down in flames. He was then at 1,000 ft. and making 200 knots.

Three Japanese fighters now had "Ike" boxed in. The two on his right prevented his turning east to Green Island, and one was on his left, so that his only course was to head north. This he did, putting his Corsair in a slight dive, shoving his throttle forward, and using his water injection–"Ike's" aircraft was one of few so fitted, designed to increase speed for a short time. He had 2750 rpm and 62 inches manifold pressure, and was jinking in a very gentle left turn. The Japanese–"Ike" thought the two on his right were Tojos–were still just within range, so "Ike" stopped jinking and tried a gentle climb. He figured that he was pulling away at a rate of only 40 knots. Consequently, he nosed over the hills in the Namatanai area on New Ireland and headed for the deck. Just as he crossed the western shore his water injection gave out. The engine missed, so "Ike" pulled back the throttle and pushed it forward again. The water injection caught for a few seconds and the engine missed again. At this point

"Ike" Kepford married Esther M. "Kraeg" Kraegel in San Diego in 1944. *Courtesy of Kraeg Kepford*

"Ike" noticed that he was making 355 knots indicated. As he was at sea level this meant that his true speed was 365 mph. "Ike" kept a course of 300° for about fifteen or twenty minutes. When he had 100 gallons left he decided that he would have to head south. He made a violent turn to the left at 270 knots indicated and the Zeke on his left, in trying to turn inside him, dug his left wing in the water and crashed. The Tojos were sucked wide on the turn and gave up the chase, so "Ike" crossed New Britain at Open Bay. After his turn, "Ike" throttled back to 2600 rpm and 48 inches. He kept this setting for ten minutes, then went to 2150 and 27 inches with his mixture in automatic lean (he had been in Rich until this point) until he sighted land. He throttled back to 1300 rpm and landed with forty gallons in his tank. He had been airborne for four hours and ten minutes. "Ike" believed that his water injection lasted for only about four minutes. Afterwards he said that the engine smelled hot but that it ran smoothly. The Corsair, which had been flown to maximum limits in this encounter, was apparently in good shape and was flown the next day.

This was the last time "Ike" saw aerial combat, and he was very shaken up by this mission even after he got back to the States. Dan Cunningham saw "Ike" when he landed:

> *"We all landed and said where's "Ike." They said he's not here. Last they heard he was heading north. He had water injection in his F4U and that's how he got away. He landed about an hour or so after we were down. God he was shaken up. I used to call him Hot Dog. I went running up to him and said how are you doing Hot Dog? Boy he just breezed by me, his eyes were all welled up. He was sure he was gone, just scared, I mean totally. I don't think he flew again in our squadron. I guess the Skipper had to chew him out and said he was getting Jap happy or something like that. He went after a float plane on his way back to base. He clobbers him, looks up, then there's all these Zekes above him and they started making runs on him. One time he I guess popped his flaps so that they overshoot him. So as this happened he clobbers them too. That's when they had him cornered. Finally he made the move and turned to get home. The Jap followed and his wing hit the water. Then as he had made some speed he got away. Then he throttled back to get home. He'd had it and was all through by the time he got home. He was a beautiful guy an aggressive guy."*

On March 4, 1944, "Ike" was recommended for another award by Tom Blackburn and received the Silver Star for his actions:

> *"Between 27 January and 27 February 1944, Lt. (jg) Kepford flew seventeen combat sorties, twelve of which were escort missions or fighter sweeps over the Rabaul area. He encountered enemy aircraft on seven occasions: on 27, 29, and 30 January, and on 3, 6, 17, and 19 February. On 27 January while escorting B-25's in a strike on Lakunai Airfield he encountered between sixty and seventy Jap fighters. He and his wingman engaged twenty five or thirty. He twice shot Zekes attacking other Corsairs, his score for this action being two Zekes destroyed and one Zeke probably destroyed. On 29 January he flew one of two Corsairs which engaged twelve Zekes which were preparing to intercept our bombers over Tobera Airfield. With no regard to his own safety he made repeated attacks on the enemy and destroyed four Zekes, thereby substantially*

"Ike" in Nebraska, pheasant hunting in November 1961.
Courtesy of Kraeg Kepford

lessening the threat to our bombers. On 30 January, he escorted TBF's in a strike on enemy shipping in Simpson Harbor. The formation met a determined interception by twenty or thirty Jap fighters. Lt. (jg) Kepford shot down a Zeke as the latter was attacking a Corsair but was himself hit by a Tony. Although the ammunition in his right wing exploded, setting the wing afire, he succeeded in destroying the Tony, using only the three guns in his left wing. On 3 February the formation of B-24's which he was escorting in a strike on Lakunai Airfield was intercepted by twenty eight Jap fighters. As the Japs attacked the bombers Lt. (jg) Kepford interposed and succeeded in shooting down one Zeke before it could complete its run. On 19 February he was assigned as part of the high cover on TBF's striking shipping in Simpson Harbor. As his wingman had had to return with engine trouble Lt. (jg) Kepford, finding our fighter cover was adequate, turned back at Cape St George. He spotted a Rufe off Cape Siar and went down and destroyed it. He was himself attacked by twenty Jap fighters four of which got within range. He shot down one and tried to outrun the others. After the chase had lasted a half hour he made a violent left turn and the Zeke on his left, in trying to turn inside him, went into the water."

"Ike" with a Brown Trout in April 1973. *Courtesy of Kraeg Kepford*

Kepford finished his combat tour with Fighting 17 in March 1944 as the Navy's top ace with sixteen confirmed victories, one probable, and one damaged. At the conclusion of hostilities he was the top Navy Corsair ace of WWII.

"Ike" was a hero upon his return to the States in April 1944. He was in newspapers throughout the States for several months, carried out many public relations engagements for the Navy with personal appearances to Chambers of Commerce and speaking to factories, such as Hedstrom - Union Co., who made ailerons for the Corsair. This helped to increase production and raise morale, and also to sell War Bonds. He also appeared on the radio, went back to Northwestern University, and home to see his family.

On June 1, 1944, he reported to VF-84 under the command of Roger Hedrick. He then reported on June 14, 1944, to Alameda, California, and Seattle, Washington, in connection with training matters.

From March until June 1944 he was attached to the Fleet Air, Alameda, Command, and for the last six months of that year served with Fighting Squadron 84. While there he suffered a couple of health problems, such as acute tonsillitis on July 28, 1944, but did not have an operation until October 10, 1944. He also had an ear problem from October 6, 1944, for ten weeks. He was detached on December 27, 1944, from VF-84 and reported to Commander Fleet Air West Coast. He was promoted to Lieutenant on May 1, 1945, and remained in that assignment throughout the remaining period of hostilities.

On September 26, 1945, he was detached from Commander Fleet Air West Coast and reported to N.A.S. San Diego for temporary duty pending release from active duty.

After the Japanese surrender, and a period of terminal leave, he was released from all active duty on November 10, 1945.

"Ike" was transferred to the Retired List of the U.S. Naval Reserve on June 1, 1956, and advanced to the rank of Lieutenant Commander on the basis of combat citations.

"Ike" and Esther "Kraeg" Kraegel were married at the Chapel of the Roses in Chula Vista, California, on September 8, 1945, while they were both stationed at San Diego, North Island. Kraeg was a W.A.V.E. (Women Accepted for Volunteer Emergency Service) and met "Ike" on a blind date.

Following the war, Kepford worked his way through the ranks to become President of Liggett and later retired as President of Liggett-Rexall Drug Co. He then became President of a metropolitan tobacco business, but he was not happy with them and resigned. He dabbled in the plastics and the gravel businesses, but decided to retire and moved to Harbor Springs in 1971. He retired early at fifty-one, as he "*had lived a hard life*" and was ready to retire at that time, despite offers from other companies.

In his retirement he was very much an outdoorsman. More than anything he loved to fish, and until Lake Michigan froze over he would stop every day and drop a line or cast in Little Traverse Bay, where he lived. He also gardened, liked to hunt, and collected Kentucky Rifles. He was woodcarving in his workshop during the last of his years.

To understand why "Ike" was so successful is best left to "Kraeg," who recalls:

> *"Ike" hated parties but people always gravitated to him. He was very comfortable with himself and accepted who he was. He loved the challenge of things and performed top drawer if challenged."*

At a reunion in the early 1980s "Ike" had this to say:

> *"One guy I've got to thank a great deal is "Butch" Davenport ("Mother"). Because "Mother" got me over. I had confidence in whatever "Butch" did. I did get initiated with a guy who knew what he was doing and I flew his wing quite a while before the Skipper would have any confidence enough to give me a section. I appreciated it very much. I appreciate the skipper I appreciate all you guys and the camaraderie. I will go to my grave remembering all of you for all you've done all the good times and memories that really mean a lot to me. For a bunch of misfits we did one hell of a job."*

In addition to the Navy Cross with Gold Star, Silver Star, Distinguished Flying Cross, and the Navy Unit Commendation to Fighting Squadron Seventeen, Kepford was awarded the American Defense Service Medal, the American Campaign Medal, Asiatic - Pacific Campaign Medal and the World War II Victory Medal.

Ira Cassius "Ike" Kepford died in Michigan on January 19, 1987. "Kraeg" still lives in Harbor Springs, Michigan.

Mel Kurlander and "Kraeg" Kepford on May 24, 2008, in Muskegon, Michigan. *Courtesy of Kraeg Kepford*

OPPOSITE: The leading ace of Fighting 17 was Lt. (jg) Ira. C. "Ike" Kepford with sixteen victories. He is shown here flying his raised canopy F4U-1A near Bougainville, in the Solomon Islands, in March 1944. *Robert Lawson Photograph Collection, National Museum of Naval Aviation / US Navy photo*

*After the chase had lasted a half hour
he made a violent left turn and
the Zeke on his left,
in trying to turn inside him,
went into the water."*

TOM BLACKBURN

Harry Andrew "Dirty Eddie" March, Jr., Fighting 17 ace with five victories. March reported to Fighting 17 on October 5, 1943. *Courtesy of the March Family*

11

HARRY ANDREW "DIRTY EDDIE" MARCH JR

5 VICTORIES

Harry Andrew March, Jr., was born in East Liverpool, Ohio, on February 2, 1919, to Harry Andrew March Sr., who was a chemist, and Lois Whitfield Campbell. He was ranked number one in junior tennis in Washington, DC, when aged fifteen, and had a National ranking as a junior. He even played the famous Bill Tilden in an exhibition match.

March received his elementary education in Washington, graduating from McKinley Technology High School in 1936. He then studied at the University of North Carolina, where he attended from September 1936 to June 1940. He graduated with a B.A. degree in Physical Education in the class of 1940. It was reported at the time:

> *"Harry March is one of the most versatile track athletes ever to represent the University of North Carolina.*
>
> *He's competed in eight different events during his varsity career and in competition has done the following times and measurements:*
>
> *880 yards (running one lap of the two mile relay) - 1:58.2*
> *440 yards - 49.8 seconds*
> *440 yard low hurdles - 53.8 seconds*
> *220 yard low hurdles - 23.4 seconds*
> *High Jump 6 feet 1½ inches*
> *Broad Jump 23 feet*
> *120 yard high hurdles 15 seconds flat*
> *100 yard dash - 9.9 seconds."*

He qualified for the Olympic team of 1940 in the 400 hurdles and was named to the All American Track Team. There is little doubt that Harry would have gone to the 1940 Olympics, which were cancelled as a consequence of the war. He won

Harry Andrew "Dirty Eddie" March, Jr., was appointed an Ensign in August 1941.
Courtesy of the March Family

the National A.A.U. Pentathlon Championship in Newark, NJ, on October 6, 1940, with a score of 2981. The events consisted of Broad Jump, Javelin, 200 metres, Discus, and 1500 metres. This was while in his senior year at the University of North Carolina, and he also held a number of records in track events.

On December 16, 1940, he enlisted in the U.S. Naval Reserve as a Seaman Second Class, and on his application listed athletic, coaching, and teaching experience in civilian life. It was noted that he was: "*Very good officer material, with an affable, sincere manner and a brawny, athletic appearance.*"

On March 5, 1941, Harry became an Aviation Cadet and began his elimination flight training on March 6, 1941, reporting to N.A.S. Jacksonville for training. He was detached from N.A.S. Jacksonville and ordered to N.A.S. Miami at Opa - Locka for further training, reporting on August 21, 1941. On September 23, 1941, he was designated a Naval Aviator, and on November 6, 1941, was commissioned as an Ensign.

Harry was then ordered to the Advanced Carrier Training Group, Pacific Fleet at N.A.S. San Diego, reporting there on November 29, 1941. He was further ordered to Fighting Squadron Six, based on the USS *Enterprise*, and reported on June 15, 1942. On Friday, August 7, 1942, the day the U.S. attacked Tulagi and Guadalcanal, March was involved in the action and noted the following:

> *"Today was the day! We took all the islands with very little opposition. I was over Guadalcanal for two hours and saw no signs of Japs at all. They probably took to the hills!*
>
> *In the afternoon they had some aircraft in on us probably from up Rabaul way. Some of the boys met twenty two twin engine bombers and about ten Zeros. We got two bombers, possibly more - and one Zero - possibly more. Oh yeah, my hop met some dive bombers and I got one of 'em. He was practically on the water trying to run away."*

Harry was involved in action again with Fighting Six, who helped frustrate a Japanese attack on a United States Task Force on August 24, 1942.

The Task Force, under way in the Solomon Islands area, learned that a strong Japanese air attack was coming. Grumman F4U Wildcat fighters of Fighting Squadron Six were sent aloft to protect the Task Force. Seventeen pilots of VF-6 shot down twenty-seven enemy aircraft, one probable was scored, and they didn't know how to count another that was forced to fly into the sea.

VF-6, composed of officers and enlisted pilots, lost two pilots and four aircraft in the action. One aircraft ran out of fuel and landed in the sea, but the pilot was recovered. Another returned to the carrier so badly shot up it was written off. The pilot, however, received only minor injuries. In the fight Harry fired a tentative burst at long range at a Mitsubishi 87 torpedo bomber, but caught it square and down it went.

According to his family, the nickname "Dirty Eddie" was something to do with his black beard he grew while based at Guadalcanal. It may have also had something to do with the conditions there, which were primitive due to the intense fighting involved with this island. He was very fond of the nickname and signed squadron photos as "Dirty Eddie."

He was promoted to Lt. (jg) on October 1, 1942, and on December 19, 1942, he was detached from Fleet Air Command, West Coast and ordered to Fleet Air Detachment, N.A.S. New York, and then on December 31, 1942, to Fighting Squadron Twenty-Four based on the USS *Belleau Wood*.

Harry March was interviewed for a radio show when he returned from deployment in February 1943. This interview was noted by his family at the time:

Interviewer: *Good morning, folks. Today we have the privilege of presenting a young man of action - Lt. Harry A. March. Lt. March is a Flight Officer of the United States Navy - and he has just recently returned from the hot spot of the Pacific - Guadalcanal. Lt. Harry A. March, USNR.*

March: *Thank you. It's a real pleasure to be here with you.*

Interviewer: *According to the record, you are credited with knocking quite an impressive number of Japanese out of the air. Apparently that occupation agrees with you.*

March: *Why do you say that?*

Interviewer: *For one reason - you're here to tell the story. Furthermore, you look like you're in tip - top health.*

March: *I feel tip - top. I ought to because all I've been doing since I got back to the States has been - taking it easy.*

Interviewer: *Can't complain about that, can you?*

March: *No complaints ---, but I have got a little guilty conscience.*

Interviewer: *From what?*

March: *I've got a lot of good friends out there in the South Pacific. I know what they're doing right this minute. I know how tough it is.*

VF-6 pilots on board the USS *Saratoga* (CV-3). "Dirty Eddie" March is 10th from left middle row. *Courtesy of the James A Halford Collection*

Interviewer: *And knowing that, you can't go on living the life of Riley here in New York - without - well, without thinking about them. Is that about it?*

March: *That's it exactly. Anyway, I guess it won't be very long before I'll be back there - so what am I worrying about.*

Interviewer: *You mean you really want to return to the South Pacific?*

March: *Those pals of mine aren't having any picnic. I promised 'em I'd be back to help out - and I will. They need all the help they can get.*

Interviewer: *I take it you have no quarrel, then, with my description of the place being the "hot spot of the Pacific."*

March: *(Lightly) Well, that's one way of putting it. I'm afraid my way of putting it - wouldn't sound too good over the radio.*

Interviewer: *Lt. March - I don't suppose there's any doubt in your mind why we asked you to appear on this broadcast. Our listeners, like all Americans at home, are intensely interested in hearing about what's going on out there in the Solomons - and we particularly want to hear about it from men like yourself - who have actually participated in combat. So let's move along and have your story. First of all, how old are you?*

March: *Twenty four just a few days ago.*

Interviewer: *Did you attend college?*

March: *Yes, I graduated from the University of North Carolina back in 1940.*

Interviewer: *Any special degrees?*

March: *I was after a Degree in Physical Education, but I settled for an AB.*

Interviewer: *Why?*

March: *Because that's when I decided to enter Naval Aviation.*

Interviewer: *Immediately after graduation?*

March: *That's right.*

Interviewer: *I understand you were quite a track man in college. Did you win any particular recognition in that line? You could be a champion for all I know - so happens I don't follow track activities in the papers.*

March: *I think you'll find in the records, that I was National Pentathlon Champion.*

Interviewer: *I sort of put my neck way out on that one, didn't I. Anyway, I think that's fine, Lt. March--apparently the qualities which gave you recognition as a winner in that field have been carried over into Naval Aviation. Now you say you entered the service right after you graduated from the University of North Carolina. When was that?*

March: *I was enlisted as a Cadet on December 16th, 1940. I was 21 at the time.*

Interviewer: *Where did you start your flight training?*

March: *I started my primary at the Naval Reserve Air Base at Anacostia.*

Interviewer: *That's just outside of Washington, D.C. - then where did you continue?*

March: *I was then ordered to the Naval Air Station at Jacksonville. I was there about five months, went from there to Miami where I got my wings and was commissioned an Ensign.*

Interviewer: *Did you state a preference for any particular type of duty?*

March: *Yes, I did. I asked for fighter duty aboard a carrier - and got it.*

Interviewer: *That, of course, is in keeping with the Navy's policy to assign men where they want to be - and for which duty they are best fitted. Of course, not every man is fortunate enough to get the duty he wants. The needs of the Navy at a given time must be considered as well as the man's fitness for such duty he requests, as shown in his training record. Anyway, evidently both you and your instructors felt the right spot for you was behind the controls of a fighter plane. Have you ever regretted your choice of duty?*

March: *I should say not. If I had it to do over again, I'd still ask for fighter duty.*

Interviewer: *Where did you take your operational training, Lt. March?*

March: *San Diego. There we trained for every conceivable type of operation. Then I was assigned to a squadron destined for further training at Pearl Harbor. We arrived there just about the day after the Battle of Midway.*

Interviewer: *In other words - sometime in June, 1942.*

March: *That's right. We trained pretty carefully for about a month - operating with other squadrons - practicing landing operations - strafing - in fact, everything in the book and a lot more.*

Interviewer: *When did you personally have your first contact with the Japs?*

March: *I was just about to come to that. Actually, my first contact with the Japs came on August 7th. Our mission was to act as air support for the Marines going in to take the airport and soften up the harbor defences set up by the Japs at Tulagi.*

Interviewer: *Now wait a minute, Lt. It has been my understanding that the Marines took over Henderson Field at Guadalcanal on August 7th.*

March: *They did. But it is also a matter of record that we were in the air protecting the landing*

The men of VF-6 pose in front of a tent in September 1942 on Guadalcanal with propeller blades marked with Japanese flags indicating the number of aerial victories scored by the squadron. "Dirty Eddie" March is 4th from the left, back row. *Courtesy of the James A Halford Collection*

parties before the Marine fliers came. Our skipper Lt. Lou Bower, from Philly led us on that first strafing attack on August 7th.

Interviewer: *I stand corrected then. Tell us more about that first attack. How did you feel about meeting the enemy for the first time in the air? Were you scared?*

March: *I was plenty scared. And anybody who says he isn't scared in a situation like that - is either abnormal mentally and emotionally - or he's a liar.*

Interviewer: *What kind of plane were you flying at the time?*

March: *A Grumman F4F.*

Interviewer: *For the benefit of our radio audience, the Grumman F4F is the Navy's single seater fighter plane - more popularly known as the Wildcat. The Naval Aviators who pilot this type of aircraft have to do their own navigation, handle the radio, and fire the 50 caliber guns.*

March: *That's the general, idea. It's strictly a one - man operation.*

Interviewer: *Tell us about it.*

March: *Well I was, as I said before, plenty scared - and a little nervous at first - but then when I found myself right square in the middle of things - I was kept too busy to think about myself. And that's the time, that I thanked my lucky stars I had trained in the Navy.*

Interviewer: *How do you mean?*

March: *Well it's pretty hard to explain.*

Interviewer: *I think I know what you're trying to say - and that is - when the real test came, you were able to meet it squarely and confidently, as a result of your training in Naval Aviation. You were trained so well and disciplined to such an extent that when the time actually came to prove what you really knew - it was a little like a practice maneuver.*

March: *Exactly, excepting this time - unlike a practice maneuver - I had to be right or else. Everything I did that first time came instinctively and easily. I had the comfortable feeling of knowing what to do and precisely when. This may sound a little boastful - but that's not the way I mean at all. What I'm trying to say is that --- I consider the training I got in Naval Aviation the best in the world. I felt I had an advantage - a big advantage over every Jap - because of my training. After all, the proof of the pudding is in the eating --- there were 36 of our fighters altogether in that attack - and we lost only three in actual combat, recovering two of the pilots at a later date.*

Interviewer: *How'd you make out? That is, how'd you make out personally?*

"Dirty Eddie" March in front of #29 early in the first tour of Fighting 17 at Ondongo in November 1943. *Courtesy of Vought*

March: *That's a pretty hard question to answer. Officially I was credited with knocking down an enemy dive bomber during one of the actions.*

Interviewer: *I'd say that's a mighty fine record for the first time up to bat. When did you actually move in over Guadalcanal?*

March: *Early morning about 05:30.*

Interviewer: *Then you yourself were one of the first men to fight in the air over Guadalcanal.*

March: *Right. We started off the battle at 05:30. The Marines landed not many hours later. And what a job they did on those Japs when they did land. No those Marines, make the Dead End Kids look like a gang of sissies. They're really tough - and I mean tough! That goes for the land troops and Marine flyers as well.*

Interviewer: *At this point, let's not fail to remind our audience that all Marine Aviators are trained by the Navy. The training they receive is identical to that of the Naval Aviator. Tell me, Lt., how do the Grumman Wildcat's stack up against the Jap Zero fighters?*

March: *Well of course it's well known that the Jap Zero is a much lighter plane. That means they can fly level faster - they can climb faster - and they can, by and large, out - maneuver us. On the other hand, they're pretty flimsy craft - they can't pull out of a fast deep dive without something going wrong - and once we hit one, it usually blows up right in the air. The Grumman Wildcat, while not as fast, is well protected - can take a lot of punishment and they can dive.*

Interviewer: *According to all reports, our success in knocking Zeros out of the air has been phenomenal. Can you elaborate on that a little?*

March: *I don't know what the actual odds are - but I'd guess there are about eight Zeros knocked down to every one Wildcat.*

Interviewer: *That's a high percentage - eight to one.*

March: *Well take this case, for example. On August 24th our squadron alone knocked off 27 Jap planes in the vicinity of the Stewart Islands - that's northeast of Guadalcanal. We lost only two planes - that's a percentage of a little over thirteen to our one. The total number of Jap*

*I was plenty scared.
And anybody who says
he isn't scared
in a situation like that -
is either abnormal
mentally and emotionally -
or he's a liar.*

planes knocked down by all of our operations that day was 96.

Interviewer: *96 in one day! I guess you'll never forget that occasion.*

March: *Not likely. Then about the 11th September, my squadron was transferred from the carrier to Henderson Field. We were based there and we lived there.*

Interviewer: *Operating with the Marines.*

March: *Yes, and I'll never forget that occasion either. There they were with only eight planes - going up to fight four and five times a day against always a superior number of Jap planes - every day - day in and day out. They were really whipped down. And then when we arrived with twenty four planes to add to their eight, you should have seen the reception we got. We were like an answer to their prayers - and were they thankful and happy about it. They cheered every one of us, and they'd meet us almost lift us out of the cockpit. I have never had a warmer reception in all my life. And I never expect to see a happier gang of tired guys anywhere. All they could say was - "Boy, are we glad to see you" and "Thank God you're here at last" and "Wait 'till Tojo comes over again expecting to meet only eight planes and we go tearin' into them with thirty two." That was an occasion I'll always remember.*

Interviewer: *How long were you stationed on Henderson Field, Lt.?*

March: *My squadron was there from September 11 until the 15th October. That's a pretty long time when you consider that almost every day you go up to fight in the air two or three times - most of the time when you're on the ground you're dodging shells and bombs. And every minute of every day - you've got to be on guard against Japanese snipers up in trees - and behind bushes.*

Interviewer: *I see our time is running a little short, Lt., but how about telling us about some of your other experiences.*

March: *Well we had a pretty decent contact on September 12th --- knocked a number of planes down - and lost only one ourselves. Then the next day we bagged twelve enemy bombers and three Zeros - and only lost one pilot. Then on the 28th - twenty five enemy bombers came over and we knocked down no less than twenty three of them.*

Interviewer: *How many planes did we lose on that meeting?*

March: *None. Not a single plane or pilot. There's the best proof in the world of the superiority of Naval Aviation Training.*

Interviewer: *In other words, you think pretty highly of it.*

"Dirty Eddie" March and "Country" Landreth. *US Naval Historical Center / M W "Butch" Davenport Collection*

March: *I most certainly do. In fact, I'm convinced that even if things were reversed - and we had to fight in Zeros - and the Japs had our Grumman's --- we would still have the upper hand in combat - because of our training.*

Interviewer: *That's a mighty fine tribute. But tell me, Lt., would you actually prefer to fight in a Zero?*

March: *No, sir. I'll take Grumman protection any day.*

Interviewer: *Well thanks a lot for being with us today, Lt. March.*

Interviewer: *We really do appreciate hearing your story because it gives us all a better understanding of what a courageous group of fighting airmen are actually responsible for the good news we read in our newspapers today --- United States in complete control of Guadalcanal.*

On his fitness report from March 31, 1943, to October 7, 1943, whilst with VF-24, it was noted:

> *"Lt. March has performed his duties as a Flight Instructor in an excellent manner. He possesses a strong character and a pleasing personality. He is a fine leader and is a person you would like to take with you when the battle is tough."*

Harry had married Elsa Smedes March as soon as Ensigns were allowed to do so, and their daughter Mary Elizabeth March was born on September 29, 1943.

On September 24, 1943, he was ordered to Air Force Pacific Fleet, and on September 28, 1943, reported to the Fourteenth Naval District, Pearl Harbor, and on to N.A.S. Barber's Point, Oahu. He was promoted to Lt. from October 1, 1943, and when he completed his Carrier Aircraft Service Unit One duty he was ordered to Fighting 17.

He was one of a handful of combat veterans that Fighting 17 relied upon when going into combat for the first time in November 1943. He was assigned Corsair #33 to start the first tour, then "Dirty Eddie" took over #29 from Lem Cooke as the first tour ended.

He named his aircraft "Baby Skeex" after his daughter Mary, who had the nickname of "Skeex" after his good friend "Dutch" Shoemaker's wife Mary. "Dutch" and many other comrades of "Dirty Eddie's" were killed at Guadalcanal.

On November 8, 1943, "Dirty Eddie" was one of five pilots led by Tom Blackburn on a strafing attack on Buka Airfield. Blackburn, "Dirty Eddie," and Whit Wharton observed a transport-type plane, probably a converted Ruth, circling to land.

The three flew right along the Buka strip at a height of 50 ft. and strafed a parked Zeke and personnel on the edge of the strip. By this time Blackburn and "Dirty Eddie" were on the tail of the Ruth, who was halfway up the strip. Both Corsairs had perfect shots at ranges of 200 down to 25 yards and the Ruth, hit in the wing roots and motors, burst into flames and crashed. Citations for awards to Blackburn and March appear to give them both credit for the Ruth. The Fighting 17 War Diary gives full credit to Blackburn, while the aircraft action report would appear to share the credit. "Dirty Eddie" was therefore given an assist in the victory, as being the accreditation closest to the contemporary reports. The citation for "Dirty Eddie's" first Air Medal gives him credit for one bomber on this date. "Dirty Eddie" was also awarded a Gold Star in lieu of a second Air Medal for destroying two enemy aircraft during the period of June 10, 1943, to January 27, 1944.

On January 28, 1944, twenty Corsairs were assigned as partial cover on the TBFs in a joint SBD - TBF strike on Tobera Airfield, New Britain. About forty to fifty Zekes and Hamps intercepted the strike.

The Corsair high cover disorganized at least part of the enemy's attack, and the low and medium cover was strong enough to turn back all fighters who got through to them, accounting for at least nine. "Dirty Eddie" shot down a Zeke in what was apparently the first attack on the cover for the Avengers. "Dirty Eddie" was at about 15,000 ft. over Kabanga Bay, weaving over the bombers with another division. About eight Zekes came down in a dive on the second division. "Dirty Eddie" turned in and up and got a good burst into a Zeke who was recovering in a wingover. The Zeke was seen to crash in flames. Lt.

(jg) Carl "Gil" Gilbert, "Dirty Eddie's" wingman, got in a snap shot at another Zeke and saw pieces fly from his tail. Almost immediately afterwards a Zeke began an attack on "Dirty Eddie" but pulled away and over on his back. "Dirty Eddie" pulled up his nose, fired, and set the Zeke on fire. At this point the bombers started their attack, with "Dirty Eddie" and his division over them. Zekes made several attacks on the formation during the retirement, but disengaged when the fighters turned towards them.

"Dirty Eddie" was awarded the Distinguished Flying Cross for this mission.

During his service with Fighting 17 "Dirty Eddie" was recommended by Tom Blackburn for the Navy Cross on March 14, 1944, with the following report:

"For extraordinary heroism while participating in aerial combat. Lt. March as a member of four squadrons which have operated in the South Pacific under frequently difficult and occasionally hazardous conditions, has seen action intermittently since June 10, 1942, in a series of campaigns ranging from Guadalcanal to New Britain, from aircraft carriers until bases were established and then from the bases themselves. In the early stages of the severe Guadalcanal campaign his flight of six F4F's attacked a force of enemy bombers which attacked our transports. During this action he shot down one of the six Vals destroyed. Again, on August 24, 1942, he was one of the five fighters who repulsed a determined enemy

"Dirty Eddie" March (6th from left) with VBF-74 shortly before the war ended. He is pictured with former Fighting 17 skipper Tom Blackburn (5th from left) and Lem Cooke (2nd from left). *US Navy Photo*

attack on the USS Enterprise and in this action he shot down one Jap torpedo plane. Following this, he operated from the USS Saratoga and Guadalcanal, where his squadron was in almost daily contact with the enemy. Then, after participating in three more actions while in VF-24, Lt. March began his second tour of combat as a member of VF-17. As a Flight Leader, during the squadron's second tour of combat, Lt. March flew twenty four combat sorties, of which eighteen were escort missions or fighter sweeps over the Rabaul Area, and on eight of which he encountered enemy aircraft. On 28 January, the bombers he was escorting in a Rabaul strike were intercepted by a swarm of enemy fighters which Lt. March attacked without regard for the odds against him. The attack was so well timed and executed that the enemy attack was repulsed. During the melee Lt. March shot down two Zekes. His untiring devotion to duty, his heroic conduct in a long series of action which mark the progress of the whole Solomons Campaign, his steady and experienced leadership, and his intelligent airmanship were in keeping with the highest traditions of the U.S. Naval Service."

On April 3, 1944, he was detached from the Pacific Fleet and ordered to N.A.S. Jacksonville, reporting on May 4, 1944. On May 6, 1944, he reported to N.A.A.S. Green Cove Springs, and then on May 16, 1945, he reported to Air Force Atlantic Fleet, N.A.S. Norfolk, and on May 21, 1945, to Bombing Fighting Squadron 74 at Camp Edwards, Massachusetts. On October 3, 1945, he was appointed Lt. Cdr., and on December 14, 1945, served on the USS *Midway*.

"Dirty Eddie" March applied to join the regular Navy, and according to a report dated November 12, 1945, was highly recommended:

"The applicant made an excellent impression on the board by means of his pleasing appearance and good presence. His candid and well considered answers to interrogation showed firm motivation and fine qualifications for transfer to the Regular service."

After the war in February 1946, Harry went to Chapel Hill, NC, to participate in the University of North Carolina indoor track meet as part of his training for the 1948 Olympics. Suddenly he became acutely ill with chills and a very high fever on February 23, 1946. He was admitted to the University of North Carolina Infirmary, Chapel Hill, NC, where a diagnosis of pneumonia was given. Despite large doses of Penicillin being administered "Dirty Eddie's" illness grew rapidly worse, and he was in need of specialist care; however, the nearest Naval Hospital was the U.S. Naval Hospital, Portsmouth, VA, which was over 200 miles away. Harry was far too ill to transfer to the Naval Hospital; therefore, he was sent by private ambulance from the University of North Carolina Infirmary to Watts Hospital, Durham, NC, a civilian hospital about twelve miles away. Despite intensive care Lt. Cdr. Harry "Dirty Eddie" March died at 04:00 on March 2, 1946. He was just 27 years old.

"Dirty Eddie" March was awarded the Distinguished Flying Cross, Air Medal with one Gold Star, Navy Unit Commendation, Presidential Unit Citation (USS *Enterprise*), Presidential Unit Citation (First Marine Division), Asiatic - Pacific Area Campaign Medal with one Bronze Star, American Defense Service Medal, and World War II Victory Medal.

He was an ace with five confirmed victories, and left a devoted wife Elsa and their young daughter Mary. Mary died on January 1, 1976, in Raleigh, North Carolina, aged 32 after battling a wasting disease for thirteen years.

Elsa never remarried, as she didn't think anyone measured up to Harry. She worked for many years as a secretary with the Extension Service at North Carolina State University in Raleigh and was actively involved with the Church until she died on May 1, 2003.

OPPOSITE:
"Dirty Eddie" March at Bougainville in 1944. *Courtesy of the National Archives*

Well I was, as I said before, plenty scared - and a little nervous at first - but then when I found myself right square in the middle of things - I was kept too busy to think about myself. And that's the time, that I thanked my lucky stars I had trained in the Navy.

Earl May while serving with VBF-10. *Courtesy of the Del and Pat May Collection*

12

EARL MAY JR

8 VICTORIES

Earl May, Jr., was born in Milwaukee, Wisconsin, on June 1, 1920, the son of Earl William May and Anna (Oehl) May. Earl's mother died in 1926 when he was just six years old. Two years later his father met and married Norma. May began shooting geese at an early age in Walworth County with his father, one of Wisconsin's leading conservation experts. Earl's friends credit his marksmanship in combat to his early days with his father.

He attended Thomas Jefferson Grammar School in West Allis, Wisconsin, from 1926 to 1934, and then went to Nathan Hale Junior High School from 1934 to 1936 and West Allis High School from 1936 to 1937. This was followed by William Horlick High School from 1937 to 1938 in Racine, Wisconsin, and Bay View High School from 1938 to 1939 in Milwaukee, Wisconsin.

On September 7, 1938, Earl enlisted in the Wisconsin National Guard and served as a Private in the 121st Field Artillery. He attended Marquette University from 1939 to 1941 in Milwaukee, Wisconsin, and then Milwaukee Extension Division from 1941 to 1942. His Major was Pre-Dental and his Minor English. He was employed by the Railway Express Agency as a clerk from 1940 to 1941. Earl's brother Del has fond memories of Earl and his sense of humor:

> *"Earl had a terrific sense of humor. I can just see him with the picture of the native girl in his wallet. I'm sure he conveniently let the wallet fall open so everyone could see the picture. In fact I wouldn't be surprised if he told strangers it was his girlfriend.*
>
> *Another thing he did when I was a young kid that has remained with me for the rest of my*

life, is I used to like raisins. I used to eat them by the box full. One day Earl told me that raisins were dead flies. Needless to say I haven't eaten a raisin since!"

On February 9, 1942, Earl enlisted in the U.S. Naval Reserve in Chicago, and on May 28, 1942, he was appointed as an Aviation Cadet and reported to N.A.S. Corpus Christi. On October 8, 1942, he was designated a Naval Aviator and the next day was commissioned as an Ensign.

On October 16, 1942, he reported to N.A.S. Miami for pre-operational training, and was then ordered to the Carrier Qualification Training Unit, Norfolk, Virginia, on November 26, 1942.

He was ordered for duty with Fighting Squadron 17 and was a founder member - or "Plank Owner" - when it was commissioned on January 1, 1943. On October 13, 1943, Earl was promoted to Lt. (jg). Earl was assigned Corsair #6 in June 1943, flying as "Jug" Bell's wingman. He stayed there for the start of the first tour. For the second tour he was assigned #27 as a section leader in "Jug" Bell's division with "Beads" Popp as his wingman.

On his first tour he gained combat experience flying patrols and escorts with Fighting 17, and flew 143.9 combat hours during this tour. Following leave in Australia, Earl returned to action on January 27, 1944, when Fighting 17 was assigned as cover on one of two B-25 squadrons striking Lakunai Airfield. Sixty to seventy Japanese fighters intercepted the strike and attacked the top cover first. "Jug" Bell and "Bitz" Bitzegaio were both hit.

Earl was the leader of Bell's second section and had several unsuccessful shots before he saw a New Zealand Air Force P-40 below him being chased by three Zekes. He went straight down, made a beam run from four o'clock, and saw one Zeke roll over and crash into the water. He recovered at 5,000 ft. and rejoined the formation. Throughout the action "Beads" Popp was on May's wing.

On January 29, 1944, Fighting 17 was assigned as cover for SBD Dauntless dive bombers in the joint SBD - TBF attack on Tobera Airfield, New Britain.

Only fifteen Zekes intercepted the strike, as a number of others were already being engaged by "Ike" Kepford and "Mac" Burriss. Earl was leading "Timmy" Gile's second section, and he and his wingman, "Beads" Popp, made several passes but became separated. Earl got on the tail of a Zeke and at very close range (only 50 ft.) fired a long burst; the Zeke crashed into the sea in flames.

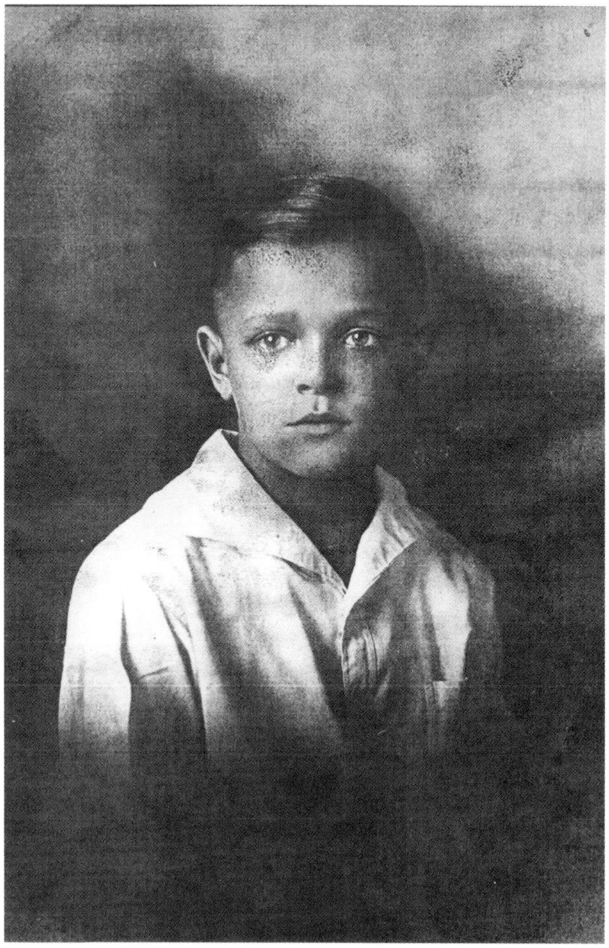

Earl May at age ten or eleven. *Courtesy of the Del and Pat May Collection*

On February 4, 1944, Fighting 17 were assigned as low and medium cover on a B-24 Liberator strike on Tobera Airfield.

About thirty Japanese fighters, including ten Kawasaki Ki 61 Tonys–distinctive with their inline engines–and three Nakajima Tojos were seen climbing as the formation crossed the coast on the approach. The Japanese seemed to make no attempt to attack the bombers until they withdrew from the strike. One Corsair, however, was attacked during the approach. The pilot, Ens. Percy Divenney, apparently

Earl May, Jr., and the "Flying Badgers" during primary training in 1942 at N.A.S. Glenview, Illinois. Earl back row 7th from left; "Hap" Bowers front row 6th from left. *Courtesy of the Del and Pat May Collection*

mistook the handle of his emergency landing gear release CO_2 bottle for the handle of his wing purging bottle because his wheels went down as he was crossing the coast. Divenney, although instructed by radio to get under the bombers, stayed up at 23,000 ft. until he and his section leader, "Chico" Freeman, saw five or six Zekes 4,000 ft. above them. They dived for a cloud layer at 17,000 ft., but when they came out of the cloud two to three minutes later they saw the Zekes still above. Divenney and Freeman again dived for cloud at 15,000 ft., and at this point "Chico" lost sight of Divenney. Shortly after Earl and "Beads" Popp had seen Divenney's plight and turned back to help protect him. They scissored above him, with Divenney taking what evasive action he could below. Earl and "Beads" destroyed one Zeke in a section run, but the Corsairs had a greater radius of turn than the Zekes, so they could not keep them off Divenney's tactically hindered Corsair with its wheels down. Divenney was badly hit and spun down with his engine smoking.

"Beads" Popp remembers the shooting down of Ens. Divenney. (According to the combat reports Fighting 17 was escorting B-24s, however "Beads" Popp was adamant it was B-25s they were escorting):

"We were escorting Marine B-25's over Vunakanau Field over Rabaul. Divenney was flying wing on 'Chico' Freeman, I was flying wing on Earl May. We were at about 20,000 feet. That model of Corsair had wing tanks in addition to main tanks. The Naval Corsair also had two CO_2 systems. One was to blow the

Earl and brother Del in 1942.
Courtesy of the Del and Pat May Collection

wheels and flaps down in the event of failure of the hydraulic system, the other one to cover the wing tank to prevent explosions in the wing if hit by enemy incendiary bullets. We took off on main tanks, switched to wing tanks and when safely airborne back to main tank when approaching main target area. Simultaneously on switching to main we would purge the main tanks with the CO_2*. There were two separate bottles; the wing tank bottle handle was yellow, the wheels and flaps was red. Unfortunately they were side by side, a grievous mistake by the aircraft designer. If you blew wheels down the only way to retract would be after you were back on the deck, have the aircraft manually hoisted and have the mechanic bleed the lines. Obviously this option was not available while airborne and certainly not in the heat of combat.*

Divenney unfortunately pushed the wrong handle and blew his wheels down. Immediately on seeing this mishap, Blackburn yelled to Divenney to firewall the plane and get under the B-25s so that they could protect him. Divenney panicked and didn't react, Blackburn then gave orders for the rest of us to stay with the bombers and forget Divenney. 'Chico' Freeman his section leader chose to ignore the Skipper's orders and turn back to cover Divenney as did

Earl May as a brand new Ensign with his proud brother Del in October 1942. *Courtesy of the Del and Pat May Collection*

my section leader Earl May. I had no choice but to stay with May and 'Chico' to protect Divenney as best we could. It was just then a matter of weaving over Divenney and kicking the rudder and shoot. I estimated there were ten to twenty Zeros. I was able to nail one by a gut shot up the tail, my first combat kill as was verified by May and Freeman, who saw the plane literally blow apart right in front of me. After what felt like hours as I was flying inverted at the time, I passed over Divenney and observed close hand his plane was on fire and Divenney was fatally wounded. I then saw tracers coming by me and looking around I counted Zeros bearing down approximately four or five. I could not see May or Freeman. Rather than do a Split - S, I dumped over the top and went straight down. I dove from 20,000 feet to less than approximately 5,000 feet. I think I was still in a high blower; I tried to recover from the dive but because of my speed my plane began to tuck. I was very close to the speed of compressibility. By the use of my tabs little by little I began to recover. My next concern was that I would go into a high speed stall. I recovered at about 3,000 feet. I looked around, no Zeros, I then noticed the B-25's approximately ten miles ahead at about 10,000 feet. I maintained my speed and flew into their formation and let them protect me. I next had problems keeping my knees from uncontrollable tremors. Finally at about the Treasuries I bid the B-25's adieu and flew to Bougainville.

When I landed and reported in, 'Chico' and Earl having seen me dive reported me being lost. I walked into the ready tent and as I arrived Blackburn was berating May and Freeman for violating his orders, resulting in for what they assumed was my being shot down and the loss of Divenney. Upon spotting me both 'Chico' and Earl joyously welcomed me. However, this did not placate Blackburn, in fact it made him madder and continued to give May and 'Chico' hell for violating his orders and leaving the B-25s. Blackburn was very proud that he never lost a bomber we were protecting to enemy aircraft."

On February 9, 1944, Fighting 17 was assigned as cover, this time for the TBF Avengers in a joint SBD - TBF strike on Vunakanau Airfield. After the dive bombers pushed over into their attack dives, Earl took his section down through a tunnel-like hole in the clouds and saw a Zeke ahead at 5,000 ft. and climbing out of range. He tried a long distance shot and watched his tracers go over the Zeke, which broke its climb. The Zeke's indecision enabled Earl to close, and he fired a long burst from dead astern and watched the Zeke explode. May and Popp then went back over the bombers.

Sixteen F4Us were assigned as cover for a B-24 squadron in a strike against Vunakanau Airfield on February 18, 1944.

"Timmy" Gile's division was part of the Roving High Cover for this mission. Paul Cordray and Earl May were flying as second section in

"Timmy's" division. As "Timmy" attacked eight Zekes, Paul and Earl also went down in a pair in beam high side runs. Earl missed, but Paul sent a Zeke spinning down, smoking and out of control. The pair then headed towards Vunakanau and got in a running fight with eight Zekes. As they made a section attack three Zekes jumped Paul, who dived down below a layer of clouds at 16,000 ft. to try to shake them off. Earl called Paul to zoom up through the cloud so that he could shoot the Zekes off his tail, but Paul did not hear and continued his dive. Feeling very uncomfortable about being alone, Earl headed East. He came up behind a Zeke which slow rolled, and Earl shot him all the way round until it caught fire at the wing roots and went down. As Earl crossed the coast of New Britain over Put Put at 11,000 ft. he spotted another Zeke and crept up to it unobserved. This Zeke also slow rolled when Earl fired, and Earl again followed him through the roll and saw him go down in flames. Earl then rejoined with the cover on the retiring B-24s and went home. Thankfully Cordray had

Earl May in Corsair #8 after a February 26, 1944, mission. *Courtesy of the Del and Pat May Collection*

"Hap" Bowers and Earl May by Earl's aircraft #27. *Alexandra Bowers*

eluded the Zekes' attack by diving to the deck and also rejoined for the return to base.

Earl was credited with two Zekes destroyed on this mission, which made him an ace.

On February 19, 1944, twenty-four Corsairs were assigned as high cover on TBF Avengers and as high and medium cover on the Dauntless dive bombers for the strike on Lakunai Airfield. An additional four Corsairs were assigned as Roving High Cover. Because of engine troubles and other eventualities, only twenty-four arrived over the target. The TBF and SBD strike was attacked by Japanese fighters on their withdrawal after hitting the target.

Earl and "Beads" Popp were in "Timmy" Gile's second section, and went into action almost simultaneously with the first section. Earl took on a Zeke in a head on attack and the Zeke exploded. He and "Beads" recovered at 3,000 ft. and headed towards Cape Gazelle. There were Zekes all over the sky, but Earl and "Beads" repulsed all attacks by scissoring. Earl shot down two more Zekes and "Beads" one, all attacks being made from astern and the section working well as a pair. Earl was credited with three Zekes, which took his final total to eight.

On his second tour Earl flew 75.4 combat hours up to February 21, 1944, and had completed twenty-one combat sorties, including sixteen missions to Rabaul.

In his two tours with Fighting 17, Earl was awarded the Silver Star and Distinguished Flying Cross. After returning to the States and a well earned leave he reported to N.A.A.S. Green Cove Springs on May 6, 1944, as an Instructor. Then, on August 28, 1944, he reported to Fighting Squadron Ten in N.A.S. Atlantic City, and on November 20, 1944, was appointed to the regular Navy.

Earl May and ground crew in front of his assigned aircraft #27. Middle man in the photo is Earl May's Plane Captain Thomas Carpenter AMM2c. On the left is Norm Growchowski. *Courtesy of the Del and Pat May Collection*

L-R: "Ginger" and Bill Landreth and Thelma and Earl May, taken in late 1944 just before Bill and Earl left for the Pacific with VBF-10 aboard the carrier USS *Intrepid*. Bill and Earl were good friends, and were each other's best man at their weddings. A few months later Bill was forced down over Honshu, Japan, and was a prisoner of war for the duration. *Courtesy of the Del and Pat May Collection*

Earl met his wife Thelma thanks to Tom Blackburn, and Earl's brother Del remembers:

> *"Earl married Thelma Wright May on September 11, 1944 in Atlantic City, New Jersey. "Country" and "Ginger" Landreth stood up at their wedding and they did the same for them. The family were surprised to say the least. Earl had one or two girlfriends in the Milwaukee area and it was just assumed one of those would someday be his wife. The surprise only lasted one or two days because within a very short time my parents received a beautiful letter from Thelma, introducing herself and stating how much she loved Earl and that she would do everything she could to be a perfect wife, which impressed Earl's parents."*

Earl was promoted to Lt. with effect from January 1, 1945, and on January 2, 1945, he reported to Bomber Fighter Squadron Ten, based on the USS *Intrepid*. He served in combat against the Japanese home islands and Okinawa campaign, being awarded a second Distinguished Flying Cross to add to the one he was awarded with Fighting 17.

Whilst Earl was serving in combat in the Japanese home islands his wife, Thelma, had an "illegal adventure" with Earl's brother Del, who remembers the incident:

> *"Around early 1945 time a funny, and then embarrassing thing happened to Thelma and me at this time. I was just fourteen years old and was driving cars all over town. Thelma was very pregnant and had to see her doctor but because she was so pregnant she couldn't drive her car. So I volunteered to drive her.*
>
> *The doctor's office was in Downtown Milwaukee and the time was just after lunch. We were driving slowly down the main street with Thelma giving me directions when Thelma suddenly told me to turn left. As soon as I started turning left she shouted "No, I mean turn right." So I slammed on the brakes and started to backup to prepare to turn right. In a moment we heard a loud bang. I looked into the rear view*

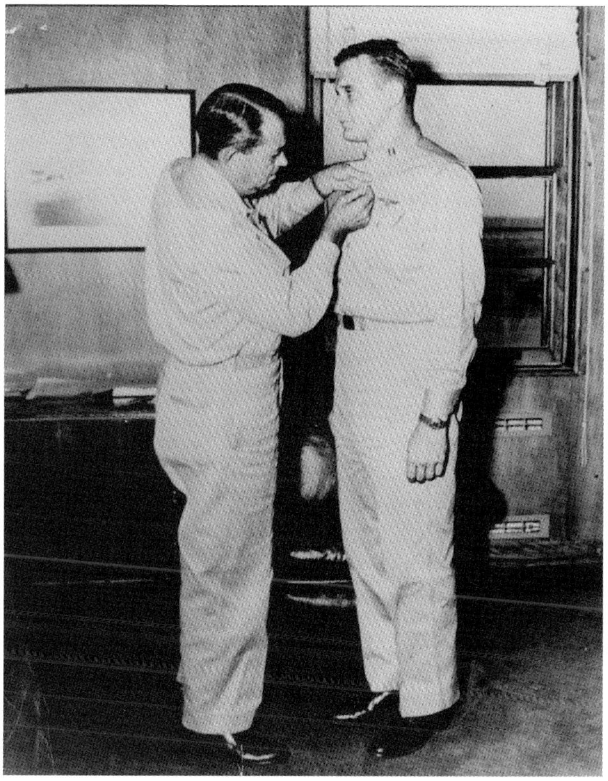

Lt. Earl May, Jr., receiving the Air Medal and Gold Star in lieu of a second Distinguished Flying Cross while serving with VBF-10. *Courtesy of the Del and Pat May Collection*

mirror and much to my horror I saw a Police Officer standing next to his overturned side - car motorcycle brushing himself off. He then charged over to my window and screamed. "What's going on here and how old are you?" I said. "I'm fourteen." Then Thelma stepped in with her persuasive southern accent and explained, pointing to her stomach, that she couldn't drive and I was the only one available. The Officer was actually very understanding and told us to proceed CAREFULLY!"

Earl was ordered to N.A.S. Glenview, reporting on December 23, 1945, and then to N.A.S. Corpus Christi on February 26, 1946. He then reported to N.A.A.S. Rodd Field, Corpus Christi, on June 5, 1946.

On October 21, 1946, Earl was appointed as a Lt. in the regular Navy. He was assigned to N.A.S. Roosevelt Roads, Puerto Rico, reporting on January 16, 1948, to Commander Air Force Atlantic Fleet.

On April 15, 1949, he reported to Aircraft Development Squadron Three and then to the Naval School All Weather Flight, N.A.S. Corpus Christi, from

Earl May (fourth from left front row), probably taken in 1946 whilst Earl was instructing at N.A.S. Corpus Christi, Texas. *Courtesy of the Del and Pat May Collection*

I counted Zeros bearing down . . . I dumped over the top and went straight down. I dove from 20,000 feet to less than approximately 5,000 feet. . . . I tried to recover . . . but . . . my plane began to tuck. . . . 'Chico' and Earl having seen me dive reported me being lost.

September 21, 1950, to November 15, 1950. "Country" Landreth remembered how Earl became a Test Pilot:

> *"Butch" Davenport was already at the test pilot school and I think he was quite instrumental in getting Earl the chance to go through test pilot school."*

On January 22, 1951, the Naval Air Test Center was advised of Earl's experience, which at the time included 1,000 hours on Corsairs and 290 hours on the F2H Banshee jet fighter:

> *"Energy and determination displayed in the performance of flying duties is in direct proportion to his personal interest in the flying assigned.*
>
> *Lt. May has displayed cool, sound judgement in all flying assignments.*
>
> *Has a keen mind and is able to analyze problems in a straight forward manner.*
>
> *Has the ability to put thought on paper in a concise manner, delineating? Between facts and opinion."*

On June 21, 1951, Earl was detached from VX-3 and ordered to N.A.S. Patuxent River, Maryland. Amongst those serving at "Pax River" at the time was the future astronaut Alan B. Shepard.

On August 29, 1951, Earl was promoted as Lt. Cdr. U.S. Navy. Lt. Cdr. Earl May died on October 10, 1951, when he crashed in an F8F-1 Bearcat at high speed from high altitude. The aircraft crashed at Saw Mill Road, Cedarville, New Jersey. It is believed he may have been unconscious due to loss of oxygen or carbon monoxide poisoning. Local residents have been caring for Earl May's crash site to this day. Earl's brother Del relates the story:

> *"I got a very unexpected and surprising phone call in 2003 from a guy in New Jersey asking if I was Earl May's brother. I naturally said I was. He asked if I knew that the people in a small town in New Jersey had been maintaining Earl's crash site since 1951! My wife and I immediately made arrangements to visit the area and the people. We've found good friends out there and have made two visits so far."*

Opposite:
Lt. Cdr. Earl May, Jr. A memorial portrait commissioned by his father and painted by Charles W. Thwaites, a Milwaukee artist.
Courtesy of the Del and Pat May Collection

Earl and Thelma May shortly after they were married in 1944.
Courtesy of the Del and Pat May Collection

Lt. Cdr. May's remains were transported to Milwaukee and buried at Wanderer's Rest Cemetery, now called Lincoln Memorial Cemetery. His parents, Earl Sr. and Norma, who died just a few weeks apart in 1965, now lie beside him. He left a widow Thelma, a son Richard E. May, a daughter Carol Ann May, and a brother Del R. May.

Millville Army Airfield Museum has a display in May's memory, and Lawrence Township Historical Society has dedicated a road sign to mark the crash site.

Earl May, in addition to the Silver Star and Distinguished Flying Cross, was awarded a Gold Star in lieu of a second Distinguished Flying Cross, two Air Medals, Navy Unit Commendation, Asiatic - Pacific Campaign Medal with three stars, American Campaign Medal, Navy Occupation Service Medal "Asia" Clasp, Philippine Liberation Ribbon with two Bronze Stars, and the World War II Victory Medal.

Thelma May passed away on September 23, 2008.

Lt. (jg) Robert "Bobby" Mims at Bougainville in 1944. Mims returned to Fighting 17 on December 5, 1943, after recovering from an illness. *Courtesy of the National Archives*

13

ROBERT "BOBBY" MIMS

6 VICTORIES

Robert "Bobby" Mims was born on March 20, 1920, in Dallas, Texas. He was the only child of John Emmett Mims and Lillian Smith.

He was educated at Rice Institute in Houston, Texas, and Southern Methodist University in Dallas, Texas, where he played football and track.

Before going into the Navy he was a student and interested in publishing for a career.

"Bobby" enlisted in the Navy on February 1, 1942, and entered active service in Dallas as a Seaman Second Class on February 26, 1942. His enlistment was terminated on May 27, 1942, when he was appointed an Aviation Cadet on May 28, 1942, and trained at N.A.S. Corpus Christi. After completing the Navy flight training program he received his commission as an Ensign to rank from October 1, 1942, and was designated a Naval Aviator on October 8, 1942. From October 16, 1942, to November 22, 1942, he undertook his pre-operational training at N.A.S. Miami.

He was assigned to Fighting 17 early in 1943, until his flying was interrupted by some medical problems. He had German measles at the end of April 1943, appendicitis from April 26 to May 6, 1943, and a peptic ulcer from May 23 to June 4, 1943. He was admitted to hospital in Portsmouth, Virginia. He returned to Fighting 17 on June 12, 1943. "Bobby" was assigned Corsair #4 in June 1943 as wingman to "Big Jim" Streig, or Tail End Charlie in Tom Blackburn's division. During training "Bobby" was flying with a good buddy when "Bobby" got vertigo coming down through the clouds and his friend flew with him. "Bobby" finally pulled out, but his friend couldn't and he went straight into the water.

"Bobby" served with Fighting 17 until September 28, 1943, when he had further medical problems, resulting in a stay at the Naval Hospital in

San Diego until November 19, 1943. He was unable to go with Fighting 17 when they went into combat for their first tour.

As a result of his medical issues "Bobby" also failed to qualify for promotion as Lt. (jg) on October 1, 1943. This was deferred until December 17, 1943, when he was back with Fighting 17.

He reported back to Fighting 17 on December 5, 1943, in time for their return to combat at the end of January 1944.

He was assigned Corsair #4 in Tom Blackburn's division as Tail End Charlie when they went into action on January 26, 1944, the first mission into Rabaul.

On the next mission on January 27, 1944, when twenty F4Us were assigned as cover on one of two B-25 squadrons striking Lakunai Airfield, sixty to seventy Japanese fighters intercepted the strike as the bombers were leaving the target.

When the Japanese attacked the medium and low cover, "Big Jim" Streig and "Bobby" dove away and lost the Zekes. Climbing back to 14,000 ft., they pulled up on the tail of a Zeke and got a good burst into his belly, which burned the Zeke. Four Zekes were seen above and two or three above and astern. This group came down and got on "Big Jim's" tail. "Bobby" turned in on one of them and with a burst from dead astern set him on fire. "Big Jim" had broken left and down (losing "Bobby" in the process) and saw a Zeke below him at 3,000 ft. He made a high-side run, saw the Zeke burn and crash, and pulled up to 5,000 ft. Tracers went by him and he dove to 1500 ft. He climbed to 5,000 ft. and headed for Cape Gazelle. He saw seven or eight Zekes climbing from Rapopo Airfield at 1500 ft. He dove on the nearest Zeke and made a beam run. Pieces flew from the plane, and he fell off to the right and crashed near the field. They then put on full power and headed for the retiring bombers, making 310 knots (indicated) at 1,000 ft. He joined up on "Bobby" and headed back to base.

After "Bobby" and "Big Jim" were separated the former dove for the water. He saw eight or ten planes (blue grey in color) circling slowly with their wheels down right on the water off Malaguna Airfield ("Bobby" was unable to identify the type). He got on one's tail and it crashed into the water. He then headed for Cape Gazelle and joined up on "Big Jim" over the bombers. "Bobby" scored two confirmed victories and a shared one with "Big Jim" on this mission.

On January 28, 1944, twenty F4Us were assigned as partial cover on the TBFs on a joint SBD - TBF strike on Tobera Airfield, New Britain. About forty to fifty Zekes and Hamps intercepted the strike.

"Bobby," number two man in Blackburn's division in the lower cover, was hit in the windshield and oil cooler on the initial attack. "Bobby" broke to the right, got a 90° deflection shot on a Zeke, and followed him from 13,000 ft. almost to the ground firing most of the time, but lost him as the Zeke went into a roll. "Bobby" was west of the field and headed for the rally point over Kabanga Bay. He was at about 100 ft. when he got on the tail of a Zeke. He fired a good burst (four guns) and saw the Zeke begin smoking. He fired again and only one gun worked, and as he pulled up a Marine F4U finished off the Zeke. "Bobby" then climbed, joined another F4U and, since his oil pressure was dropping, headed home. On landing his plane was caught in a slip stream and his plane nosed over. "Bobby" was credited with a shared Zeke with a Marine pilot and one probable Zeke.

February 6, 1944, was a big day for "Bobby." He was one of four pilots assigned to the Roving High Cover led by "Big Hog" Tom Blackburn. Fighting 17 were escorting B-25s on a strike to Lakunai Airfield.

The account of Blackburn's actions reveals the nature of the combat. He (with his division) made the first attack on four of six Zekes who were over Rapopo headed for the strike at 22,000 ft. He dove at 45° from 25,000 ft., fired from the five o'clock position, and the Zeke exploded. He recovered in a right chandelle to 23,000 ft. and saw a group of Japanese fighters heading northwest after the bombers. Blackburn reformed his division and followed. Over Lakunai at 20,000 ft., the division jumped several Zekes who were climbing and heading south. Blackburn made a high side run from the left and saw the Zeke burn. Before he completed his recovery he made a pass at another Zeke and

Bobby and Doris Mims on their wedding day. *Courtesy of Betsy Bryant and Susan Ritter*

followed him down in a diving spin for about 4,000 ft. (his wingman saw the plane burn).

Blackburn recovered to the left in a tight climbing spiral to 2,000 ft. He picked up a group of Zekes and Hamps and pursued them to the north. He got in some bursts and his wingman burned one Zeke. Blackburn again reformed his division, and the F4Us headed northeast after the bombers. As the division was above the clouds over Duke of York Island, they jumped eight or ten Zekes who were climbing for altitude. Blackburn caught one unaware and saw him smoke and pieces fly off. "Bobby," his section leader, had dropped back, and the other F4Us headed after him. The reformed division was pursued by four Japanese fighters (Zekes or Hamps), but climbed away from them at 160 knots. When they had gained altitude the F4Us turned back. Two of the Japanese fighters had disappeared, and the other pair dove away in opposite directions. He joined up with his division but sent his second section home because of oxygen shortage. Tom Blackburn recalls the mission:

Bill Meek, Bobby Mims, and "Ike" Kepford at Bougainville in 1944. *Courtesy of Vought*

Bobby Mims as an Ensign in 1942. *U S Navy photo*

"Toward the latter part of the aerial opposition phase over Rabaul we tailed in some Thirty to thirty five mixed Zeros and Hamps and "Bobby" was leading the second section. He and I worked as a team and attacked these Japs from opposite sides in succession and each of us got four flamers out of it."

Harold Bitzegaio recalls his part in this mission:

"He was going to catch the Japs as they came back so he and "Bobby" Mims and I was Tail End Charlie and we shot down seven airplanes. The Skipper got four and "Bobby" got three and I got one if I remember right.

But that was quite exciting to start at 30,000 feet and fight your way to the ground. That was the time "Bobby" unplugged his oxygen mask and passed out and the Skipper and I were trying to get his attention and we thought maybe he was hurt. But finally we got down to 8 or 9,000 feet and "Bobby" woke up and joined up and we came back."

Blackburn scored three Zekes, one Hamp, and two probables; "Bobby" scored one Tojo, two Zekes, and two Zeke probables. This mission made "Bobby" an ace with six victories and concluded his scoring with Fighting 17.

His final tally was six confirmed and three probable victories, and he flew 68.8 combat hours up to February 21, 1944.

Tom Blackburn recommended Bobby for the Distinguished Flying Cross on February 29, 1944:

"Between January 27, 1944 and February 26, 1944, Lt. (jg) Mims flew twenty seven combat sorties, fourteen of which were escort missions or fighter sweeps over the Rabaul area. He encountered enemy aircraft on nine occasions: on 26, 27, 28, 30 and 31 January, and on 4, 6, 17, and 19 February. On 27 January the formation of B-25's which he was escorting in a strike on Lakunai Airfield was aggressively intercepted by sixty or seventy Jap fighters. He and his section leader destroyed one Zeke in the initial attack, and Lt. (jg) Mims destroyed another which had attacked his section leader. Having become separated from the latter he nevertheless continued in the melee and attacked eight Japs over Simpson Harbor, destroying one of them. On 28 January the formation of TBF's which he was escorting in a strike on Tobera Airfield was intercepted by about sixty Jap fighters. Although his windshield was smashed by a Jap bullet in the initial attack he engaged the interceptors, probably destroyed one Zeke and shared another with a Marine pilot. On 6 February he flew one of four Corsairs which preceded a B-25 strike on Lakunai Airfield. The Corsairs made contact with twenty Jap fighters, and disregarding the five to one numerical superiority of the enemy, made repeated attacks destroying eight, probably destroying five thereby facilitating the task of our bombers. In this action Lt. (jg) Mims shot down two Zekes, one Tojo, and probably destroyed two Zekes."

The Distinguished Flying Cross Citation as follows:

> *"For heroism and extraordinary achievement in aerial flight as pilot of a fighter plane in Fighting Squadron 17 during action against enemy Japanese forces in New Britain, Solomon Islands, from January 27, to February 26, 1944. Participating in numerous strikes against enemy installations in this area, Lt. (then Lt. (jg)) Mims struck repeatedly at his targets and, despite frequent powerful enemy fire, succeeded in personally destroying three enemy fighters and contributed to the destruction of two additional by his flight. Attacked by a numerically superior force of enemy aircraft during a fighter sweep over Lakunai airfield, he closed with the hostile planes and, pressing home his attacks with skill, personally blasted three of them from the sky and probably destroyed two more. His airmanship and devotion to duty throughout these hazardous operations were in keeping with the highest traditions of the United States Naval Service."*

Upon his return to the States after his combat tour with Fighting 17, "Bobby" served at N.A.A.S. Green Cove Springs from May 10, 1944, but was admitted to the Naval Hospital in Jacksonville on May 11, 1944, until May 25, 1944.

He then returned to N.A.A.S. Green Cove Springs from May 25, 1944, to July 31, 1944, where he was a Combat Team Instructor, and then served with VF-10 from September 4, 1944, to January 1, 1945. He requested non-flying duty on November 22, 1944, and on January 1, 1945, was appointed a temporary Lt. Once his request to come off flying duty was considered he was assigned to Air Force Atlantic Fleet from January 6, 1945, to January 12, 1945. He then reported to N.A.S. Jacksonville on January 17, 1945, under instruction as a Landing Signal Officer until March 28, 1945.

"Bobby" reported to N.A.S. Miami on April 3, 1945, as Assistant to the Section Control Officer, and was then assigned to the USS *Hancock* (CV-19) from May 17, 1945, to October 29, 1945, and from June 1945 to August 1945 was in action in attacks against the Japanese home islands.

After the war was over "Bobby" finished his active service and left the Navy at Camp Wallace, Texas, on November 5, 1945.

After the war he married Doris Elaine Crockett, who was a distant relative of Davy Crockett. They had two girls, Betsy and Susan, and they divorced in the late 1950s when the girls were six and seven. "Bobby" had little contact with his family after then.

"Bobby" went into the oil business after the war and was very successful, a big "wheeler dealer" who put deals together to drill for oil and in the leasing business. He made $300,000 in one particular deal.

Unfortunately "Bobby" had an alcohol addiction. He didn't go to the war with an alcohol problem but came back with one. He was known as a "hell raising kind of a guy" by his squadron-mates.

On February 29, 1952, on his fitness report it was noted that "Bobby" had some medical problems and recommended his flight status cease due to not being physically qualified for flying.

Having been specially commended for his performance in actual combat by the head of the executive department, "Bobby" was, on March 1, 1953 placed on the retired list of the USNR with the rank of Lt. Cdr.

"Bobby" was married several times after Doris, but continued to have problems with alcohol addiction. On April 9, 1963, "Bobby" was convicted of a felony. On April 15, 1963, he was sentenced to fifteen years and was fined $10,000. The sentence was reduced on December 13, 1964, to five years, and the fine was suspended. Apparently he boarded an airliner whilst quite drunk, and in middle of the flight tried to attempt to take over the aircraft and had an altercation with the pilot. He was sent to the Federal Correctional Institution in Seagoville, Texas, where he died of a heart attack on September 19, 1966.

"Bobby" Mims, Fighting 17 ace with six aerial victories, is buried at Restlands Cemetery, Dallas, Texas.

In addition to the Distinguished Flying Cross he was awarded the Navy Unit Commendation, 3rd Fleet Unit Citation Letter of Commendation, American Campaign Medal, Asiatic - Pacific Campaign Medal with five Gold Stars, and the World War II Victory Medal.

Opposite:
Bobby Mims Fighting 17 ace with six victories. *Courtesy of Vought*

. . . disregarding the five to one numerical superiority of the enemy, made repeated attacks destroying eight . . .

John M. "Smitty" Smith, fourth ranked U.S. Navy Corsair ace with ten victories; three were achieved with Fighting 17 and seven with VF-84. *Courtesy of the John M Smith Collection*

14

JOHN MALCOLM "SMITTY" SMITH

10 VICTORIES

John Malcolm Smith was the fourth ranked Corsair ace of the Navy, a superb fighter pilot, and a typical Tom Brokaw's "Greatest Generation" type. Roger Hedrick, his Commanding Officer with VF-84, said:

> *"John was an outstanding fighter pilot and had ten confirmed victories. He was a modest man and dearly loved flying."*

His sister Marie also remembered her older sister Pat telling her that John told her before leaving for war that he did not expect to return. He put all of his military pay into a joint checking account with Marie and told her to use it to go to college, all without telling their father. John M. Smith was born on April 7, 1922, in Owatonna, Minnesota. He was the second son of Wilber J. Smith and Anne Foran Smith, and was their fourth child out of six. His father was an electrician and founder of Smith Electric, a business later continued by his eldest son, W.T. Smith. That company remained in business in Owatonna until 2005.

His mother was a housewife descended from Irish and Scottish immigrants who came to the New World in the mid-nineteenth century. His paternal grandfather, born on September 11, 1888, was a wagon maker married to Belle Carter, of English and Cornish extraction, whose families came to America in the early1800s. His great-grandfather (also named John Smith) was from Lancashire, England; he came over in 1850 and had a farm and orchard in Wisconsin. John M. Smith was of English, Cornish, Welsh, Scottish, and Irish ancestry.

John Smith's mother died on February 4, 1927, when he was not yet five years old. His older sister, Margaret Anne, took over the task of raising her siblings, assisted by their grandmother, Belle Carter, who lived with the family until her death in 1940.

John Smith attended St. Mary's Catholic Grade School in Owatonna, and graduated from Owatonna High School in 1939. There were no funds for college in those Depression years, so he worked as a collector for the Internal Revenue Service in St. Paul after high school.

Following the entry of the United States into World War II, John M. Smith enlisted in the U.S. Navy on July 22, 1942, at Iowa City, Iowa, as a Seaman Second Class. On June 15, 1943, his enlistment was terminated in order to accept appointment as an Ensign on June 16, 1943, to rank from June 1, 1943. He was able to train as a pilot despite the lack of a college degree, as the former requirement for such a degree had recently been relaxed. He first trained at the Naval Reserve Station at Glenview, Illinois, then received his flight training at the U.S. Naval Air Training Center at Corpus Christi, Texas.

He was assigned as a replacement pilot to Fighting 17, the "Skull and Crossbones Squadron," based in the Solomon Islands. Ensign John "Smitty" Smith reported to the squadron on December 8, 1943. After a period of evaluating new pilots "Smitty" was assigned as "Timmy" Gile's wingman flying aircraft #21. For most of the second tour this is where he was assigned.

On January 26, 1944, Fighting 17 started its second combat tour of duty flying from its new base at Bougainville on missions over the Solomon Islands and the Japanese stronghold of Rabaul in New Britain, Japan's major fortress in the southwest Pacific. Their opponents were elite air units of the Imperial Japanese Navy land- based at Rabaul. "Smitty" entered the combat arena on Fighting 17's first mission of their second tour when thirty-two F4Us were assigned as cover for the SBDs in a joint SBD - TBF strike on Lakunai Airfield, New Britain.

"Timmy" Gile's division was at 16,000 ft. over the Dauntless dive bombers as they started their attack dives when they were jumped by a group of Zekes. The division dived and levelled off at about 7,000 ft., with "Timmy" heading for a melee over St. George's Channel off Rapopo. "Timmy" made attack runs at four Zekes, and in a quarter stern run from eight o'clock set the fourth Zeke on fire.

"Timmy" looked for his second section and could not find them, so he and his wingman John "Smitty" Smith headed out after the SBDs. Twelve Zekes followed, and one closed the range on "Smitty," got on his tail, and shot and hit him. "Timmy" chandelled and ran at the Zeke, who was forced to disengage and return to Rabaul. "Timmy" and "Smitty" joined up and returned to base, as "Smitty's" aircraft had a hydraulic failure.

On January 29, 1944, "Smitty" was part of the assigned cover for the SBDs for the SBD and TBF strike on Tobera Airfield, New Britain. Due to the success of a Fighting 17 Roving High Cover attack on twelve Zekes the low and medium cover were only intercepted by about fifteen Zekes. "Timmy" Gile was leading the low cover and turned back several attacks, but became separated from his division.

"Smitty," who was "Timmy's" wingman in the action, was hit, but not seriously. As he was scissoring with "Timmy" he spotted a Zeke on a Corsair's tail. He executed a 360° turn, making an attack on the Zeke during his turn. However, he was unable to pull in tight enough, so pulled up in a wingover to gain height advantage and ran back in the Zeke's tail, chasing it for about a minute and firing bursts throughout. As "Smitty's" windshield was smeared with oil he could not estimate the exact damage inflicted, but he saw pieces fly from the Zeke. As "Smitty" broke off he saw it flop on its back and was diving from 1,000 ft. He then rejoined with another Corsair back over the dive bombers and returned to base. He was credited with one Zeke probable.

The next day, January 30, 1944, he was part of twenty-four F4Us assigned to cover B-25 Mitchell medium bombers for their strike on a supply dump in the Rabaul area, near Lakunai. The Japanese intercepted the strike after the bombers had finished their bomb runs. "Smitty" was in the second division of Roger Hedrick's flight, along with Paul Cordray, James Miller, and Don Malone. "Smitty" was flying without his usual division leader "Timmy" Gile on this day.

The division made contact with the Zekes at about 16,000 ft. In the ensuing melee Paul Cordray

John M. Smith as a young Ensign in the summer of 1943. *Courtesy of the John M Smith Collection*

had a Zeke on his tail with "Smitty" firing a burst at this Zeke, seeing bullets strike into its nose. "Smitty" was credited with one probable Zeke.

On February 17, 1944, "Smitty" had a busy day and was credited by "Beads" Popp for saving his life. "Beads" was "Smitty's" closest friend, and they both went on to serve with VF-84 after their service with Fighting 17. Twenty Corsairs were assigned as high and medium cover for the dive bombers in an SBD and TBF strike on shipping in Simpson Harbor. Thirty to forty Japanese fighters intercepted the formation just before it reached the target. "Smitty" was flying wing on "Timmy" Gile, together with Earl May and "Beads" Popp in the high cover. They spotted twelve to fourteen Zekes climbing over Blanche Bay and arriving at a position astern of the bombers. The division turned back into them and made several section attacks at about 12,000 ft. "Smitty" lost his section leader after a chandelle, and almost immediately saw a Zeke at his altitude approaching from his port side, as though he were trying to join up. "Smitty" made a beam attack and fired a long burst, and the Zeke spun down in flames. "Smitty" recovered and looked for someone to join up on. He saw no Corsairs, so he dived to 8,000 ft. and made a beam attack on another Zeke, who rolled over and dived away, obviously damaged. "Smitty" then climbed and headed towards the rally point off Cape Gazelle. Over Ralunana Point he spotted a Nakajima Oscar slightly below him. He made a stern attack, closing to about 1,000 ft., and fired into the Oscar's tail, which spun down with fuel streaming from its wing roots. "Smitty" climbed away and started to the rally point to join up with the bombers. A Zeke got on his tail and fired into his wings. "Smitty" broke off to shake off the attack and got back to the bombers.

"Beads" Popp recalls his near fatal mistake of trying to loop with a Zeke during this action:

> *"We were in a four plane division at about 8,000 feet over Rabaul. I was Tail - End Charlie. "Timmy" Gile was division leader, John Malcolm Smith was his number two (Gile's wingman), Earl May (my section leader) number three and I was number four.*
>
> *A single Zero made a dive on us and continued by looping in front of the division. Gile pulled up, took a shot, broke off, followed by Smith, took a shot, broke off, followed by May, took a shot, broke off. By that time I was almost on my back, but I had the Zeke in my sights. I took a couple of shots at him, then I almost stalled out at the top of the loop. By the time I recovered I was losing air speed and had lost my altitude, giving me very little operational chances. I had no area in which I could dive, all I could do was kick the rudder and shoot, kick the rudder and shoot. Fortunately at that time a lone Marine Corsair flown by a Major Wilbur plus John Smith who had seen my predicament and came post haste to give me assistance. We formed a three man Thach Weave and finally were able to extricate me from my mess. I believe I smoked a Zeke, however, neither I nor the other two were able to confirm it. I never even got a probable."*

I suppose you are wondering whether I am still a "virgin". Well the answer is no. I've shot down three Zeros.

L-R. #1 "Win" Rowley, #2 John M. Smith (Smitty), #3 "Heck" Kramer, and #4 James C. Dixon (Jimmy). Harvey Matthews is on the bottom. *Courtesy of the Matthews Family*

Smith was credited with one Zeke destroyed, one Zeke damaged, and one Oscar probable.

The next day February 18, 1944, sixteen F4Us were assigned as low and medium cover on the first of two squadrons of B-24s striking Vunakanau Airfield. There was practically no interception of the strike itself. The Roving High Cover, however, had lots of business. The two divisions on Roving High Cover reached the target a half hour before the bombers. They approached from the south over Wide Bay at 32,000 ft. and made a wide circle of the area with Roger Hedrick's division at 29,000 ft. and "Timmy" Gile's division at 26,000 ft.

Over Blanche Bay "Timmy" spotted eight Zekes at about level with his division and in a climbing turn. The Zekes were in two "beautifully" formed four aircraft divisions. The Zekes and Corsairs continued climbing, each formation seeking altitude advantage. The Corsairs got to 30,000 ft. first and the division started section runs on the Zekes, who then dived away. The action then developed into a running fight. "Timmy," with "Smitty" on his wing, made three unsuccessful attacks, followed by chandelles to gain height advantage. Over Keravat they caught a Zeke at about 25,000 ft. The Zeke Split-S'd, but "Timmy" and "Smitty" were able to make an attack run from

John M. Smith while serving with VF-84 at N.A.A.S. Twenty-Nine Palms in the fall of 1944. *Courtesy of the Matthews Family*

five o'clock. The Zeke caught fire and spun down. This was credited to "Timmy" Gile. Two Zekes then appeared on "Smitty's" tail, so the section made a 180° turn and went into a flat dive. The Zekes turned back and "Timmy" chandelled after them. "Smitty" thought that this maneuver was part of a scissors, so he crossed beneath "Timmy" and turned back on an opposite course. He lost contact with "Timmy" and started a climb over Cape Gazelle. He saw a Zeke approaching in a slight left turn on an opposite course. Both the Zeke and the Corsair thought that each other was friendly and started to join up. Luckily "Smitty" corrected his error first by spotting the Zeke's tail at about 1,800 ft., so he set up for a 70 mil deflection shot lead from one o'clock. "Smitty" held his fire until the range had closed to 800 ft. and then gave the Zeke a long burst, which stayed in the same turn throughout. "Smitty" chandelled and saw the Zeke smoking and spinning down, so he followed, fired again, and pulled away when the Zeke began to burn. Smith was credited with one Zeke destroyed.

The last time Fighting 17 met the Japanese in aerial combat was the following day, February 19, 1944, when twenty-four Corsairs were assigned as high cover on the TBF torpedo bombers and as high and medium cover on the SBD dive bombers in a strike on Lakunai Airfield. The strike was intercepted by Japanese fighters when it retired from the target.

The first division of the high cover was led by "Timmy" Gile and had to fight its way through about twenty Zekes and probably Nakajima Ki 44 Tojos to get to the rally point off Cape Gazelle. "Smitty" scored first when, at 14,000 ft., he caught what he thought to be a Tojo, and in a stern quarter shot set it on fire. Almost immediately after this pass the section ("Timmy" with "Smitty" covering) made a similar attack on a Zeke, with "Timmy" getting in a long burst, and the Zeke caught fire, spun down, and was seen to crash. By this time the Japanese had withdrawn, and "Timmy" and "Smitty" continued their weave over the TBFs. Smith was credited with one Tojo destroyed.

He finished his tour with Fighting 17 with three confirmed, three probables, and one damaged, and would soon add to this total in further air combat with VF-84.

Up to February 21, 1944, John M. Smith flew eighteen days and completed twenty combat sorties with fifteen missions to Rabaul and 63 hours of combat.

On 25 February John wrote home to his youngest sister, Marie:

> *"I've been flying over Rabaul and based in the Solomons. It isn't any secret now so I can tell you. We've been in, what anyone will tell you, some of the toughest aerial fights of the war. In fact you will probably read a great deal about Fighting Squadron Seventeen, alias Skull and Crossbones gang, alias Blackburn's Irregulars, in the near future. We've established several all time records as far as enemy planes shot down. I suppose you are wondering whether I am still a "virgin". Well the answer is no. I've shot down three Zeros. That isn't very remarkable in this squadron - in fact it's way down on the list but it's better than none anyway. I've also damaged or probably shot down about six more but those don't mean a thing.*
>
> *We've been in combat about five weeks now. At the beginning it was very rough. We were knocking them down like flies and they were getting some of us too. I've returned home three times with bullet holes in my airplane and twice with scratches in my leg where bullets just touched! I didn't even require iodine. Now however we escort bombers to Rabaul and don't see a single Jap in the sky. That suits me fine. We're as safe as if we were in church now.*
>
> *Talking about church, if you don't think this makes a Christian out of a guy, you're crazy. I've prayed more and been more thankful for people praying for me, in the last five weeks than at any similar length of time in my life. This all sounds very dangerous - well in the beginning it was but that's all over now and there is nothing more to worry about."*

John and Fighting 17 returned home after being relieved on March 7, 1944. After a period of leave many of its pilots, including John M. Smith, formed the nucleus for the formation of VF-84 in May 1944. It was a new squadron which was to operate Corsair aircraft aboard the Essex class carrier USS *Bunker Hill* (CV-17). The Squadron Commander was Roger Hedrick, promoted from his former Executive Officer role with Fighting 17. The squadron commenced a period of training until it was ready for combat in early 1945.

The *Bunker Hill* was a part of Task Force 58 in the last stages of the Pacific War. Its battles included support of landings on Iwo Jima and Okinawa, the sinking of the *Yamato*, the largest battleship in the world, and raids on the Japanese home islands.

On February 16, 1945, "Smitty" flew a strike against Yaizu Airfield. He shot down a Kate for his fourth victory. He also recorded in his log book a Dinah and Kate destroyed on the ground. He was awarded the Air Medal for this mission.

"Smitty" was awarded a Gold Star in Lieu of his second Air Medal for five combat missions. The citation stated:

> *"For distinguishing himself by meritorious acts while participating in aerial flights in operations against the enemy in the vicinity of Tokyo, Iwo Jima, Okinawa and Kyushu. As pilot of a carrier based fighter plane during the period February 16, 1945 to March 19, 1945 he participated in five missions against enemy shipping, airfields and installations, inflicting extensive damage. His skill and courage were at all times inspiring and in keeping with the highest traditions of the United States Naval Service."*

Smith was awarded his third Air Medal after flying ten combat missions:

> *"For meritorious achievement in aerial flight as pilot of a fighter plane in Fighting Squadron Eighty Four during operations against enemy Japanese forces in the vicinity of Tokyo, Iwo Jima, Kyushu and Okinawa from*

February 16 to April 3, 1945. Completing his tenth mission during this period, Lt. (jg) Smith contributed materially to the success of his squadron in the infliction of extensive damage on enemy shipping, airfields and installations. His courage and devotion to duty in the face of grave hazards were in keeping with the highest traditions of the United States Naval Service."

Smith received his fourth Air Medal after fifteen combat missions:

"For meritorious achievement in aerial flight as pilot of a fighter plane in Fighting Squadron Eighty Four, attached to the USS Bunker Hill, in action against enemy Japanese forces in the vicinity of Tokyo, Iwo Jima, Kyushu and Okinawa from February 16 to April 13, 1945. Completing his fifteenth flight during this period, Lt. (jg) Smith, inflicted extensive damage on enemy shipping, airfields and installations and contributed to the success of his squadron. His skilled airmanship and courageous devotion to duty in the face of grave hazards were in keeping with the highest traditions of the United States Naval Service."

Smith was awarded a Gold Star in lieu of his second Distinguished Flying Cross:

"For heroism and extraordinary achievement in aerial flight as pilot of a fighter plane in Fighting Squadron Eighty Four, attached to the USS Bunker Hill, in action against enemy Japanese forces in the Tokyo area on February 17, 1945. As division leader of a fighter group escorting a bomber formation over 120 miles of enemy territory, Lt. (jg) Smith delivered a rocket and strafing attack on an aircraft engine plant in the face of intense and accurate anti - aircraft fire and assisted in escorting the bombers back to their carrier through extremely hazardous weather. His skilled airmanship and courageous devotion to duty were in keeping with the highest traditions of the United States Naval Service."

In March 1945, "Smitty" was on the photo reconnaissance mission that discovered the super battleship *Yamato*, which had not been seen since the Battle of Leyte Gulf the previous year. When this great ship sailed towards Okinawa, "Smitty" covered torpedo bombers on their 7 April attack that sank this ship before it could interfere with the invasion. "Smitty" also strafed and rocketed Japanese destroyers and a light cruiser on this action. He was awarded his third Distinguished Flying Cross for this mission. The citation stated:

"For meritorious acts while participating in an aerial flight in operations against the enemy on April 7, 1945, off the southwestern coast of Kyushu. He directly preceded the torpedo planes, and despite intense medium and heavy anti-aircraft fire he made rocket and strafing attacks on the screening destroyers, thereby contributing substantially to the success of the torpedo planes which were able to make numerous hits on the battleship. His skill and courage were at all times inspiring and in keeping with the highest traditions of the United States Naval Service."

Smith received his fourth Distinguished Flying Cross for completing twenty combat missions:

"For heroism and extraordinary achievement in aerial flight as pilot of a fighter plane in Fighting Squadron Eighty Four, attached to the USS Bunker Hill, in action against enemy Japanese forces in the vicinity of Tokyo, Iwo Jima, Kyushu and Okinawa from February 16 to April 22, 1945. Completing his twentieth mission during this period, Lt. (jg) Smith contributed materially to the infliction of extensive damage on enemy shipping, airfields and installations. His skill and courage were in keeping with the highest traditions of the United States Naval Service."

On April 28, 1945, during his second mission of the day he shot down three Nakajima Nates to become

OPPOSITE:
Ens. John M. Smith at Bougainville in 1944. Smith reported to Fighting 17 on December 8, 1943. *Courtesy of the National Archives*

I've returned home three times
with bullet holes in my airplane and
twice with scratches in my leg
where bullets just touched!
I didn't even require iodine.

an ace, and was awarded his fifth Distinguished Flying Cross for this mission. The citation states:

> *"For heroism and extraordinary achievement in aerial flight as division leader in Fighting Squadron Eighty Four, attached to the USS Bunker Hill, in action against enemy Japanese forces in the vicinity of Kikai, Nansei Shoto, April 28, 1945. Leading his division on a target combat air patrol, Lt. (jg) Smith encountered one enemy fighter plane which he shot down and, when his division ran into twelve hostile aircraft later in the flight, skillfully destroyed two of them in rapid succession. His airmanship, courage and devotion to duty were in keeping with the highest traditions of the United States Naval Service."*

On May 11, 1945, on combat air patrol over Kikai, "Smitty" scored one Zeke and two Tojos to bring his total to ten confirmed victories. He was awarded the Silver Star for this mission. The citation as follows:

> *"For heroism while participating in aerial flight against the enemy on May 11, 1945 in the vicinity of Kikai, Nansei Shoto. Leading his flight on target combat air patrol he skillfully deployed the group to enable them to successfully intercept and shoot down a number of enemy fighters. His division encountered a group of enemy fighters and he personally shot down two of them. Later on he encountered another enemy fighter which he shot down. His courage and skillful leadership were at all times in keeping with the highest traditions of the United States Naval Service."*

This was his final score, as after landing the USS *Bunker Hill* was struck by two kamikazes off Okinawa, causing massive explosions and fires that burned out of control for many hours. Three hundred and forty-six American sailors were killed, including nineteen officers of VF-84, most of whom were killed in the pilot's ready room, which John Smith had just left. This put the *Bunker Hill* out of the war. John Smith later told family members what happened:

> *"On the morning of 11 May I shot down the final three planes of my career and landed aboard the Bunker Hill. Immediately after returning from a flight pilots would normally go in to the ready room and debrief the flight. I had just left the ready room when a kamikaze struck the ship; the explosion destroyed the ready room and killed a large number of VF-84 pilots. I was in the corridor outside the ready room and was knocked down by the explosion; had I remained in the room I would have been killed."*

After his successful combat duty with Fighting 17, John Smith became the joint top ace of VF-84 and tied for fourth ranked Navy Corsair ace of WWII with ten confirmed victories. He left the Navy on November 3, 1945, with an honorable release to inactive duty.

One of John's sisters, Marie, now a Sister of St. Joseph, remembers her brother coming home on leave:

> *"When Johnny was home on leave he would spend a great deal of time visiting the families of fallen comrades in the area. I would always want to go in with him but he never let me go into the house with him. This was all when gas was rationed and cars and roads were not nearly what they are now."*

After one such visit the family of a fallen sailor, who had been buried at sea, wrote to John:

> *"Words cannot begin to express our appreciation for you taking the time and expense in coming to see all of us, so just plain "Thank You John." We know now what Bill meant when he would say "My best buddy and I are going fishing." Thank you John for having been that buddy."*

Following his service John enrolled at St. Mary's College in Winona, Minnesota, under the GI Bill in

1946. He attended St. Mary's for three years, and then went to Creighton University Law School in Omaha, Nebraska, for his L.L.B., which he obtained in 1950. After passing the Bar he was employed by the Mutual Service Insurance Company and was admitted to the Nebraska and Minnesota Bars.

He met Therese Frances Martin, who was a student at St. Theresa's College in Winona, whilst at college, and they were married on July 29, 1950, in Emmetsburg, Iowa. They made their home in Owatonna, Minnesota, and they had seven children: sons Bernard, Steve, Robert; and daughters Anne, Molly, Tracy, and Kasey. John was a devoted family man. John's son Barney related a story about his father:

> *"Dad met mom in college after the war. Dad was at St. Mary's in Winona, Minnesota and mom was at St. Theresa's, also in Winona. They became engaged there but decided to wait until after dad finished law school to get married. Dad went to Creighton in Omaha and mom went back to Emmetsburg, Iowa to teach while dad finished law school. Dad had stayed in the Reserves after the war and had become Commander of a Reserve squadron. Dad would have his squadron fly a triangle from Omaha to Emmetsburg to Minneapolis as a training exercise. One flight, in the middle of winter, just as his squadron passed over Emmetsburg, his engine quit suddenly. Fortunately, there is a lake in the middle of Emmetsburg which was frozen over. He did a "dead stick" landing on the ice with his wheels up, and walked away from it."*

Smith told the local newspaper that this was the first time that a Corsair had "let him down." Barney remembers another story about his father:

> *"While in the Reserves the pilots would engage in target practice, by shooting at a "sock" towed behind an aircraft. A hit would leave a dye mark on the sock so the competing pilots could see which group won. The other pilots decided to play a trick on dad, so they all put the same colored charges in their planes. Dad still recorded more hits than all the rest of them together."*

John continued flying in the Reserves after the war and was recalled to active duty during the Korean War from December 14, 1951, to October 9, 1954. By then he was an Attorney, and spent the Korean War as Security and Legal Officer for the Twin Cities Naval Air Station. He and his family lived at the base, and later in Minneapolis, when the Korean War ended, John Smith was faced with the decision of staying in the Navy or returning to civilian life.

He decided to return to civilian life, but remained in the Navy Reserve, flying out of the Naval Air Station in the Twin Cities, where he became Wing Staff Commander. He was Commanding Officer of nearly 1,000 Naval Air Reservists attached to the Training Detachment and Commanding Officer of two fighter squadrons. In 1957 one of these squadrons, Jet Fighter Squadron 811, won the Noel Davis Trophy awarded annually by the Navy Department for the most efficient aviation division of the U.S. Naval Reserve. A letter from the Department of the Navy stated in part:

> *"On behalf of the entire Naval establishment, I commend you and all the members of Fighter Squadron 811 for your exemplary performance in winning the Noel Davis Trophy presented each year to the most efficient fighter squadron in the Naval Air Reserve Program.*
>
> *The initiative and hard work of all members of your squadron in achieving such a high degree of proficiency deserves the gratitude of every citizen of our country. I extend to you the traditional and highly deserved Well done."*

In later years, after N.A.S. Twin Cities closed, he served at Glenview, Illinois, outside of Chicago, where he had trained shortly after first joining the service. After over thirty years on active and reserve duty, John retired from the reserves in August 1972 with the rank of Captain.

In the meantime, after the Korean War he had returned to Owatonna and opened a law practice

I had just left the ready room when a kamikaze struck the ship; the explosion destroyed the ready room and killed a large number of VF-84 pilots. I was in the corridor outside . . . and was knocked down by the explosion; had I remained . . . I would have been killed."

with Charles E. Cashman, a childhood friend from Owatonna and a decorated veteran of the United States Navy in the Second World War, serving on a destroyer escort in the Pacific. Their practice, known as Cashman and Smith, was a general practice of law. The partnership continued until Charles Cashman became a probate court judge in 1960.

John was a practicing attorney in his home town of Owatonna, Minnesota, from 1954, and in 1958 was elected Steele County Attorney. He served one term. He was a member of the Minnesota Trial Lawyers Association, the Association of Trial Lawyers of America, the Steele County, Fifth District and Minnesota State Bar Associations, and was President of the Steele County group from 1956 to 1964.

John Smith was well known throughout the area as a fine, effective, honest, and professional attorney. He was often appointed by the court to represent indigent clients who could not afford to pay for a private attorney. While he would have been entitled to be paid by the county for representing such clients, he never submitted a bill–he felt everyone was entitled to legal representation even if they could not afford it, and he refused to bill the county to provide that representation. On one occasion he was court-appointed to represent an immigrant boy in juvenile court. A police officer stopped this teenager, who was driving a moped while transporting five of his brothers and sisters. No one in the courtroom could keep a straight face, especially when John Smith told Judge Cashman that "*my client wishes to throw himself on the mercy of the court.*"

On another occasion son Rob Smith was required to go to court for a traffic violation. Judge Cashman made a great show of explaining to Rob his rights, that he had the right to a competent representation, and that if he did not have competent representation an attorney would be appointed to represent him. Rob decided to stay with his father as his attorney.

One of his most well known cases, which was put before the Minnesota Supreme Court, was Busch v. Busch Construction, Inc., 262 N.W.2d 262 (Minn. 1977). This decision is one of the most important product liability decisions of the postwar era, and the principles established in that case have been cited and followed many times since.

John was a fundamental part of life in Owatonna and participated in numerous civic organizations. He was director of Owatonna Civil Defense in 1955, and a member of the Owatonna Chamber of Commerce Board of Directors from 1969 to 1971. In 1965 he was honored as Boss of the Year in Owatonna by the Owatonna Area Chamber of Commerce.

He was a member of the Marian High School Building Commission in 1956, and served as a member of the St. Mary's - Marian Catholic School Board of Education, 1966 to 1971, and as Chairman from 1969 to 1971. He was treasurer of the Catholic Education Memorial Fund and a member of Knight of Columbus Council, serving as Grand Knight in 1959 to 1960. He was a member of the St. Joseph Church finance committee and the Christian Board of Education for Dodge and Steele Counties.

Politically active and a lifelong Democrat, John served on the Executive Committee of the Steele County Democratic - Farmer - Labor Party, and was active in a number of campaigns, including those for fellow Navy veterans John F. Kennedy and Eugene McCarthy. He was a delegate to the First Congressional District and State Conventions from 1960 through 1966, and was an alternate delegate to the National Democratic Convention in 1964.

An avid outdoorsman, hunter, and fisherman who loved golf, boating, and snowmobiling, John M. Smith died suddenly while jogging on June 9, 1981, of a heart condition. His law practice, now known as Smith, Tollefson & Rahrick, continues to this day in Owatonna with his second son Stephen.

John M. Smith was authorized to wear the following decorations: the Silver Star, Distinguished Flying Cross with four Gold Stars and the Air Medal with five Gold Stars, Presidential Unit Citation, Navy Unit Commendation, Asiatic - Pacific Campaign Medal with five Gold Stars, American Campaign Medal, National Defense Service Medal, Navy Reserve Medal, and WWII Victory Medal.

Opposite:
John M. Smith, who later made ace with VF-84.
Courtesy of the John M Smith Collection

F. J. "Big Jim" Streig at Bougainville in 1944. *Courtesy of the National Archives*

15

FREDERICK JAMES "BIG JIM" STREIG

5.5 VICTORIES

"Big Jim" described his thoughts on the squadron at the 1984 reunion:

> *"We are family, been like brothers all the way through. All of us will never forget anyone and we're still the same today as we've always been. We owe it all to the leadership we had in the squadron, the organization, the camaraderie that we developed and I don't think they'll ever find another group of combat pilots that are as close organized as we are."*

Frederick James "Big Jim" Streig was born on April 24, 1921, in Sacramento, California. His father was from Voldek, Germany, and when the war broke out he didn't want to fight the Germans, as it meant he could have been fighting his cousins. He was happier when he was sent to fight the Japanese.

He was educated at Hollister High School, Salinas Junior College, and the University of California. He joined the Navy Reserve on January 9, 1942, for flight training and was stationed at Oakland and Dallas. In April 1942 he became an Aviation Cadet at N.A.S. Corpus Christi and was commissioned an Ensign on October 1, 1942. In November 1942 he reported to N.A.S. Miami, and then to the Carrier Qualification Training Unit, N.A.S. Norfolk in January 1943, and then on to Fighting 17.

"Big Jim" had his first taste of aerial combat on November 1, 1943, when he was one of eight pilots on combat air patrol over U.S. ships in Empress Augusta Bay, Bougainville.

A formation of about forty Zekes and Vals were sighted and "Big Jim," together with Tom Killefer flying in the second section in Tom Blackburn's division, followed Blackburn down on the leading group of Zekes. They missed

"Big Jim" Streig and Tom Killefer at Ondongo in November 1943. *Courtesy Robert Lawson Photograph Collection, National Museum of Naval Aviation/ U.S. Navy photo.*

Two Fighting 17 aces, "Ike" Kepford and "Big Jim" Streig. *Courtesy of Vought*

on their first pass and pulled up to 17,000 ft. "Big Jim" located a Zeke in the left flanking formation at 14-15,000 ft. He and Killefer made a 60° deflection high side run, and the Zeke burst into flame at the root of the right wing and crashed. Their section then turned back to Mutupena Point, sighted a Zeke over Mt. Bagana heading north, got directly on his tail and fired at a range of 250 yards. The Zeke caught fire and crashed. The pilot was seen to bail out. "Big Jim" and Killefer then followed another Zeke north almost to Buka, but could not overtake him. The section then returned to base. They were given a share of a Zeke and Killefer scored another Zeke destroyed.

His first full victory occurred on November 11, 1943, during the Battle of the Solomon Sea, when the division, consisting of Paul Cordray, Brad Baker, "Big Jim" and Dan Cunningham, was vectored out. At about 00:45 "Big Jim" spotted a Tony on his port bow on an opposite course and at the same level. "Big Jim," together with Dan Cunningham on his wing, immediately turned and pursued the Tony in a 30° dive, overtaking him rapidly. The Tony levelled at 10,000 ft., then pushed over in a 45° dive to 200 ft. "Big Jim" levelled out behind him and fired from 300 yards astern. After a short burst the Tony exploded. The division then reformed and climbed to about 20,000 ft. The action had occurred about ten miles north of the Task Force. "Big Jim" Streig recalls this action:

> *"I was on a combat station at about 20,000 feet northeast of the carrier and the radar picked up a bogey coming in from the northeast. I was sent out to intercept him and investigate and I had a four plane division. We caught up with the bogey and he immediately dove and headed for the water and we took off after him and chased him down to an altitude of about 500 feet and then made a run behind him and blew him up on the water. He didn't get back but he had already radioed our position to the Japanese."*

"We are family, been like brothers all the way through.

"Big Jim" Streig, Fighting 17 ace with 5.5 victories. *US Naval Historical Center / M W "Butch" Davenport Collection*

The action was notable, as it was the first time that a Kawasaki Ki 61 Hein or Tony had been shot down in the South Pacific Islands.

"Big Jim" Streig further describes his part in this eventful mission:

> *"As we were climbing back weaving in and out of the clouds and we looked up to the left and we saw these square wing tipped planes and I thought to myself, the F6F's are up there. All of a sudden I realized the F6F's were on the deck and there weren't any up there.*
>
> *We looked again and we saw the whole Japanese force coming in from Rabaul and Buka toward the carriers and at that time I was about 15 - 16,000 feet. I called the C.I.C. (fighter control) on Bunker Hill and told them to hold their hats because the spam was about to hit the fan! We immediately pulled up and started to climb and got above them and intercepted them and I got one more and two more probables and started running out of fuel and had to go back to the beach. They couldn't take me on the carrier because there was so much going on. My wingman at that time was Danny Cunningham and he had thrown an exhaust stack through his cowling and gone back and I was up there by myself. So I headed back toward Ondongo and managed to reach Vella Lavella got in the landing pattern and landed and I was going down on the taxiway and my engine quit. I just got back, thank goodness.*
>
> *There was probably close to 150 airplanes coming out to intercept the Task Force. We were airborne for about 3½ to 4 hours of which about 2½ hours was hectic combat before I left it. Some of it still went on after I departed but I had made two climbs to altitude and used a lot of fuel."*

When attacked the Zekes turned towards the Corsairs. "Big Jim" shot at two but missed and did a chandelle to the left, losing his wingman in the process, then made a head on run at three Zekes who dived out away from him. "Big Jim" saw another group of eight or twelve Zekes at about 24,000 ft. and nearer the ships. He climbed to 26,000 ft. and made a high side run on a Zeke, coming in on his tail in a 20° dive. He saw his bullets go into the cockpit and the Zeke pulled up sharply, went into a spin, and crashed into the sea.

Several Zekes and Hamps were now on "Big Jim's" tail and he climbed, using all the power that his Corsair had available to 28,000 ft. The Zekes stalled out at 26,000 ft. From his position of altitude advantage "Big Jim" made several passes at the Zekes and Hamps, all of his attacks being head on. He caught a Zeke breaking away and shot a foot and a half off his rudder, then fired at a Hamp, seeing pieces fly off a wing. After this last pass he turned home and landed at Barakoma, Vella Lavella, at 04:35 with just fifteen gallons of fuel left on board. (Cunningham was forced to leave immediately before "Big Jim" shot down his second aircraft).

"Big Jim" was credited with a Tony and a Zeke destroyed and a Hamp and Zeke damaged.

"Big Jim" was promoted to Lt. (jg) with effect from January 1, 1944. After leave in Australia he returned to action at the end of January 1944.

He was part of Tom Blackburn's flight on January 27, 1944, assigned as cover on one of two B-25 squadrons striking Lakunai Airfield, New Britain.

Sixty to seventy Japanese fighters intercepted the strike as the bombers were leaving the target.

When the fighters attacked the medium and low cover, "Big Jim" and "Bobby" Mims dived away and initially lost contact with the Zekes. Climbing back to 14,000 ft., they pulled up on the tail of a Zeke and fired an accurate burst at its belly which made the Zeke catch fire. Four Zekes were seen above and two or three above and astern. This group came down and got on "Big Jim's" tail. Covering "Big Jim," Mims turned in on one of them and with a burst from dead astern set him on fire. "Big Jim" had broken left and down and got separated from "Bobby" in the process, but then saw a Zeke below him at 3,000 ft. He made a high-side run and saw the Zeke catch fire and crash. He then pulled up to 5,000 ft. and saw tracer bullets fly by him, so he dived to 1500 ft. Pulling up to 5,000 ft., he headed for Cape Gazelle when he saw seven or eight Zekes climbing from Rapopo Airfield at 1500 ft. He dived down on the nearest Zeke and made a beam attack. Pieces flew from the Zeke, which then fell off to the right and crashed near the field. "Big Jim" opened up to rejoin the bombers, joined up on Mims and headed back to base. "Big Jim" was credited with two Zekes and a Zeke which he shared with Bobby Mims, which made him an ace and concluded his scoring with Fighting 17.

Up to the time enemy opposition was cleared from the skies of Rabaul, "Big Jim" had flown 156.9 hours in two tours of combat. For the second tour he flew eighteen combat sorties in fourteen days with eight missions to "Fortress Rabaul."

"Big Jim" Streig in 1969, just prior to his retirement from the U.S. Navy. *U S Navy photo*

"Big Jim" arrived home after his combat with Fighting 17 as an ace with 5.5 confirmed victories. He was awarded the Distinguished Flying Cross with two Gold Stars and Air Medal with six Gold Stars.

His next deployment was from May 1944 until December 1945 at N.A.A.S. Green Cove Springs as Operational Flight Instructor and Aviation Equipment Officer. After the war "Big Jim" married Vera Mae Dodge and had four sons: James, Richard, Frederick, and Eric.

From March 1946 until December 1947 he was V-2/V-4 Division Officer and Senior Watch Officer on the USS *Antietam* (CV-36). He was on active duty in the Navy Reserve until October 1, 1946, and transferred to the Regular Navy on October 2, 1946. From January 1948 until June 1950 he was based at N.A.S. Alameda as Flight Operations and Assistant Operations Officer, and also transport pilot.

From July 1950 until August 1952 he was with VR-5 as Transport Pilot and Assistant Operations Officer, and from September 1952 until June 1953 at the Reserve Officer's Training Corps Unit of the University of California, Berkeley. In July 1953 "Big Jim" attended General Line School at Monterey, California, until February 1954, when he reported to C.I.C. Officer School, Glenview until July 1954. From September 1954 until April 1956 he was Air Operations; Acting Navigator; Communications Officer and Nuclear Weapons Employment Officer on USS *Shangri La* (CVA-38).

"Big Jim" was promoted to Commander on July 1, 1956, whilst he was serving with VW-12 as Personnel Officer; Airborne Early Warning Aircraft Commander. From January 1959 until March 1961 he served as Aircraft Maintenance Officer at N.A.A.S. Saufley Field, Pensacola.

From March 1961 until January 1962 he was assigned to Chief of Naval Air Basic Training (CNABATRA) Staff Pensacola as Staff Aircraft Maintenance and Material Officer, and was there during the April 1961 Bay of Pigs crisis and in "Lock Down" with President Kennedy at the critical time of the crisis.

From February 1962 until July 1965 "Big Jim" served as Commander-in-Chief, U.S. Atlantic Fleet Nuclear Operations (CINCLANT), and from August 1965 to June 1969 as Commander Western Sea Frontier (COMWESTSEAFRON) on Staff in Logistics Plans and Programs.

"Big Jim" was awarded the Navy Commendation Medal with the citation:

> *"For meritorious service while serving as Plans and Programs Officer on the staff of Commander Western Sea Frontier from August 30, 1965 to June 30, 1969. At the onset of increased hostilities in the Western Pacific, Commander Streig was instrumental in developing the concept and organization of Pacific Command Movements Priority Agency (PAMPA), and agency responsible for expediting priority material to the Pacific theatre. as Commander Western Sea Frontier's logistics representative on the Alaska - Canada - United States Emergency Defense Planning Committee, Commander Streig provided sustained effective liaison with our allies and other friendly nations. As Staff Logistics representative on the Western United States (WESUS) Joint Defense Planning Staff, he effected harmonious and essential relations with other military services in joint defense efforts. These contributions were vital to Commander Western Sea Frontier in order to accomplish his logistic mission in support of Commander in Chief U.S. Pacific Fleet and were in keeping with the highest traditions of the United States Naval Service."*

Cdr. F. J. "Big Jim" Streig in 1968. *US Navy*

"Big Jim" Streig retired from the Navy on June 30, 1969, after a distinguished career.

After retiring from the Navy he went back and completed his degree in history and taught as a teacher at the high school level. He also did a lot of work for the 4H Organization. He retired from this in 1975.

He attended the Fighting 17 reunion at E.A.A. Oshkosh in 1994 and died following a long illness on August 31, 1995, in Alameda, California. He is buried in Golden Gate National Cemetery.

In addition to the Distinguished Flying Cross with two Gold Stars and Air Medal with six Gold Stars, "Big Jim" was also awarded the Navy Unit Citation (two awards), Navy Unit Commendation, Navy Commendation Medal, American Campaign Medal, Asiatic - Pacific Campaign Medal with three Gold Stars, WWII Victory Medal, Navy Occupation Service Medal, China Service Medal, National Defense Service Medal (with one Star), Philippine Independence Medal, and Navy Expert Pistol Shot Medal.

OPPOSITE:
"Big Jim" Streig with his #3 Corsair. *US Naval Historical Center / M W "Butch" Davenport Collection*

We caught up with the bogey
and he immediately dove
and headed for the water
and we took off after him
and chased him down to an altitude
of about 500 feet
and then made a run behind him
and blew him up on the water.

FREDERICK JAMES "BIG JIM" STREIG

"Russ" Novak whilst at Lincoln High School, Manitowoc, Wisconsin, in 1935 had a Milwaukee Sentinel paper route. *Courtesy of the Marvin Russell "Russ" Novak Collection*

OTHER ACES WHO SERVED WITH FIGHTING 17

16

MARVIN RUSSELL "RUSS" NOVAK

5 VICTORIES

Marvin Russell "Russ" Novak is listed in nearly all of the official sources as an ace with five confirmed victories. He was born on September 28, 1918, in Manitowoc, Wisconsin. His parents were John and Emily Hlinak-Novak, and he had a sister Estelle Novak-Rosinsky and a brother David J. Novak, who was a crane operator who served as a Seabee in the Pacific Theater in WWII.

He was educated from 1923-29 at McKinley School and later in 1930 at Madison School. In 1931-1932 he studied at Woodrow Wilson Jr High School, and then from 1932-1936 at Lincoln High School, Manitowoc, Wisconsin, where he graduated in 1936. Whilst there he played football, did track and field, and set records in the 100 and 220 yard dash and Long Jump. He also played the clarinet. The summers of 1930-1935 were spent with Grandma Hlinak, working and helping out at the farm.

In 1936-1937, whilst living at home he took 1st year college extension courses and played semi-pro football with the Manitowoc Gaels; years later he was inducted into their Hall of Fame. He later worked at Aluminum Goods. In 1938-1939, while a sophomore at University of Wisconsin, Madison he played on the freshman football and track teams, where he broke records in the 100 and 220 yard dash and the long jump.

As a senior in 1941 he majored in Hispanic Studies, and back home in Manitowoc was taking college courses and learned to fly through the Civilian Pilot Training Program. He took his first solo flight in a Cub, and in 1941 bought a 1941 Aeronca with Hal Zweifel and Don Steiger.

He joined the Navy in October 1941 in Chicago, Illinois, and reported to Naval Air Station (N.A.S.) Glenview in January 1942 until March 1942. He was then assigned to N.A.S. Dallas from March 1942 to

April 1942, and then from May 1942 to September 1942 at N.A.S. Corpus Christi, Texas. He completed his operational flight training at N.A.S. Miami and received his wings as an Ensign on October 9, 1942.

"Russ" Novak served with Fighting 17 from January 1943 until August 1943, all through their training period. After being detached from Fighting 17 he was assigned to VF-14 in Atlantic City in August 1943. While serving there "Russ" Novak escorted a Miss America contestant. He relates the story:

> *"It was in September 1943 we were becoming familiar with the F6F Hellcat fighter built by Grumman and flying out of N.A.S. Atlantic City. The station was built in the middle of a forest of trees and about 30 miles west of Atlantic City itself. This was no place for long low approaches as we had to quickly drop in on the runway which was short enough. We visited the city by bus and enjoyed walking up and down the boardwalk. One day, the station got a call for officers to escort Miss America contestants. Most of the officers were off on liberty, and I was one of the lucky Ensigns to be selected. It was my honor (in dress whites) to escort Miss New Jersey on and off the stage for her appearances and also to be her friend for the week before. We did go to a couple of coffee houses as I thought she should remain sober, and I thought that she was under 18 anyway. We did the boardwalk for some pleasant conversations. She didn't win in the finals but Miss New Jersey was very cute and personable. This was one of many pleasant experiences while in the squadron."*

Novak then served from November 1943 to February 1944 at Quonset Point, and from March until December 1944 he was on board the U.S.S. *Wasp* (CV-18), where he served with distinction and became an ace with five confirmed victories.

Flying an F6F-3 Hellcat on June 19, 1944, on a combat air patrol he shot down a Tony or Judy and assisted in shooting down another Japanese aircraft.

University of Wisconsin – Madison, Flying Fraternity Fullback "Russ" Novak. *Courtesy of the Marvin Russell "Russ" Novak Collection*

He received the following Air Medal citation for this action.

> *"For distinguishing himself by meritorious achievement in the line of his profession as pilot of a carrier based fighter aircraft while engaged in aerial combat with a large and determined enemy force, west of the Marianas Islands. On 19 June 1944, he ably assisted in disrupting an attack of twelve enemy torpedo*

Opposite:
Track and field star "Russ" Novak at Lincoln High School in 1935/36 where he set records in the 100 and 220 yard dash and long jump. *Courtesy of the Marvin Russell "Russ" Novak Collection*

"Russ" Novak in 1941 with the Aeronca aircraft which he and his friend Hal Zweifel bought whilst at college. *Courtesy of the Marvin Russell "Russ" Novak Collection*

planes escorted by four enemy fighter planes on our surface forces. By his determination, skill in combat, and his courageous attack, he was largely responsible for the complete rout of the enemy force throughout this action, and destroyed one enemy plane. He displayed exceptional coolness under fire and his conduct was in keeping with the highest traditions of the naval service."

On June 22, 1944, "Russ" Novak assisted in shooting down a Kawanishi H8K Emily flying boat whilst on combat air patrol.

During his tour on the U.S.S. *Wasp* "Russ" Novak recalled a July 4, 1944, fighter sweep over Iwo Jima where he shot down two Zekes:

"I was on an early fighter sweep flight over Iwo Jima in Bill Knight's flight. Going in our initial strafing dive, we were met by intense anti-aircraft fire. A real 4th of July, fireworks all over. We damaged some aircraft on the field. Climbing for altitude we came across about a dozen Zeroes. Bill went after one and I went after another. We both dove after them as they tried to escape. I shot mine down as he pulled out at low altitude.

Climbing back up again, I spotted another Zero in front of me, and I got on his tail. Before I could get the gun camera on and fire at him, he turned belly up and out popped the pilot. Plane went into water kerplunk. I didn't fire

Opposite:
Ensign Marvin Russell "Russ" Novak in 1942 at home in Manitowoc, Wisconsin. *Courtesy of the Marvin Russell "Russ" Novak Collection*

On 19 June 1944, he ably assisted in disrupting an attack of twelve enemy torpedo planes escorted by four enemy fighter planes on our surface forces. . . . he was largely responsible for the complete rout of the enemy force . . .

Air Medal citation

at the pilot whose chute had opened as he was going to be pretty wet and lonesome in the ocean.

We rendezvoused and returned to base. After landing, my Plane Captain asked how it went. I said nothing to it - no problems. It was then he showed me a 5 inch hole in my hood just forward of the instrument panel. The armor plate must have been the saving feature."

Flying an F6F-5 Hellcat during a combat air patrol on September 21, 1944, around Luzon in the Philippines, Novak was credited with shooting down a Judy as a probable victory.

Whist on rest and recreation "Russ" Novak recalled another story:

"After attacks on the Philippines, the U.S.S. Wasp and Air Group 14 arrived at Manus in the Admiralty Islands (near Australia) for ships supplies and pilots R & R, arriving on my birthday September 28, 1944. We were anchored in a beautiful bay and the weather was B-Beautiful also warm and sunny. Liberty boats took us to shore facilities and the "O" Club. I passed on the club because I went searching for the 20th Special Seabee Unit supposedly located there. After I had left my home town of Manitowoc, Wisconsin to join the Navy, I left my brother Dave working at the local shipyard. Next thing I knew he had joined the Seabees as crane operator. They gave him an EM 1 rating.

So hearing that the unit was at Manus, I'm casually smoking away while nosing around the area where they were moving bombs around. Naturally it was a non-smoking area. But I did locate my brother high up in a crane. We spent a nice day visiting. He showed me around his Quonset quarters and we had the evening meal at his mess. He took me up to the nest high up on the crane and asked me if I had ever been that high before, and I said yes about 43,000 feet in a Corsair – just kidding.

This was a rare opportunity to meet my brother miles away in the war zone and I really appreciated it."

"It was in September 1943 . . . The station was . . . 30 miles west of Atlantic City itself. . . . One day, the station got a call for officers to escort Miss America contestants. Most of the officers were off on liberty, and I was one of the lucky Ensigns to be selected. It was my honor (in dress whites) to escort Miss New Jersey on and off the stage for her appearances and also to be her friend for the week before. . .

May 18, 1945, Lt. Marvin Russell "Russ" Novak marries Ann Elizabeth Hamner in Jacksonville, Florida. *Courtesy of the Marvin Russell "Russ" Novak Collection*

On October 26, 1944, Air Group 14 was ordered to strike the Japanese Fleet. "Russ" Novak remembers this engagement:

> *"Our ship the U.S.S. Wasp had reversed course from going to Ulithi to going back to find the Jap fleet. I remember being in BJ's flight, but with a bad engine, was very late in taking off. All aircraft from several air groups were already heading west. I finally caught up with them and not finding my flight, I took a high covering position on some bombers below. The Jap fleet was tally hoed a couple hours later west of the Philippines.*
>
> *I saw Art Downing's three plane SB2C bomber section leading the attack. He was making a wide sweep around from West to East. About every twenty seconds there appeared three black AA puffs of smoke slightly behind the flight. This appeared to happen five or six times before Downing went into his dive. Talk about luck-no one was hit. Downing then called on fighters to strafe which is when I went into my dive strafing a cruiser on the left of the Yamato battleship. It looked to me that Downing was going after the Yamato and he did get a direct hit on her bow. I pulled out and jinked away, climbing for altitude. Tracers started coming over my bow so I two blocked it and turned away. We mixed it up with a couple of Zeroes before they disappeared. This was one of my many fearful moments. I rendezvoused to the East over Panay and returned to base with the other aircraft. Time of flight 5.5 hours."*

Following his tour of duty Novak returned home in December 1944, and after leave was

L-R: VF-14 buddies Paul Coari, John Cantrell and "Russ" Novak at Eniwetok in 1944. *Courtesy of the Marvin Russell "Russ" Novak Collection*

"Russ" Novak and 17 month old daughter Sharon in San Juan, Puerto Rico, in December 1947. *Courtesy of the Marvin Russell "Russ" Novak Collection*

assigned to N.A.S. Jacksonville for combat team training until May 1945. While serving there he married Nancy "Ann" Elizabeth Hamner on May 18, 1945. In June 1945 he was assigned to VBF 97, and then in October 1945 to the U.S.S. *Kearsarge* until October 1946. Daughter Sharon Kaye was born on May 14, 1946, in Jacksonville, and on July 1946 he was sworn into the regular Navy and also had assignments at N.A.S. San Juan and Roosevelt Roads Puerto Rico, N.A.S Corry Field, U.S.S. *Princeton*, and upon the outbreak of the Korean War the U.S.S. *Boxer*. In July 1947 "Russ" Novak's six month old son, Jonathan, died of hepatitis. On November 4, 1949, "Russ" and Ann were blessed with a son, Richard Alan. On August 1, 1951, Novak was promoted to Lt. Cdr., and upon the outbreak of the Korean War he served as Executive Officer of VA-65 on the U.S.S. *Boxer* (CV-21), where he flew an AD4 Douglas Sky Raider attack bomber. He served there from April to October 1952. He received his second Air Medal with the citation:

> *"For meritorious achievement in aerial flight as pilot of an attack bomber in Attack Squadron Sixty Five, Carrier Air Group Two, based on board the U.S.S. Boxer, during operations against enemy aggressor forces in Korea from 31 March to 18 June 1952. Completing twenty missions during this period, Lt. Cdr. Novak carried out destructive attacks against the enemy in the face of hostile anti-aircraft fire. His courage, skilled airmanship and devotion to duty throughout were in keeping with the highest traditions of the United States Naval Service."*

His third Air Medal citation in June 1952 stated:

From March to October 1952 during the Korean War, Lt. Cdr. "Russ" Novak was Executive Officer of VA-65 based on the U.S.S. Boxer (CV-21). *Courtesy U.S. Navy photo via Marvin Russell "Russ" Novak.*

Lt. Cdr. Marvin Russell "Russ" Novak in 1961. *Courtesy U.S. Navy photo.*

"For meritorious achievement in aerial flight as pilot and division leader in Attack Squadron Sixty Five, Carrier Air Group Two, based on board the U.S.S. Boxer, during operations against enemy aggressor forces in Korea on 23 and 24 June 1952. Leading his division in a series of devastating attacks against strongly defended enemy hydroelectric power plants at Songpa-ni and Sokhyon, Lt. Cdr. Novak personally scored direct hits on the targets in the face of intense hostile anti-aircraft fire, inflicting heavy damage and destruction upon the power facilities. By his courage, skilled airmanship and unswerving devotion to duty, he contributed materially to the success of his squadron and upheld then highest traditions of the United States Naval Service."

Novak's tour of duty ended in October 1952, which meant he would be home in time for Christmas.

Following the Korean War, "Russ" Novak went to General Line School in Monterey from

"Russ" Novak's service included being assigned to the U.S.S. *Ticonderoga* (CVA-14) in 1957. *Courtesy U.S. Navy photo via Marvin Russell "Russ" Novak.*

After landing, my Plane Captain asked how it went. I said nothing to it . . . then he showed me a 5 inch hole in my hood just forward of the instrument panel.

L-R: Chuck Houston and Ann and "Russ" Novak at the VA-65 Reunion. *Courtesy of the Marvin Russell "Russ" Novak Collection*

January 1953 to June 1953. He was then assigned to the Bureau of Aeronautics from August 1953 to August 1955. In October 1955 he reported to N.A.S. Ford Island, where he served until January 1957. From February 1957 until September 1957 he was assigned to VAW 11 at North Island and also served on the U.S.S. *Ticonderoga* (CVA-14).

His final assignment was at N.A.S. North Island, San Diego, from June 3, 1961, to June 30, 1963, when he retired from the Navy as a Lt. Cdr.

The years following his retirement from the Navy were spent employed as a social worker with the San Diego County of Social Services until he retired in 1978. He is currently living in San Diego, California.

Marvin "Russ" Novak was authorized to wear the following decorations: the Air Medal with two Gold Stars, Presidential Unit Citation (Korean), Navy Unit Commendation, Asiatic - Pacific Campaign Medal, Korean Service Medal, United Nations Service Medal, Philippine Liberation Ribbon, and the World War II Victory Medal.

Opposite:
Lt. Cdr. Marvin "Russ" Novak flew F4U Corsairs with VBF 97 after World War II. *Courtesy U.S. Navy photo via Marvin Russell "Russ" Novak.*

Lt. Edward Bennett Turner with his F6F Hellcat on the U.S.S. *Wasp* **in 1944.** *Courtesy U.S. Navy photo via the Edward Bennett Turner Family.*

OTHER ACES WHO SERVED WITH FIGHTING 17

17

EDWARD BENNETT TURNER

7 VICTORIES

Edward Turner was born on February 15, 1917, in Cherokee Springs, South Carolina. He attended Asheville Agricultural School and had left his college studies at Wofford College in Spartanburg, South Carolina, to join the Navy on January 27, 1941. Following completion of flight training at N.A.S. Pensacola he served as a Flight Instructor, and was then assigned to Fighting 17 for five months from March to August 1943, then reported to VF-14 on the U.S.S. *Wasp* (CV-18) in September 1943.

In what would become known later as "The Great Marianas Turkey Shoot," Lt. Turner scored his first victory in air combat when the U.S.S. *Wasp* was under heavy enemy attack. He intercepted an incoming Japanese flight and shot down a Zeke fighter in the Philippine Sea west of Guam.

He received the following citation for the Air Medal for this engagement:

"For meritorious achievement in aerial flight as pilot and division leader in Fighting Squadron Fourteen, attached to the U.S.S. Wasp, during operations against enemy Japanese forces in the First Battle of the Philippine Sea, on June 19, 1944. Intercepting a hostile force of two fighters and four torpedo planes maneuvering to strike our surface units, Lieutenant Commander (then Lieutenant) Turner engaged the enemy in furious combat, disrupting the offensive and contributing to the excellent coverage provided our Task Force. His devotion to duty throughout reflects the highest credit upon Lieutenant Commander Turner and the United States Naval Service."

Lt. Turner received a Gold Star in Lieu of a second Air Medal with the following citation for his actions on September 12, 1944.

Edward Bennett Turner as a young Ensign in 1941. *U.S. Navy photo via the Edward Bennett Turner Family.*

"For distinguishing himself by meritorious acts while participating in aerial flight against the enemy as pilot of a carrier based fighter plane. On 12 September 1944, in the vicinity of the Central Philippine Islands, he scored a direct bomb hit on a medium sized freighter in a masthead bombing attack in the face of anti-aircraft fire. His skill and courage throughout this action were in keeping with the highest traditions of the United States Naval Service."

On October 14, 1944, Lt. Turner was given shared credit for damaging a Zeke over Okinawa. The following day the U.S.S. *Wasp*, along with the other ships in the Task Force, was attacked by enemy Japanese aircraft based in the Philippine Islands. Lt. Turner intercepted and shot down an Irving only five miles from his ship. The citation for a Gold Star in lieu of a Third Air Medal is as follows:

Edward and Wylene Turner in 1942. *Courtesy of the Edward Bennett Turner Family*

Tyre C. Weaver, Jr., of River View and Lafayette, Robert C. Ripley of Believe It or Not fame, and Ed Turner, director of the Palmetto Air School, LaGrange, are shown together as they were entertained at luncheon given in honor of Weaver at the Waldorf-Astoria in New York in 1945. Weaver appeared on Ripley's radio show and told the dramatic story of his war experience when he was shot down over Germany. Weaver and Turner flew in a private plane to New York where they were granted permission to land at LaGuardia Field. *Courtesy of the Edward Bennett Turner Family*

On 12 September 1944, in the vicinity of the Central Philippine Islands, he scored a direct bomb hit on a medium sized freighter in a masthead bombing attack in the face of anti-aircraft fire.

> *"For Meritorious achievement in aerial flight as pilot of a fighter plane in Fighting Squadron Fourteen, attached to the U.S.S. WASP, during action against enemy Japanese forces in the vicinity of Formosa on October 15, 1944. Engaging a numerically superior force of enemy aircraft in combat, Lieutenant Turner succeeded in destroying a hostile fighter plane. His devotion to duty was in keeping with the highest traditions of the United States Naval Service."*

On October 18, 1944, Lt. Turner was in a flight of three F6F Hellcat divisions that arrived over Mabalacat, north of Manila. They were attacked by a large flight of Japanese fighters and were immediately involved in a dogfight. When the smoke had cleared fifteen of the enemy had been shot down and seven others damaged. Lt. Turner was credited with four Zekes and an Oscar to make him an ace in one day.

For his heroic deeds on this mission Lt. Turner was awarded the Navy Cross. The citation as follows:

> *"For extraordinary heroism as pilot of a fighter plane in Fighting Squadron Fourteen, attached to the U.S.S. Wasp, in action against enemy Japanese forces in the vicinity of the northern Philippine Islands, on October 18, 1944. Intercepting a strong force of hostile fighters, Lt. Cdr. (then Lt.) Turner engaged the outnumbering enemy in fierce combat, shooting down four and forcing a fifth to the ground where it crashed and burned. By his skill and devotion to duty, Lt. Cdr. Turner contributed to the success of his squadron in the fulfillment of a vital mission and upheld the highest traditions of the United States Naval Service."*

He finished his distinguished WWII service as an ace with seven confirmed victories.

Edward Turner returned to civilian life following World War II and was a member of the Warbirds aerobatic exhibition team at La Grange Airport in Georgia, where he owned and operated a flight instruction school under the GI Bill. He remained active in the Naval Reserve until he retired as a Lt.

Edward B. Turner (right) on his 80th birthday with his son Jeff C. Turner (Left). *Courtesy of the Edward Bennett Turner Family*

"Hero's Overlook" in Augusta, GA. Edward Turner's citation on a brass plaque that earned them their medal(s). He is standing in front of his plaque which describes his five enemy planes downed in one day for which he earned the Navy Cross. *Courtesy of the Edward Bennett Turner Family*

Cdr. in 1967. In 1955 Ed Turner started the Turner Music House after he moved his family to Augusta, Georgia. Just as on the farm in South Carolina, Mr. and Mrs. Turner and their six children all worked at the piano store. Brenda, Sherrie, Karen, Ed, Jeff, and Lisa Turner all wanted to work at the family store since they were in grade school. After Ed retired in 1975, Ed Turner, Jr., and Sister Lisa took over the running of the store and still bring the same family values to their business, just like their mom and dad did in the 50s and 60s! Daughter Lisa remembers the humble side of her dad.

> *"Although known an outgoing, larger than life country gentleman who was very well respected by his friends and colleagues, he rarely talked about his war exploits. Many of his longtime friends never even knew he served his country in World War II. The fact that he was an ace and highly decorated combat pilot was shocking to many, especially at his funeral when the Augusta Chronicle mentioned his war record. He was that humble of a man."*

He died on February 21, 1998.

OPPOSITE:
Lt. Edward Bennett Turner after he returned from the flight where he earned the Navy Cross. His handwriting across the top "5 in one flight" relates to shooting down 5 Japanese aircraft on this mission on October 18, 1944. *Courtesy U.S. Navy photo via the Edward Bennett Turner Family.*

Edward B. Turner at "Hero's Overlook" in Augusta, GA. "Hero's Overlook" is a beautiful memorial to Augusta veterans who served in WWII and earned medals. Each veteran has a beautiful brass plaque stating the citation that earned them their medal(s). He is standing in front of his plaque which describes his five enemy planes downed in one day for which he earned the Navy Cross. *Courtesy of the Edward Bennett Turner Family*

Turner engaged the enemy in furious combat, disrupting the offensive and contributing to the excellent coverage provided our Task Force.

CITATION FOR THE AIR MEDAL

"Ike" Kepford and Tom Blackburn at the Fighting 17 reunion in 1983 at Oceana. *Courtesy of the Matthews Family.*

18

Color Gallery

Lou Antonacci's Corsair in "Ike" Kepford's markings with an F-14 Tomcat of the "Jolly Rogers" VF-84 at the Fighting 17 reunion in 1983. *Courtesy U.S. Navy, Fighting Squadron 84 via the Chasnoff Family and Andy Jagger.*

Fighting 17 reunion in 1983. L - R Tom Blackburn, Cdr. J. S. Daughtry, Jr. (VF-84), Jamie Blackburn, and "Ike" Kepford. *Courtesy U.S. Navy, Fighting Squadron 84 via the Chasnoff Family and Andy Jagger.*

Tom Blackburn and the Skipper of VF-84 the present day Jolly Rogers at the Fighting 17 reunion in 1983. *Courtesy U.S. Navy, Fighting Squadron 84 via the Chasnoff Family and Andy Jagger.*

"Ike" Kepford signing his name to Lou Antonacci's aircraft. Tom Blackburn had already signed it. This Corsair is still flying with the Fighter Collection at the Imperial War Museum, Duxford, England although it is now in Fleet Air Arm Colors. *Courtesy U.S. Navy, Fighting Squadron 84 via the Chasnoff Family and Andy Jagger.*

"Ike" Kepford and "Butch" Davenport in 1985. *Courtesy Courtesy of Kraeg Kepford.*

L - R: Robert "Andy" Anderson, Roger Hedrick and "Ike" Kepford at the Fighting 17, reunion on May 26, 1984. *Courtesy Hap Harlow.*

Marshall Beebe, Roger Hedrick and Tom Blackburn. *Courtesy Hap Harlow.*

There was a flyover and then the families threw their wreaths into the river after the service on the Yorktown. The Corsair was raised from the depths of Lake Washington near Seattle, Washington, where it had lain forty years following a crash. *Courtesy of the Gile Family.*

On October 13, 1985, a Corsair FG-1D identical to the one that he flew was dedicated on the deck of the Yorktown to "Timmy" Gile. It was also dedicated to "Chuck" Pillsbury who died while serving with Fighting 17. *Courtesy of the Gile Family.*

The Corsair is still on the Yorktown at Patriots Point museum in Charleston, South Carolina but has now been moved below decks on permanent display. *Courtesy of the Gile Family.*

From left to right: "Timmy" Gile's widow, June T. Gile, daughters Robin, Toni, Susan and Shelley at the dedication ceremony. The aircraft was rebuilt with funds raised by Yale classmates to commemorate the two distinguished graduates. *Courtesy of the Gile Family.*

FG-1 Corsair in "Ike" Kepford's markings which is operated by the Fighter Collection at the Imperial War Museum in Duxford, England. This is the same plane which flew at the 1983 reunion. It has now been repainted as a Fleet Air Arm Corsair. *Courtesy Courtesy Howard Cook.*

Memorial to Earl May in Cedarville, New Jersey, the scene of his crash in 1951.
Courtesy of the Del and Pat May Collection.

"I got a very unexpected and surprising phone call in 2003 . . . He asked if I knew that the people in a small town in New Jersey had been maintaining Earl's crash site since 1951!

EARL'S BROTHER DEL

A display of Roger Hedrick's medals. *Courtesy of the Hedrick Family.*

FG-1D "VF-17 Remembered" painted up to represent #17 of Fighting 17 flown by Lt. Cdr. Roger Hedrick. This aircraft was owned at the time by Paul Morgan. Paul was tragically killed in a flying accident in 2001. *Courtesy Courtesy Howard Cook.*

FG-1D "VF-17 Remembered" painted to represent #17 of Fighting 17 flown by Lt. Cdr. Roger Hedrick. Vintage Fighters owned by Charles Osborn and managed by Brad Hood restored this plane which won an E.A.A. Grand Champion award. *Courtesy Brad Hood Director/Chief Pilot - Vintage Fighters.*

Tom Blackburn's "Big Hog" at Duxford, England, prior to a change of color scheme. *Courtesy Courtesy Howard Cook.*

A Corsair in the painted in the colors of "Big Hog" flown by Lt. Cdr. Tom Blackburn which used to be operated by the Old Flying Machine Company at Duxford, England. *Courtesy Courtesy Howard Cook.*

FG-1D painted up to represent #29 of Fighting 17 flown by Lt. (jg) Ira Cassius "Ike" Kepford. Kepford was the U.S. Navy's top Corsair ace with sixteen confirmed victories. Vintage Fighters owned by Charles Osborn and managed by Brad Hood restored this plane which won an E.A.A. Grand Champion award. *Courtesy Paul Bowen, www.airtoair.net*

This Corsair used to be operated by the Old Flying Machine Company and flew in the colors of Tom Blackburn's "Big Hog" at Duxford, England. *Courtesy Courtesy Howard Cook.*

The Skull and Crossbones lives on with the 21st Century version - the VFA-103 Jolly Rogers flying the FA-18F Super Hornet. Taken in the North Arabian Sea in the summer of 2009, while the squadron was aboard the U.S.S. Dwight D. Eisenhower (CVN-69). *Courtesy U.S. Navy Photo / Brian M. Garrison Fighting 103 Commanding Officer.*

Another View of VFA-103 Jolly Rogers flying the FA-18F Super Hornet in the North Arabian Sea in the summer of 2009, while the squadron was aboard the U.S.S. Dwight D. Eisenhower (CVN-69). *Courtesy U.S. Navy Photo / Brian M. Garrison Fighting 103 Commanding Officer.*

Another View of VFA-103 Jolly Rogers flying the FA-18F Super Hornet in the North Arabian Sea in the summer of 2009, while the squadron was aboard the U.S.S. Dwight D. Eisenhower (CVN-69). *Courtesy U.S. Navy Photo / Brian M. Garrison Fighting 103 Commanding Officer.*

GLOSSARY

A/A Anti-aircraft fire
AWOL Absent without leave

B-24 Consolidated Liberator four engine bomber
B-25 North American Mitchell medium bomber
Bail out Jump out of aircraft
Betty Japanese twin engine bomber
Birdcage Early model F4U-1 Corsair
Bomber One Main landing strip on Espiritu Santo
Bogies Fighter direction code - unknown aircraft
Boresighted Enemy in perfect firing position
Break Signal to an airborne comrade to make an instantaneous turn in the direction indicated with the intention of avoiding being shot at
Bunker Hill Essex class carrier CV-17

CAG Carrier Air Group
CASU Carrier Air Service Unit
Chandelle Steep high speed climbing turn
C.I.C. Commander in Chief
CL Light cruiser
Cocker Base Fighter Direction Officer for Empress Augusta Bay
C.O. Commanding Officer
COMAIRPAC Commander Air Force Pacific Fleet
COMAIRSEPAC Commander Air Force South East Pacific Fleet
COMAIRSOLS Commander Air Forces Solomon Islands
COMAIRSOPAC Commander Air Forces Southern Pacific
COMFAIRSOUTH Commander Fleet Air South
COMFAIRWESTCOAST Commander Fleet Air West Coast
COMFIGHTRON Commander Fighting Squadron
COMTASKFORCE Commander Task Force
CV Large aircraft carrier
CVE Small escort carrier
CVL Light carrier

Dane Base Fighter direction station
DC-3 U.S. Transport plane
DD Destroyer
Deflection Shot The angle of a shot in gunnery measured between the line of sight to the target and the line of sight to the aiming point
Dogfight An aerial battle between opposing fighter aircraft-aerial combat

E-Base Elimination base
Ens. Ensign

F2A Brewster Buffalo, early monoplane fighter
F2F, F3F Grumman biplane fighters
F4F Grumman Wildcat
F4U Vought Corsair
F6F Grumman Hellcat
FDO Fighter Direction Officer
Firewall Maximum throttle
Flak Anti-aircraft fire
Flathat Low level flying
Full bore Maximum engine power

G's Force of gravity
Grab ass Dogfighting
Grey out Pass out
Groundloop Loss of lateral control on the ground resulting in the plane making a sudden turn or change of direction. From this a wheel or gear strut may break and the plane could suffer considerable damage

Hack Officers punishment
Hamp Japanese fighter
High blower Engine supercharger setting used at high altitudes
High side run Steep diving attack pattern from side
Hop Mission

IFF Identification Friend or Foe (radar)
IJAAF Imperial Japanese Army Air Force
Immelmann Aerobatic maneuver (Roll off the top)
Independence CVL-22 light carrier

Jack Japanese radial engine fighter

Kate Japanese torpedo bomber

Lead The action of aiming ahead of a moving target. Refer to deflection shot
Lion Base Cruiser Task Force
LSO Landing Signal Officer
Lufbery Circle Horizontal ring of fighters for mutual defense
Lt. Lieutenant
Lt. (jg) Lieutenant Junior Grade
Lt. Cdr Lieutenant Commander

MAG Marine Air Group
MIA Missing in action
MILS Gunnery term of angular measurement
MG's Machine guns

NAB Hospital Naval Air Base Hospital
NAAS Naval Auxiliary Air Station
NAS Naval Air Station
NATS Naval Air Transport Service

O'clock The position of another plane sighted in the air as called out by its o'clock position from the observer. 12 o'clock straight ahead
Oleo Shock absorbers
OS2U U.S. Navy observation plane
Overhead Steep diving run from above target

P-38 Lockheed Lightning twin engine fighter
P-40 Curtiss Tomahawk single engine fighter
P-47 Republic Thunderbolt single engine fighter
P-51 North American Mustang single engine fighter
Pancake Land
PBY Consolidated Catalina twin engine seaplane (Dumbo)
Plank Owners Member of ship or squadron compliment from date of unit's commissioning
Pollywog A seaman who has not crossed the equator
Pour on the coal Full throttle
Princeton CVL-23 light carrier

PT boats Motor torpedo boats
PV-1 U.S. twin-engine patrol bomber

R & R Rest and Recreation
Revetment Embankment for protection from shells, bombs, etc. usually horseshoe shaped
Rufe Japanese seaplane version of Zero fighter
Ruth Japanese heavy bomber

Saratoga CV-3
SB2C-1 Curtiss Helldiver divebomber
SBD Douglas Dauntless divebomber
SCAT Southern Cross Air Transport (Army Air Force Transport Service South Pacific)
Scuttlebutt Rumors
Shakedown First operations of a new ship
Shellback A seaman who has crossed the equator
Skip bombing Low level bombing, bomb skips into target from water
SNJ North American advanced trainer
Sonia Japanese light bomber/dive bomber
Split-S Violent half roll to an inverted position

Tail End Charlie Last plane in a formation
TBF Grumman Avenger torpedo plane
Tiny Tim U.S. Air to ground rocket
Tojo Japanese radial engine fighter
Tony Japanese in-line engine fighter
Topsy Japanese Army transport aircraft
Tracer A bullet containing a pyrotechnic mixture to make the flight of the bullet visible

Val Japanese divebomber
VB Bomber - aircraft type and squadron designators
VF Fighter - aircraft type and squadron designators
VT Torpedo - aircraft type and squadron designators
VP Patrol - aircraft type and squadron designators

Washing Machine Charlie Jap night bomber over Solomon Islands
Windmill Propeller rotating on dead engine

Zeke (Zero) Principal Japanese fighter

BIBLIOGRAPHY

Blackburn, Tom. *The Jolly Rogers*. New York: Orion, 1989.

Bowman, Martin. *Vought F4U Corsair*. The Crowood Press Ltd. 2002.

Cook, Lee. *The Skull and Crossbones Squadron - VF-17 in World War II*. Schiffer Publishing Ltd. 1998.

Cook, Lee. *Fighting Seventeen: A Photographic History of VF-17 in WWII*. Schiffer Publishing Ltd. 2011.

Dwiggins, Don. *The S. O. Bees*. The New American Library of Canada Ltd. 1963.

Foster, Col. Frank, and Lawrence Borts. *U.S. Military Medals 1939 to 1994*. Fountain Inn, S.C.: M.O.A. Press, 1994.

Kepchia, John B. *Missing in Action over Rabaul*. The Palace Printer, 1986.

Nason, Joseph G. *Horio, You Next Die!* Pacific Rim Press, Inc. 1987.

Olynyk, Frank J. *U.S.N. Credits for the Destruction of Enemy Aircraft in Air - to - Air Combat in World War II*. Aurora, OH: Frank J. Olynyk, 1982.

Popp, Wilbert P. "Beads." *The Survival of a WWII Navy Fighter Pilot*.

Sakaida, Henry. *The Siege of Rabaul*. Phalanx Publishing Co., Ltd. 1996.

Tillman, Barrett. *Corsair: The F4U in World War Two and Korea*. Annapolis: U.S. Naval Institute Press, 1979.

Documents
Archival Official Military Personnel Files:

Howard McClain Burriss, Doris Clyde Freeman, Harry Andrew March, Jr.

National Personnel Records Center, Military Personnel Records:

Tom Blackburn, Oscar Chenoweth, Paul Cordray, Dan Cunningham, Merl William Davenport, Clement Dexter Gile, Roger Hedrick, Ira Cassius Kepford, Earl May, Robert Mims, John M. Smith and Jim Streig. VF-17 Action Reports and Combat Statistics.

VF-17 War Diary

VF-84 Squadron History and Action Reports

VF/VBF-10 Squadron History.

Recommended Reading
Abrams, Richard. *F4U Corsair at War*. New York: Scribners, 1981.

Green, William. *Famous Fighters of the Second World War*. New York: Doubleday, 1962.

Gurney, Gene and Friedlander, Jr., Mark P. *Five Down and Glory*. G. P. Putnam's Sons. New York. 1958.

Guyton, Boone. *Whistling Death*. Atglen, PA. Schiffer, 1994.

Johnson, Frederick A. and Watanabe, Rikyu. *F4U Corsair*. New York: Crown, 1983.

Maloney, Edward T. and Feist, Uwe. *Chance Vought Corsair*. Fallbrook, CA: Aero.

Musciano, Walter A. *Corsair Aces The Bent - Wing Bird Over The Pacific*. New York: Arco.
Styling, Mark. *Corsair Aces of World War Two*. London: Osprey, 1995.

Veronico, Nicholas A. and Campbell, John M. and Donna. *F4U Corsair*. Osceola, WI: 1994.

Videos
Dare County Regional Airport "Then and Now." Cable AD. Kill Devil Hills, N.C.

Fighting Seventeen, The Jolly Rogers. Kenwood Productions, Minneapolis, 1990.

VF-17 at Oshkosh 1994. RAD Productions, Beverly Hills, 1995.

VF-17 Remembered. RDR Video Productions. Northbrook, Illinois, 1984.

World War Two Pacific Heroes. U.S. News Video, 1991.

ACKNOWLEDGMENTS

Since I first started researching Fighting 17 in 1993 I have had the continued support, encouragement and help of a great many people. I would like to acknowledge the magnificent cooperation and assistance of all the members of Fighting Squadron Seventeen and their families, who have provided photographs, information, tapes, and other valuable documents to make this book possible. I am indebted to "the Skipper", Tom Blackburn, for encouraging me to pursue my research into his great squadron. His passing drove me on further to fulfil the publication of the squadron history to the best of my ability.

"Country" and "Ginger" Landreth took me under their wing and helped me to press on over the years, and I thank them for their help, support and faith. "Country" has been an inspiration to me for seventeen years in my quest to document Fighting 17's many achievements.

I would like to thank the veterans and families whose contact resulted from Tom's roster in 1993–many of whom I first met at Oshkosh in 1994 and at two further reunions–for their ongoing support and assistance to this day. "Andy" and Betty Jagger, Wilbert Peter "Beads" and Jean Popp, Wally and Maureen Schub, Rear Admiral Roger Hedrick, Mills and Marilee Schanuel, Mel "Kurly" Kurlander, Hal and Barbara Jackson, Jack and Alice Chasnoff, Dan and Ruthie Cunningham, Robert "Windy" Hill, Tom and Carolyn Killefer, "Hap" and Alice Bowers, Harold and Betty Bitzegaio, "Big Jim" and Vera Streig, Lennard "Red" Edmisten, George and Laurie Mauhar, Joy Anderson Schroeder, Boone Guyton, Kraeg and Tim Kepford, Therese Smith, "Hap" and Marje Harlow, Charles E. Dixon, Jim and Jan Dixon and Don McQueen, Sid Buff, Lisa Turner Maddox, Ed Turner Jr., and the Turner family, and Marvin Russell "Russ" Novak and Sharon Novak. This includes not only the pilots, but the men who served alongside Fighting 17 and who worked with them in training or ground support roles to make their success possible.

The family members and others associated with Fighting Seventeen have made a huge contribution, providing records, letters, anecdotes and photographs, many of which have not been published before. So many have helped, and I would like to extend my sincere thanks to Alexandra Bowers, John Chasnoff, Del and Pat May, Rick and Cathy Einar, Dora Taylor, Lloyd Taylor, Alida Christinaz, Mike DeBorde, Steve Smith, Barney Smith and the Smith family, Toni and Rob Sennott, Phil Schanuel, John and Mary Deveney, Mark Blackburn, Paul Blackburn, Randolph Soggs, Jack Burriss, Kelly Burriss, Bob Burriss, Jay Burriss, Mac and Dorothy Burriss, Judy Chasnoff Smith, John and Adele Chenoweth, Chip Chenoweth, John M. Cordray, Sr., John M. Cordray, Jr., Don and Sue Arvin, Carol Lifton, Rick Hedrick, Jerry Halford, Betsy Bryant, Katherine Ritter, Susan Ritter, Jamie Blackburn, Dave and Janice Streig, Mark and Janece Streig, Robin Litwin, Paul Matthews, Cindy Spriggs, Kimberley Cunningham, George R. Edwards, Linda Landreth Phelps, Keith Hoey, Sidney Buff, Phyllis Garrett, and Christine Silengo. All have helped me above and beyond the call of duty.

Great assistance was provided to me by Robert Lawson, whose photograph collection is at the National Museum of Naval Aviation, Pensacola; Roger Mott; Bob Pisz; Curt Lawson and Bill Addison at NMNA; Frank Olynyk for his victory credit information; the staff at the National Personnel Records Center in St. Louis, Missouri, and National Archives and Records Administration; Ariana Jacob at the Department of the Navy, Naval History and Heritage Command, Archives Branch; and Harold Rubin at the American Fighter Aces Association.

My thanks to aviation artist Jack Fellows for contributing his excellent work for this book and Paul Bowen for his wonderful photo of Corsair #29 in Fighting 17 colors.

My thanks to Brad Hood of Vintage Fighters and Jerry Yagen of the Fighter Factory, award-winning restorers of vintage aircraft including "Bent-Wing Birds", and Tony Staley A.A.U. Sports Manager.

Thanks also to Cdr. B. M. "BG" Garrison, Commanding Officer, Strike Fighter Squadron 103 for the present day "Skull and Crossbones" photographs.

Bob Biondi at Schiffer publishing for his encouragement with all the books and also his support for this latest one.

My thanks also to my family, Martin and Millie Cook, Audrey and Derek Barnett, and to my wife Jackie, a constant source of inspiration and support during what has been a long arduous process getting the book completed. To my daughters Charli, Natalie, and Lani for putting up with the "Dad's on the laptop again" moments – lots of them!

To my brother Howard and his wife Peta for their constant support, inspiration, advice and meticulous attention to detail with this project.

I hope I have managed to include everyone who has helped, but to anyone who has assisted me and I have missed a profound thank you.

AUTHOR'S NOTE

The author would be extremely interested in hearing from families or relatives of men who served with Fighting 17 or anyone who may have relevant photographs, information, letters or stories relating to Fighting 17, the Skull and Crossbones Squadron. Any material will be fully credited to its original source.

Lee Cook

jacleecook@yahoot.co.uk